Euripides and the Instruction of the Athenians

Justina Gregory

Ann Arbor

THE UNIVERSITY OF MICHIGAN PRESS

Copyright © by the University of Michigan 1991
All rights reserved
Published in the United States of America by
The University of Michigan Press
Manufactured in the United States of America
1994 1993 1992 1991   4 3 2 1

Library of Congress Cataloging-in-Publication Data

Gregory, Justina.
    Euripides and the instruction of the Athenians / Justina Gregory.
        p.   cm.
    Includes bibliographical references and index.
    ISBN 0-472-10230-3 (alk. paper)
    1. Euripides—Criticism and interpretation. 2. Greek drama
(Tragedy)—History and criticism. 3. Political plays, Greek—
History and criticism. 4. Didactic drama, Greek—History and
criticism. 5. Athens (Greece)—Intellectual life. I. Title.
    PA3978.G68   1991
    882' .01—dc20   90-27859
                                                                         CIP

Acknowledgments

Portions of chapters 1, 4, and 5 appeared in article form in *Hermes* 107, 1979 ("Euripides' *Alcestis*"), *Yale Classical Studies* 25, 1977 ("Euripides' *Heracles*"), and *Eranos* 84, 1986 ("The Power of Language in Euripides' *Troades*"). I am grateful to Franz Steiner Verlag and Cambridge University Press, publishers of *Hermes* and *Yale Classical Studies*, and to Stig Y. Rudberg, editor of *Eranos*, for permission to reprint.

Smith College allowed me time off from teaching in 1986–87, as well as financial assistance in the form of a grant from the Andrew W. Mellon Fund. Audrey Ryan and Anne Deutsch helped in preparing the typescript. I would particularly like to thank John Graiff, head of interlibrary loan at Neilson Library, for his efforts on my behalf.

Ellen Bauerle, my editor at the University of Michigan Press, gave me much help and advice. The Department of Classics of the University of Edinburgh extended a hospitable welcome and made available to me the resources of its library.

For information, comments, and criticism I am indebted to Paula Arnold, Victor Bers, George Dimock, Richard Garner, Lisa Kallet-Marx, David Kovacs, Ann Michelini, Krishna Winston, and several anonymous referees. The remaining errors of fact and judgment are my own.

To Patrick

Contents

Introduction

The earliest assessments of tragedy we possess—one by a fourth-century philosopher, the other by a fifth-century comic poet—bear witness to the organic connection between tragedy and the Athenian polis. Aristotle, to be sure, refers to it only in passing. In the *Poetics*, while discussing the element of "thought" in tragedy, he remarks that the older poets (that is, the fifth-century tragedians) made their characters speak *politikōs*, "in a political vein," whereas those of his own day make their characters speak *rhētorikōs*, "in a rhetorical vein."[1] Although he does not elaborate on this tantalizing observation, in the *Nichomachean Ethics* (1093a27–1094b11) he describes as "political" the discipline that spans ethics and public policy and that pertains to the moral education of the community.[2] If (as seems likely) Aristotle is using the term in the same sense in both passages, then his remark offers a preliminary indication that the political and ethical components of Greek tragedy will be closely conjoined.

Aristophanes, on the other hand, considers the political role of tragedy directly and at length. The climax of the *Frogs* is an *agōn* or poetry contest that takes place in the underworld under the auspices of the god Dionysus. The shades of Aeschylus and Euripides are vying for the title of best tragedian; the realm of Hades, it seems, bears a curious resemblance to Athens, where tragedians competed for first prize at the City Dionysia. Just as at Athens public benefactors were rewarded with free entertainment and favored seating in the Prytaneum or city hall, so in the underworld the winner of the contest will enjoy "meals in the Prytaneum and a seat next to Pluto" (*Frogs* 764–65).

Euripides, arguing his own cause, claims to have freed tragedy from the cumbersome staging and obscure language favored by his rival. He explains that he has substituted a leaner, more tightly structured, "democratic" form (952) that is relevant to the spectators' daily life and allows them room for discrimination and judgment. Aeschylus presently demands, "On what grounds should we admire a tragedian?" Euripides is unhesitating in his reply: "For his skilfulness and his admonitions, because we improve the people in the cities" (1009–10).

Aeschylus has no quarrel with this formulation. He concurs with Euripides on the didactic function of tragedy: "For children it is the schoolteacher who instructs; for grown-ups, it is the poet."[3] It is an acknowledged goal of tragedy to teach what is good and useful (chrēsta, 686, 1056, cf. 1035, 1421); the two poets diverge, however, on the appropriate means. Aeschylus maintains that whereas he has incited the Athenians to courageous action through his productions of tragedies "full of Ares" (1021 ff.), Euripides has made people worse instead of better, because his characters exhibit moral weaknesses that have inspired the audience's imitation. Though Aeschylus admits that his rival's portrayals are true to life he believes that moral edification, not truth, is the business of tragedy. "The poet should hide what is bad," says Aeschylus, "not represent or produce it" (1053–54). The verb "produce," didaskein, also means "teach." Aristophanes is taking advantage of ordinary linguistic usage to buttress his claim that the playwright is also a teacher.[4]

The association between poetry and teaching is a recurrent motif in the Frogs. The parabasis leads off with the statement that it is right for the chorus to offer "good advice and instruction to the city" (chrēsta tei polei xumparainein kai didaskein, 686–87). At a later point in the play Aeschylus associates his own inspirational and instructive practice with that of a distinguished group of predecessors: Orpheus, Musaeus, Hesiod, and Homer (1032–36). In identifying the poets as the fountainhead of practical and moral wisdom he is on firm historical ground. "There is an important element in early, archaic, and classical verse that might be called, broadly, 'educational' or 'culturally formative.' Homer, Hesiod, Solon, Xenophanes, Theognis, to name a few, all address themselves, in greater or lesser degree, to the information and admonition of their audiences."[5]

But Aristophanes has in mind something more precise than cultural formation. In the course of the contest between the two rivals, it emerges that the improvement of the polis is the goal of the poet's instruction; it is in that sense, according to Aristophanes, that tragedy aspires to the political. As we have seen, the chorus offers its good advice to the city, and Euripides asserts that the tragedian should make the people better in the cities. Defending himself against Aeschylus' accusations, Euripides inquires indignantly in what way his passionate female protagonists *harm the city* (1049). Dionysus ultimately informs the two tragedians that he intends to bring back with him to the upper world "whichever one of you can give *the city* some useful advice" (1420–21)—a charge that each does his best to satisfy.

These passages make assumptions that may appear startling to modern readers, but are taken for granted by the two contestants; presumably they reflect fifth-century preconceptions about poets and poetry. There is no concern that aesthetic and political purposes might inhibit one another; rather, artistry and admonition are said to operate in tandem (cf. 1009–10). The domain of private life is not envisaged as separate from the public realm; both dramatists agree that sexual conduct, for example, has the potential to damage the city. Both recognize too that as dramatists they are doubly accountable: not only should they help the Athenians become better citizens, they must themselves serve as examples of responsible statesmanship. Both assume that the representations of tragedy will provoke a mimetic response in the audience. Aeschylus, to be sure, reduces this notion to its most absurd because most literal form: Athenian women have committed suicide in emulation of Euripidean prototypes, he claims, and prosperous citizens have managed to evade their civic responsibilities by dissimulating their wealth on the model of Euripides' ragged kings (1050–51, 1065–66). Euripides does not admit that his characters have caused harm, but neither does he challenge the basic premise. As we have seen, the two poets disagree only on whether the community is better served by portraying conflicts and passions in all their complexity, or by presenting a simple and idealized account of human nature.

It is hard to imagine anyone more favorably situated than Aristophanes to comment on the social function of tragedy. As a contemporary of Sophocles and Euripides, as an Athenian citizen who was himself a playwright, he enjoyed an insider's privileged perspective. Therefore his account of tragedy's didactic function and political orientation tends to inspire respect. But we must also keep in mind that Aristophanes was above all a writer of comedies, with a penchant for parody, exaggeration, and sheer fantasy. It is possible that the didactic account of tragedy set forth in the *Frogs* was not intended to be taken seriously.

Several considerations tell against this view. In the first place, a successful joke depends on a degree of cultural consensus; it is the comic turn given to shared assumptions that most reliably raises a laugh. The "didactic theory" may be no more than a convenient peg on which to hang the contest between Aeschylus and Euripides, with its elaborate stage business and its mischievous caricatures of both playwrights.[6] Nevertheless, the audience must accept the basic point that tragedy does indeed offer instruction in order to find amusing its subsequent ludicrous applications.

There is no reason why a comic poet (not unlike a modern cartoonist) cannot be "funny . . . [and] serious at the same time."[7] To succeed on both counts is, in fact, the fond prayer of the chorus in the *Frogs* (389–90). Aristophanes seems to combine the two modes in his treatment of tragedy, assigning tragedy a responsible social role even as he relentlessly parodies and caricatures its practitioners.[8] Finally, if it is permitted to consult the social and historical context for the tragic performances as a kind of control on Aristophanes, even a brief survey will turn up numerous indications that lend credence to his account.

The Social and Historical Context

Tragedy was a genre unique to Athens; its development coincided with the city's transformation into a major power and the equally rapid evolution of Athenian democracy.[9] The fifth century opened with the wars against Persia, which brought Athens to the forefront of the Greek states and displaced Sparta from its previous position of leadership. The subsequent founding of the Delian-League consolidated Athenian hegemony. Athens kept a tight hold on its confederates, assessing an annual tribute and crushing all attempts at revolt, and the other members of the League discovered in short order that they were not so much Athens' allies as Athens' subjects. Increased tensions with Sparta led to an outbreak of hostilities in 461. A peace treaty concluded in 445, and designed to last for thirty years, did not endure: the year 431 saw renewed hostilities between Athens and Sparta. The conflict would continue, with only minor interruptions, until 404.

Even as Athens launched military initiatives on many fronts, the establishment within the polis of a democratic system of government proceeded apace. Cleisthenes had laid the groundwork in the previous century, with his reorganization of the citizenry into new political units that cut across traditional affiliations based on locality, cult, ancestry, and class. Ephialtes introduced changes that curtailed the authority of the aristocratic law court and strengthened the legal and political authority of the ordinary citizens. Pericles made widespread participation in the business of government a practical reality when he introduced monetary compensation for jurymen and, in all likelihood, for citizens serving in other official capacities as well.

The theater was not an invention of the democracy, but by the fifth century it had become closely identified with the official life of the democratic polis. Presented annually at the state-sponsored festival of Dionysus, the plays integrated some of the democracy's most characteristic practices into their production.[10] The theatrical program was selected by a polis official, the eponymous archon, and the productions were financed by wealthy individuals as a *leitourgia* or public service on the same order as outfitting a warship or sponsoring an athletic event.[11] Reflecting the democratic principle of accountability, an assembly held after the event offered a chance to investigate any irregularities connected with the festival.

The composition of the chorus, the judges, and the audience contributed to the democratic ambience. Ordinary Athenians (out of the ordinary, to be sure, in their ability to sing and dance) made up the chorus, and the prizes were awarded by a panel of judges chosen by lot—that favorite instrument of the democracy. The plays were viewed by an audience whose attendance, once Pericles established a fund to offset the price of admission, was subsidized by the state; as a further official inducement to attend, city business was suspended for the duration of the festival.

A religious as well as a civic occasion, the festival of Dionysus drew in the same broad constituency that participated in the many other religious festivals that articulated the Athenian year.[12] There is every reason to believe that the theater audience spanned the full spectrum of society: men, women, and children; aristocrats, commoners, and slaves; poor and wealthy; city-dwellers and rustics; citizens, metics, and foreigners.[13]

The theater was democratic in a way that approaches the modern use of the term—it was comprehensive as the assembly and the law court, those other great political gathering-places, were not.[14] This circumstance offered the dramatist a unique opportunity to address himself to representatives of the entire population on issues that concerned them both individually and as members of the various groups that claimed their allegiance.

If Athens was the school of Greece, as Thucydides' Pericles asserts (Thuc. 2.41.1), then the theater had a strong claim to be the school of Athens. Yet this figure should not suggest (as it might in a modern context) the indoctrination of an impressionable populace by the establishment's designated spokesmen. The social policy of Athens was self-consciously liberal rather than prescriptive; the members of the audience harbored strong, diverse, and noisy opinions of their own; and the message they received at the festival of Dionysus contained as much of query and admonition as of flattery and praise.[15]

The quality of instruction was already discernible in the festival's opening events — ceremonies that constituted a powerful statement of "civic ideology."[16] The festival of Dionysus — held in late March, when the seas were open for sailing after the winter storms — was the occasion for the members of the Delian League to bring their annual tribute to Athens.[17] The tribute was displayed in the theater — a sight calculated to appeal to Athenian pride and patriotism. But another preliminary feature of the festival was a parade through the Theater of Dionysus by the war-orphans who had been raised at public expense — a ceremony that no less insistently underscored the sacrifices and burdens of empire.[18] The civic ideology adumbrated in the opening ceremonies was not a simple one.

Even if the evidence is only circumstantial, it seems reasonable to associate the plays presented in such a framework with the same civic program. But tragedy had the resources to convey a far broader range of political concerns than those implicit in the festival's opening pageantry, and to treat them with more complexity, finer shading, and greater variation.

The Political Contribution of Tragedy

That tragedy possessed a political component is now generally acknowledged. There remains, however, considerable uncertainty about the level at which it can be seen to operate.[19] The theory that tragedy's political consciousness manifests itself in overt references to specific contemporary events now has few supporters.[20] The very structure of tragedy militates against such a practice: there is no feature like the *parabasis* of comedy, which suspends the action and breaks the dramatic illusion in favor of direct address to the audience.[21] The matter too discourages topical reference: with one exception, the characters and plots of the surviving dramas are derived from the world of legend, from Homer and the poems of the epic cycle.[22] If these tales from the heroic age make allusion to the concerns of fifth-century Athens it can only be indirectly, through inference and comparison. Tragedy's contemporary message is "general not particular, and objective not personal . . . inherent in the detached reality of the drama as a whole."[23]

A more promising line of inquiry opens up with the suggestion, consciously paradoxical, that tragedy derives its political influence precisely from its unpromising structure and material. Tragedy, on this interpretation, exploits the tensions inherent in the contrast between past and present; it juxtaposes the characters of legend with the world of the fifth-century polis in order to bring into focus the divergent values of the inherited culture and the new social order.[24]

The Greek ethical vocabulary was forged in an aristocratic milieu that equated merit with birth and wealth, and that prized individual assertion and accomplishment over communal effort. In such a society results counted for much and intentions for little; there were no mitigating circumstances for failure. Social esteem, more than any internal measure, was the determinant of individual worth. This aristocratic code contributed to the successful functioning of a society at war—the kind of society depicted in the *Iliad* and dominated, as Aristophanes puts it (*Frogs* 1036), by "battle-lines, deeds of valor, men's armament."[25]

Scarcely had these standards been articulated than they began to undergo modification to serve changing social needs. The *Odyssey* already reflects a different set of circumstances, and in the next century the lyric poets would reshape Homer's language to articulate the concerns proper to their own age.[26] Yet a conservative and reverential impulse ensured that such modifications as took place were all but invisible. The ethical vocabulary itself did not change, but the traditional terms were transferred to different contexts, thereby acquiring different significations even as they preserved a sense, or illusion, of continuity.[27]

Democratic Athens introduced far-reaching innovations, both social and political, that might have seemed to call for some wholesale readjustment of the aristocratic code. The structures put in place by Cleisthenes encouraged the Athenians to define themselves as members of a network of social groups—local, tribal, civic—whose demands could not necessarily be reconciled with one another or with traditional standards of individual honor.[28] Another Cleisthenic mechanism, that of ostracism, seemed designed to deal precisely with the threat that an exceptional individual might pose to the community: provided that six thousand citizens turned up at a special assembly and the majority scratched his name on a potsherd, an individual could be banished from Athens for ten years without ever having been accused of any definite crime.[29] The qualities that constituted excellence in the archaic hero could prove problematical for a society like that of democratic Athens, which depended for its successful functioning not on outstanding individual accomplishment but on the unified efforts of a majority of citizens.

Another fundamental change concerned the distribution of political authority. Although the aristocrats enjoyed a monopoly of the highest military offices, they had to share power with the ordinary citizens. It was the common people who by their votes in the assembly had the last word on public policy; they who served on the juries, and manned the ships that formed the basis of the city's power.[30] Such a society assumed no natural hierarchies; birth and wealth no longer served as reliable indicators of merit, while exceptional achievement could be perceived as a threat to the collective. The inherited aristocratic code was out of alignment with contemporary social reality. Yet despite all social transformations, the authority of tradition still held strong. The Athenians still respected the standards enshrined in the paradigms of myth and poetry, still looked to the past as a source of validation.

At this juncture the whole society stood in need of guidance from that traditional source of wisdom, the poets. Aristocrats and commoners alike could benefit from a scheme of values retaining the glamor and authority of the heroic past, yet accessible and appropriate to the present. It is in attending to this demand that tragedy — including the tragedy of Euripides — reveals its political dimension.[31]

So wholesome an aim may surprise in a poet generally reckoned a literary and social subversive.[32] This view of Euripides has encountered strong support in the twentieth century among critics who found something familiar and deeply sympathetic in the image of an artist alienated from his society.[33] The image itself, to be sure, has its source in antiquity, in the comic Euripides memorably caricatured by Aristophanes. These caricatures, accepted at face value and pieced out with motifs from Euripidean drama, gave rise to the Euripides of the biographical tradition: a morose solitary disappointed in his private life and unpopular with his fellow citizens.[34]

This Euripides in turn was assimilated to the evolutionary account of tragedy promulgated in the nineteenth century and still widely influential. In the assessment of the German scholars of the Victorian age, Aeschylus represented the beginning, Sophocles the zenith, and Euripides the decline.[35] Such an ordering posits a simple hierarchical succession where ancient audiences would have perceived complex and tangled interrelationships, both literary and chronological. For Sophocles produced tragedies simultaneously with Aeschylus as well as with Euripides; he influenced and was influenced by Euripides, whom he outlived. Aeschylus' plays, moreover, were revived after his death, at the same time that Sophocles and Euripides were producing their mature work.[36]

If we aspire to recover something of the Greeks' perspective on Euripides we must make strenuous efforts to shed modern habits of thought—including a bias in favor of evolution and alienated artists—while constantly checking categories and assumptions against the ancient testimony. Certainly the ancient witnesses can be interpreted in many different ways. But there can be no doubt that both Aristotle and Aristophanes regarded Aeschylus, Sophocles, and Euripides as a trinity set apart from other playwrights, and sharing more similarities than differences.[37] A study of political elements in Euripides will tend to reaffirm this ancient alignment, for it will focus attention on characteristics of Euripidean tragedy that could be matched in Aeschylus and Sophocles.[38] It can of course be objected that what emerges is a somewhat flattened picture of Euripides, and there is no question that a concentration upon other elements of his dramaturgy would yield a different result. Nevertheless, this study will have fulfilled its purpose if it serves as a corrective to the conventional modern account of Euripides and helps to reinstate him in the historical context he shared with his fellow tragedians.

Political Elements in Euripides

We may distinguish three strands of political reflection in the plays of Euripides, although in practice they will often be found to intertwine. The most obvious (and also the most frequently studied) is the evocation of democratic institutions and practices.

Although there exists no single fifth-century synthesis of democratic political theory, many passages in the extant literature combine to show that Athenian citizens were cognizant of the special features of their political system and took enormous pride in its bene-fits.[39] To those who met its stringent requirements for citizenship, Athens' radical democracy promised liberty and equality – abstrac-tions that translated into access to the political process, the guarantee of free speech, and the impartial protection of the law. These features became the staples of fifth-century celebrations of Athens, of which the best known is the funeral oration that Thucydides puts into the mouth of Pericles.[40] They also found their place in tragedy, incorpo-rated into the dramatic action by Aeschylus in his *Suppliants* and by Eu-ripides in *Children of Heracles* and his own *Suppliants*. It is these two plays, together with isolated passages from other tragedies that strike an overtly patriotic or democratic note, that are generally featured in discussions of Euripides' political thought.[41] The *Ion* has been ana-lyzed for its treatment of autochthony and the Athenian colonization of Ionia; the political assemblies of the *Orestes* and *Hecuba* have also at-tracted notice.[42] Yet institutions and practices are not the only registers of a society's political tenor. This handful of plays by no means ex-hausts the political significance of Euripidean drama.

Athens' changing relations with the external world constituted an aspect of the political that Euripides' generation was especially well situated to apprehend. Born in 484 B.C., Euripides grew to adulthood in a city still elated by its unexpected victory over Persia. In 455 Euripi-des competed for the first time in the City Dionysia; soon after, proba-bly in 454, the Delian League moved its treasury from Delos to Athens. That move has traditionally been interpreted as symbolizing a new stage in the relationship between Athens and its allies – a proclama-tion that the alliance begun as a defensive coalition against Persia had been transformed into an instrument of Athenian power.

The city that prided itself on its democratic institutions ordered its foreign policy according to a different set of political principles.[43] The same citizens who rejoiced in their internal freedom did not hesitate to impose their rule upon others; so far from perceiving any contradic-tion, they seem to have regarded the empire as the guarantor of Athe-nian independence. Thucydides' Alcibiades warns the citizens that ruling others is their insurance against being ruled themselves (6.18.3), and Thucydides later makes the comment that it was difficult for the

Athenians to lose their liberty, because ever since they had expelled their own tyrants they had been accustomed "not only not to be subjects, but for more than half of that time [actually] to exercise rule over others" (8.68.4; cf. 7.75.7). True to their admonitory function, the dramatists repeatedly called Athenian imperialism into question. Aristophanes' lost comedy, the *Babylonians*, caustically portrayed "the effect of democracy on the allies."[44] Sophocles made oblique reference to Athens as a tyrant city in his *Oedipus the King*.[45] And the morality of power emerges as one of the major themes of Euripides' *Hecuba*.

The most pervasive aspect of the political in Euripides is also the most difficult to isolate. It is sounded in the characteristic tonality he imparts to themes of perennial, indeed universal interest; this tonality is not confined to specific passages, but is audible throughout each play. Euripides is anything but innovative in his choice of subject matter; his themes are well attested in the literary tradition and indigenous to tragedy as a genre. The relationship between life and death; the nature of moderation; the claims of justice; the definition of nobility: the uses of language and intellect—these are the dominant motifs of Euripides' *Alcestis*, *Hippolytus*, *Hecuba*, *Heracles*, and *Trojan Women*. I shall try to show that these traditional subjects acquire a contemporary and political dimension at his hands; that each becomes, with varying degrees of emphasis, the carrier of a democratic ideology.

Such a claim is not susceptible of proof, only of repeated and, it is hoped, cumulatively persuasive illustration. It is best tested through the detailed textual interpretation of each individual play—an approach that avoids the danger of discussing single terms in isolation from their contexts and the equal danger of generalizing about the ideology implicit in "Greek tragedy." Within the scope of a single tragedy it is possible to see issues made vivid through ethos and example, subjected to the challenges and debates that are intrinsic to the structure of Greek drama. The rather amorphous notion of "democratic ideology" acquires shape from the thematic material particular to each play, while the text itself acts as a control against unwarranted schematization.

It is a common complaint that Euripides resists critical generalizations; unpredictability, it has been said, is the single constant of his work.[46] No one would have the temerity to claim that any selection of Euripides' plays is "representative." Rather, the five plays here chosen for analysis illustrate a spectrum of Euripides' political thought. While each of the tragedies stakes out its own political ground, collectively they will be seen to display an outlook so consistent that it may fairly be taken as Euripides' own.

The plays also share a certain consistency of subject matter. Each has a starting point eminently traditional and entirely characteristic of tragedy as a genre: an encounter with *Ananke* or necessity.[47] Necessity might be described as a grim subset of *Tyche* or Fortune, that well-known wrecker of mortal plans and expectations.[48] Whereas *Tyche* was merely unpredictable, *Ananke* was unfavorable almost by definition. At a minimum it entailed compulsion, at its worst it imposed fearful suffering and loss. *Ananke* recommends itself to the dramatist, however, as a point of departure—not just for its emotional potential, but because it sets the stage for ethical reconsideration. Whereas human beings at the height of prosperity have no reason to question the standards that have contributed to their success, misfortune brings a new thoughtfulness and often a change of heart—if not for the victims themselves, at least for the spectators of their suffering.

For Euripides the most fundamental aspect of *Ananke* is mortality itself, which forms the subject of the *Alcestis*. Others are war (*Hecuba*, *Trojan Women*) and divine hostility (*Hippolytus*, *Heracles*). Euripides takes advantage of the opening provided by *Ananke* to draw together the ethical and the political and to suggest—always in the indirect and allusive manner of tragedy—a series of lessons to the Athenians. He incorporates into his tragedies a modified set of standards for the democratic age. It is this process that forms the subject of this study.

NOTES

1. *Poetics* 1450b7–8. The translation is Halliwell's (1987). This passage raises two related questions: which poets does Aristotle include among the *archaioi*, and what is implied by the antithesis *politikōs/rhētorikōs*? That the "older poets" both here and at 1453b27 must include Euripides, for reasons both chronological and stylistic, was demonstrated by Denniston 1929. It is a mark of the pervasive influence of the nineteenth-century view of Euripides as a case apart from Aeschylus and Sophocles that both Else 1957 and Lucas 1968 are inclined to exclude Euripides from the company of the *archaioi* even though both cite Denniston and acknowledge the force of his arguments (Else 418, n. 29; Lucas *ad* 1453b27). Lucas *ad* 1450b8 suggests that *politikos* "implies a less exclusive interest in persuasiveness and point scoring" and singles out Euripides as partic-

ularly "rhetorical"—a characterization that helps explain his inclination to group Euripides among the *neoi*. Yet Lucas also acknowledges that "there is some overlap between" the two categories of "political" and "rhetorical." That is, he seems to recognize that for the *archaioi* political content was inseparable from its rhetorical expression—as is in fact the case for all three tragedians. For the connection between the element of "thought" and rhetorical argument see Halliwell 1986, 154–55, and 1987, 96.

2. For discussion and additional Aristotelian references see Else 1957, 265–66, and Macleod 1982, 132.

3. *Frogs* 1054–55. This translation follows Stanford 1958 in taking *hostis* as equivalent to *hos* and *didaskalos* as its antecedent.

4. The point emerges even more clearly at 1026, where Aristophanes juxtaposes both senses of *didaskein* in one line.

5. Woodbury 1986, 248–49. He notes that Aristophanes is the first specifically to link poetry with the term *didaskein*, and discusses changes in the concept of "teaching" and "teachers," linked to the activity of the sophists, that may have contributed to this development. For the didactic role assigned to Homer by later tradition and some overtly didactic elements discoverable in the Homeric texts, see Verdenius 1970. For a thoughtful general discussion of poetry and teaching in the Greek tradition see Blundell 1989, 12–15.

6. "Didactic theory" is adopted as a pejorative label by Heath 1987; invoking Aristotle, Heath defines the primary aim of drama as the production of emotive enjoyment (9–10 and passim). Heath's work is an important corrective to the tendency (which I cannot claim to have escaped) to assess the plays as if they were intellectual treatises while scanting their emotional, visual, and auditory effect. But Heath seems to stretch the evidence when, in establishing a literary genealogy for his "hedonistic poetics," he suggests that Hesiod's Muses link the pleasurable closely with the fictional (5–6). In order to attack the "didactic theory," he must insist on an increasingly strained differentiation between the hypothetically noneducational intentions of the dramatists and the indubitably educational effects of their plays (44–47, 72–78). Heath's own summary of the theory he seeks to demolish (39–44) shows how widely it was accepted in antiquity. Finally, Aristotle's *Poetics* can be interpreted to take into account the moral or didactic element (cf. Halliwell 1986). Heath does not convince me that the playwrights did not aim at instruction at once through intellectual and emotional means.

7. For the quotation and analogy see de Ste Croix 1972, 357. Cf. also Forrest 1985, 231.

8. For Aristophanes' view of tragedy, ingeniously inferred from his comments on comedy, see Taplin 1983.

9. The rapidity of these developments and the stabilizing influence of tragedy is stressed by Meier 1988, 31 ff.

10. For a full account of the circumstances of production see Pickard-Cambridge 1968, 79–99. The connection between tragedy and the democratic context is stressed by Rösler 1980, 8 ff.; cf. also Longo 1990.

11. The three liturgies are listed together by [Xen.] *Ath. Pol.* 1.13.

12. For an account of these festivals see Cartledge 1985; also Burkert 1985, 225–46. With the exception of the "festivals of inversion" (Burkert, 231; he includes the women's festivals of Skira, Arrephoria, and Thesmophoria, and the slaves' festival of Kronia) they involved the entire population.

13. The question of the makeup of the audience is controversial: some scholars (e.g., Wilson 1982, 158–59) still deny that women and slaves attended the theater. There is, however, no statement in the ancient sources that women and slaves were not included in the audience, and there is at least one unambiguous statement that they were (*Gorgias* 502d6, where Plato says that the theater is "a type of rhetoric directed to the *dēmos*, which consists at once of children and women and men, and slaves and free"). The evidence is collected and discussed by Pickard-Cambridge 1968, 263–66. Whether there was anything like proportional representation of each sector of the population is, of course, a matter of sheer guesswork. Rösler 1980 contends that the majority of the audience consisted of (male) urban, middle-class citizens; Meier 1988, 8 ff., stresses tragedy's special relevance to the (male) citizen body. Winkler 1985 posits the ephebes as both chorus and target audience, although to make his argument he must blur drama's earliest manifestations with its developed fifth-century form.

14. For the contrast between the audiences of oratory and tragedy see Ober and Strauss 1990, 238–39.

15. For Athenian liberalism see Thuc. 2.37.2, 2.39.1–2. For the conduct of the audience see Pickard-Cambridge 1968, 272–73. For the admonitions delivered by the dramatists cf. *Frogs* 1009–10.

16. The term is used by Goldhill 1987, among others. Goldhill does not provide a definition of "ideology," but seems to use it in the same sense of "unofficial belief system" as does Ober (1989, 38–40), who offers several working definitions, and Henderson (1990, 277–78).

17. For the context of the festival see Pickard-Cambridge 58–59; also Goldhill 1987, 60–61.

18. Goldhill 1987 sees the preliminary rituals (including, in addition to the display of tribute and the parade of orphans, the libations to Dionysus poured by the ten generals and the crowning of benefactors of the polis) as involving purely "a projection of power" (61), with a contrasting questioning and "transgressive" element (68–69) provided by the plays. Meier's analysis (1988, 68–70) is in my view more exact: he draws attention to the emphasis on sacrifice as well as on power implicit in the opening ceremonies.

19. Cf. the comments of Meier 1988, 242, on the shallowness of the search for topical references characteristic of many "political" interpretations of tragedy, and the rather too broad and deep generalities of the school of Vernant. Meier's own thesis that tragedy operates at the level of "nomological knowing" (set forth briefly in 1983, 154 ff., and developed in 1988, 43 ff.) is compelling, although his own analyses of the individual tragedies of Aeschylus and Sophocles remain rather general. He does not discuss Euripides.

20. Cf. Taplin 1986, 167: "I would strongly maintain that Greek tragedy is through and through political, in the sense that it is much concerned with the

life of men and women within society, the *polis*, but that this particular concern does not necessarily involve any direct reference to the immediate politicking of the Athenian audience at any one particular time." The latter hypothesis was painstakingly and ingeniously applied to the plays of Euripides by Delebecque 1951 and Goossens 1962. In a more subtle but, in my view, equally untenable modification of this position, di Benedetto 1971 posits an emotional development in Euripides directly related to the progress of the Peloponnesian War.

21. These and other structural contrasts between tragedy and comedy are discussed by Taplin 1977, 130–34, and 1986.

22. Aeschylus' *Persians* is of course the exception. It is the only surviving example of historical tragedy – an experiment evidently soon abandoned as too harrowing for the audience. That, at least, is the reason suggested by Herodotus' account (6.21.2) of the production of Phrynichus' *Capture of Miletus*, which led to the banning of the play and the fining of its author.

23. Zuntz 1955, 5. His study of *Suppliants* and *Children of Heracles* remains exemplary.

24. This paragraph summarizes the suggestive and influential position set forth by Vernant 1970, 283, and Vernant and Vidal-Naquet 1981, 4–5 and 9–10.

25. It will be apparent that this summary is based on Adkins 1960, 5–7, and passim; also 1972, 10–21, and passim. (Adkins' account in turn builds on the work of E. R. Dodds, as noted by Garner 1987, 11). Adkins' study of the interplay between "competitive" and "cooperative" standards as reflected in literature from Homer to Aristotle has been criticized on the grounds that he ignores the overlap between the two systems (Long 1970, 123–25) and discusses isolated terms without sufficient reference to their contexts (Dover 1983, 38–40). Nevertheless Adkins' criteria, under one guise or another, underlie most of the discussions of Greek ethical thought that have appeared over the last twenty-five years – including the anthropological approach of Vernant and Vidal-Naquet, which has so largely eclipsed Adkins' lexical analysis (cf. Vernant 1970, 283, on the "confrontation of two systems of value"), and the sociological methodology of Ober (cf. Ober/Strauss 1990, 243, on "the conflict between the values of competition and consensus"). Adkins' contribution to the continuing discussion of Greek values deserves to be recognized; his categories remain useful, I believe, as a basis for analysis so long as they are deployed with caution.

26. For the different morality of the two Homeric poems see Reinhardt 1960, 14–15. For adaptations of Homer in lyric poetry see Murray 1980, 126–31.

27. For the Greeks' awareness of this process of linguistic transvaluation cf. Thuc. 3.82.4–83.6; also Eur. *Hec.* 608 and Plat. *Rep.* 560e.

28. For Cleisthenes see Meier 1983, 91–143. For a discussion of Athenian social organization see Vickers 1973, 106–9, and Fisher 1976, 5–30.

29. For the institution see Arist. *Ath. Pol.* 22.

30. Cf. [Xen.] *Ath. Pol.* 1.2. Having stated that it is the men who serve in the navy who give strength to the polis, the author goes on to note that the *dēmos* sensibly does not attempt to gain control of the highest military offices

(1.3). Since the generalships and cavalry commands were decided by election, not lot, and since literary and epigraphic evidence from the fifth and fourth centuries confirms that these offices were dominated by members of aristocratic families (cf. Davies 1981, 122–24), critics both ancient and modern have questioned whether the real power did in fact lie with the people (for discussion see Ober 1989, 20–21). It remains, however, undeniable that the *dēmos* enjoyed far more authority under Athenian democracy than under any other ancient political system. Sinclair 1988, 221, reasonably concludes that the system worked because of its "balance and perspective. . . . Athenians . . . seem to have been content with the possession of power and with the exercise of it in ways that enabled them to employ the talents of ambitious individuals while keeping their leaders under close scrutiny. . . . " Ober's study (focusing, however, on the fourth century) shows how the public discourse of the orators helped maintain this balance.

31. The urgency of the Athenians' need for tragedy is emphasized, even overstated, by Meier 1988, 7 ff.

32. For an excellent critique of this tendency see Kovacs 1987, 9 ff. Kovacs insists on the importance of reading Euripides "straight" and relating his concerns to the rest of the tragic tradition. Although I do not share his view of Euripides as an artist who is nowhere ironical and everywhere conservative, and I differ also (as detailed in the notes to Chapters 2 and 3) on individual points of interpretation, I concur with his general approach.

33. Reinhardt 1957 has been influential in shaping the received view of the alienated Euripides. Cf. de Romilly 1986, 5–17 and 221–26, for a lucid discussion of Euripides' "modernity" from the perspective of his own time and ours.

34. For the influence of comedy and Euripidean tragedy on the biographical tradition see Lefkowitz 1979.

35. See Behler 1986 for an account of the origins of this evaluation in the writings of the brothers Schlegel, and Henrichs 1986 for the contribution of Nietzsche. Michelini 1987 gives a perceptive account of trends in Euripidean scholarship in the nineteenth and twentieth centuries, while herself succumbing to the temptation to set up Sophocles as the norm against which Euripides reacted (54–55 and passim). But Euripides can scarcely be convicted of violating the norms of a tradition that was still in the making at the time he was producing his plays. He himself did much to form it, and in fact exerted a more decisive influence on the subsequent history of the genre than did either Aeschylus or Sophocles.

36. For Aeschylus cf. Aristoph. *Ach.* 10–12, where Dicaeopolis describes his emotion upon seeing a play of Aeschylus and the scholiast confirms that there were revivals of Aeschylean tragedy; also *Frogs* 868–69, where Aeschylus remarks that his own poetry has not died with him, whereas Euripides' has.

37. The canonical grouping is noted by Halliwell 1987, 4, n. 3., citing *Frogs* 785–94. Aristotle too tends to link the three tragedians, especially Sophocles and Euripides: cf. *Poetics* 1453b28–31, 1454b31–36, 1455a18, 1456a25–32. (This is not to deny that Aristotle prefers Sophocles to Euripides, only to point out that he tends to discuss them as a pair. For the vexed question of the identity of

hoi archaioi in the *Poetics*, see n. 1 above.) Halliwell 1986, 10, concludes that Aristotle manifests "a relative lack of interest in Aeschylus' work . . . [and] a positive admiration for the work of *both* the other major fifth-century tragedians (more qualified, but still strong, in the case of Euripides). . . . "

38. For discussion of political elements in Aeschylus and Sophocles respectively, see Macleod 1982 and Knox 1983.

39. The absence of such a synthesis is noted by A. H. M. Jones 1957, 42, who proceeds to reconstruct one on the basis of the hostile assessments of democracy that do survive. Farrar 1988 attempts an account of early democratic thinking based on Thucydides and the fragments of Anaxagoras and Democritus.

40. Thuc. 2.35–46. For a schematic representation of democratic *topoi* see Loraux 1986, 181.

41. For a catalog of such passages see Butts 1947, 171–75. On *Suppliants* see Zuntz 1955, Collard 1975A, and Burian 1985; for *Children of Heracles*, see Zuntz 1955 and Burian 1977.

42. On *Ion* the best studies are those of Walsh 1978 and Loraux 1981B. Euben 1985 focuses on the theme of political corruption in *Orestes*, and Kovacs 1987 discusses "dynasts and democrats" in *Hecuba*. De Ste Croix 1972, 356 n. 1, makes a typical selection of "political" passages in Euripides. In addition to the plays mentioned above he lists the praise of equality in *Phoenician Women*, the discussion of wealth as a criterion of worth in *Electra*, and the anti-Spartan sentiments of *Andromache*.

43. De Ste Croix 1972, 16–17, discusses the different ethical standards implicit in Thucydides' account of internal and external affairs.

44. At *Ach.* 642. As Norwood 1930 demonstrates, it is rash to conclude from the slight and scattered ancient evidence that the *Babylonians* portrayed the allies as branded slaves. That the comedy was sharply critical of Athenian treatment of the allies is, however, implicit in *Ach.* 500–503.

45. Cf. the classic discussion by Knox 1957, 53–77.

46. Whitman 1974, v.

47. For chance and necessity as themes of Greek tragedy, see Arrowsmith 1959, 54, and Conacher 1967, 3–4.

48. See Nussbaum 1986 for a far-ranging study of *tychē* in the moral thought of Plato, Aristotle, and the tragedians.

1

Alcestis

The relationship of life and death seems to have been a recurrent preoccupation with Euripides. "Who knows if life is really death," runs a fragment from the *Polyidus* (638 N^2), "while death is viewed as life down below?" Two other fragments from lost plays echo similar sentiments.[1] The topic was so closely identified with Euripides that Aristophanes could parody it in the *Frogs* (1477–78) with a crescendo of improbable identities: "Who knows if life is really death, breath brunch, and sleep a sheepskin?"

Although we have no way of knowing how the theme of life as death was developed in the lost *Polyidus*, *Phrixus*, or *Erechtheus*, there can be no doubt of its centrality to the *Alcestis*. Euripides constructs the *Alcestis* around a suspension of the normal operations of death, the better to demonstrate the advantages of the usual arrangement. In so doing he recasts a lesson from Homer for the uses of the democratic polis: if the *Iliad* assumes that mortality is a precondition for heroism, the *Alcestis* will teach that it is essential to ordinary existence as well. He also borrows a theme from Pindar and Bacchylides, transferring the adjuration to live for the day, so typical of the epinician genre, to a context that charges it with newly egalitarian meaning.

The final choral ode of the *Alcestis* is a meditation on the necessity of death. There is nothing more powerful than *Anankē*, the members of the chorus affirm. Neither magic Orphic formulas nor herbal medicines—"the drugs that Apollo gave to the sons of Asclepius" (970–71)—have ever prevailed against it.

These words are emphatic and seem to admit of no exception. At the same time they stand in contradiction both to the premise of the play—which is that Admetus, for one, has the power to evade his death if he can only find a substitute—and to the final episode, in which Admetus' proxy Alcestis is recovered from the underworld, and Death, or Necessity, seems doubly defeated.

The inconsistency leads to the heart of this much-disputed play. For all its sharply observed psychological detail, the *Alcestis* is neither a character study nor the portrait of a marriage.[2] For all its admixture of grotesquerie it is not a "pro-satyric" drama—a genre unmentioned by the ancients and devised by modern criticism to categorize this single play.[3] Death and its relation to life are the true subjects of the drama—a tale set in the realm of a mythical Thessaly and played out in the private domain, but resonating against the political and social concerns of fifth-century Athens.

Since mortality is its subject, the play demands to be viewed in the context of the assumptions about death transmitted by epic and lyric poetry. It is impossible to overstate the influence on tragedy of the literary tradition, which was regularly evoked by the dramatists themselves in the form of quotation, allusion, or paraphrase, and which furnished them not only with plot material but with an entire worldview to be adopted or modified, rebuked or extolled.[4] The critic seeking to identify the distinctive contribution of each dramatist is well advised to keep in mind the pervasive influence of tradition and to be on the alert, accordingly, not so much for novelty as for the selection, adaptation, or displacement of traditional motifs.

The Necessity of Death

By intuition and common understanding, death for the Greeks meant not only the end but also the opposite of life. Death was dark, unchanging, and eternal; life was luminous, mutable, and finite. The Greeks recognized mortality as the most fundamental of the constraints set on human beings. On the level of etymology it was what differentiated human beings from the gods: mortals (*thnētoi, brotoi*) were subject to extinction, while the gods (*athanatoi, ambrotoi*) could never die.[5] On the level of experience, the fact that human existence was marked off by death was understood to have profound implications for the way mortals lived their lives. Mortality made demands—and offered opportunities—the undying gods could never know.

A number of basic statements about mortality recur in the archaic texts. Death, it is said, is inevitable, irreversible, and unpredictable.[6] These characteristics, familiar and obvious though they may seem, require constant reiteration. They flicker in and out of human consciousness; only in flashes is death apprehended as personal terminus. At such moments the facts of death, no matter how well known, present themselves as utterly fresh and shocking.

In Book 9 of the *Iliad*, Achilles reflects the overwhelming impact of a personal intuition of mortality as he explains to a delegation of his fellow Greeks why he does not intend to rejoin the fighting around Troy. All the heroes understand the risks of the battlefield, but Achilles moves from that understanding to an unexpected conclusion:

Fate is the same for the man who holds back, the same if he
    fights hard.
We are all held in a single honour, the brave with the weaklings.
A man dies still if he has done nothing, as one who has done
    much.[7]

It has been freshly brought home to Achilles that all men must die. As a corollary, he concludes that death annuls the honor and glory gained through individual effort and reduces everyone to the same estate. He sees no reason, therefore, to continue furnishing proofs of his heroism by the deeds of valor that his society anticipates, that Odysseus has just requested of him, and that he has up to this point also demanded of himself. Instead, he is inclined to abandon the war and sail home to Thessaly, where he can live out his life in tranquillity, if without honor.

Another factor in Achilles' decision not to fight is the realization that death is a permanent condition. Other heroes find some compensation for the risks they incur in the prospect of material honor in life and glory in death, but Achilles sees no mitigation (*Il.* 9.405–9):

                        Of possessions
cattle and fat sheep are things to be had for the lifting,
and tripods can be won, and the tawny high heads of horses,
but a man's life cannot come back again, it cannot be lifted
nor captured again by force, once it has crossed the teeth's
    barrier.

As we shall see, Achilles' vision of death as a leveller is not conventional for his society. Even for Achilles, the impulse to choose long life over glory is quickly abandoned. By the close of the scene he has modified his position and has agreed to stay on at Troy, and eventually he will rejoin the fighting with an eye to "noble glory" (*Il.* 18.121), even though he knows that he is hastening his own death thereby. Achilles' reply to Odysseus was, however, one of the best-known passages in the *Iliad*, and it is possible that ancient audiences, like modern readers, remembered the hero's initial threat more vividly than his subsequent retraction.[8] Euripides, at any rate, seems to have kept Achilles' vision in mind when he came to shape his own portrayal of death in the *Alcestis*.

For Achilles as for other, lesser mortals, death is inevitable and irreversible. He is, however, unique in being able to foresee the circumstances of his own death: his mother, Thetis, has warned him that he will die if he stays at Troy, but enjoy a long and peaceful life if he returns home (*Il.* 9.410–16). For this reason Achilles does not draw attention to the third attribute of death frequently attested in archaic texts: its unpredictability.

The Greeks had a clear conception of what constituted a normal life span: Solon (27 [West]) puts it at seventy, and goes on to list the activities and abilities characteristic of each decade. But everyone knew that there could be no guarantee of living out a normal span of years: all too often a loved one would die untimely.[9] This consideration contributes to that wistful sense of tenuousness that often finds its way into archaic texts. A man will die when the Fates so dispose, warns Callinus (1.8–15); it is possible to escape from battle unscathed only to die at home. "We live," says Semonides, "like beasts, just for the day, not knowing how the god will bring each thing to its end."[10] And in a passage that will leave its mark on the *Alcestis*, Bacchylides (3.78–84) advocates a double perspective for mortals. A man, he says, should imagine at once that the next day will be his last, and that he has fifty years of prosperity still ahead.

Imagined Alternatives

Iteration of the facts of mortality represented one way to come to terms with death. Another response was to imagine alternatives — ways of modifying death's characteristics or even eluding it altogether. Death might, for instance, be envisaged as predictable. So it was in the past, according to Aeschylus; once upon a time human beings could predict their own demise, until Prometheus took away that foresight and put "blind hope" in its place.[11] Alternatively, death might be construed as an outcome to be avoided by ingenious individuals acting either on their own behalf or another's. Mythology is rich in examples: there is Odysseus who traveled to the underworld on his way home from Troy, Sisyphus who succeeded in putting Death in chains, Theseus who descended alive to Hades to rescue his friend Pirithous, Heracles who fetched the dog Cerberus up to the world of the living, Orpheus who tried unsuccessfully to rescue his wife Eurydice, and Asclepius whose skill extended to reviving the dead, until Zeus put a decisive end to his medical career.[12] On a less fanciful plane, the same impulse to get the better of death may be reflected in the conceit that the hero will win "undying fame," *kleos aphthiton*, through outstanding accomplishment. Some part of him at least will be immortal: his reputation will survive even though his body has perished.[13]

Such imaginative evasions suggest that the Greeks felt considerable antipathy toward death. Death was the one deity who lacked a cult; he is "pitiless/," according to Homer, "and therefore he among all the gods is most hateful to mortals."[14] However, death does not invariably wear a hateful aspect. Solon reckons that death at seventy is appropriate, even seasonable.[15] And when life becomes unendurable through disgrace or misfortune, sickness or suffering, death is viewed as a remedy and invoked as healer or *Paean*.[16] Moreover, at least one notable Homeric passage makes the point that the prospect of death is instrumental in shaping a noble life. As the Trojan warrior Sarpedon exhorts his friend Glaucus before battle, he suggests that there is an indissoluble relationship between mortality and heroic accomplishment (*Il.* 12.322–28):

> Man, supposing you and I, escaping this battle,
> would be able to live on forever, ageless, immortal,
> so neither would I myself go on fighting in the foremost
> nor would I urge you into the fighting where men win glory.
> But now, seeing that the spirits of death stand close about us
> in their thousands, no man can turn aside nor escape them,
> let us go on and win glory for ourselves, or yield it to others.

We might expect Sarpedon to argue that men with nothing to fear would display conspicuous bravery in battle. In fact he maintains the opposite: that if noblemen like Glaucus and himself were set free from the prospect of death they would feel no impulse to distinguish themselves by "fighting in the foremost." Sarpedon's perspective on mortality is different from Achilles'; he voices the conventional assumptions that Achilles in Book 9 at least temporarily rejects.[17] For Sarpedon the inevitability of death acts as a spur to heroic action, for he assumes (in contrast to Achilles) that death is hierarchical, fixing the distinctions that were operative in life. It is precisely the threat of extinction that induces men to take risks that may indeed culminate in death, but will also define a life worth living, a life worth remembering. Sarpedon testifies that without the prospect of death, heroes would have no impetus to behave like heroes.

Technē and Tychē

Undying fame represented, at best, only a symbolic victory over death. For the most part the archaic tradition affirmed that death was inescapable, while also furnishing a few examples of mythological characters who managed to escape the common fate through sheer ingenuity.[18] But as the archaic sensibility gave way to the classical, ingenuity came to be perceived as characteristic not just of a few gifted individuals but of the entire human race.

This ingenuity found its clearest expression in a capacity for self-improvement. Traditional Greek thought—reflected, for example, in Hesiod's myth of the Five Ages—saw the generations of mankind as deteriorating from an initial Golden Race.[19] Fifth-century philosophers like Protagoras and Democritus, however, gave a different account. They surmised that mortal existence must have begun on a rudimentary and primitive level, with human beings themselves bringing about improvements over time. In the beginning, according to these revisionist theories, men discovered only the crudest solutions for their most pressing needs: agriculture furnished them with a consistent food supply, fire with a source of heat, clothes and housing with protection against the elements. Later, from a surplus of resources, they developed other arts or *technai*.[20]

To those who adopted this hopeful and progressive point of view, it seemed at least conceivable that human beings could find ways to better all aspects of their condition—that they could learn, in the catchword of the time, to control Fortune, *Tychē*, by means of ingenuity, *Technē*.[21] As the question of the limits of such efforts arose, mortality presented itself as a not altogether fanciful test case. If inventiveness could find an antidote for every natural ill, might even death be brought under human control?

That conservative thinkers viewed such speculations with deep disquiet is suggested by a choral ode of Sophocles' *Antigone*. In that play, produced some three years prior to the *Alcestis*, Sophocles couples the praise of human achievements that had become a commonplace of sophistic thought with a traditional caution against ingenuity gone astray.

The first stasimon of the *Antigone* takes the form of a catalog of human development. Human beings have mastered the sea with ships and the earth with plows; they have snared the birds of the air and the fish of the sea, and tamed the wild animals of the mountains. Nor is human accomplishment limited to domination of the environment. Men have also developed social skills: language, judgment, the arts of government. So much progress has been made that only death remains unconquered, and even here medicine has done much to push back the frontiers. The real danger, as Sophocles' chorus sees it, is that man in his cleverness will overstep the boundary between good and evil:

> He can always help himself.
> He faces no future helpless. There's only death
> that he cannot find an escape from. He has contrived
> refuge from illnesses once beyond all cure.
>
> Clever beyond all dreams
> the inventive craft he has
> which may drive him one time or another to well or ill.
> When he honors the laws of the land and the gods' sworn right
> high indeed is his city; but stateless the man
> who dares to dwell with dishonor. Not by my fire,
> never to share my thoughts, who does those things.[22]

Only in passing does Sophocles allude to death as a test case for human *technē*. But Euripides takes up the notion in the *Alcestis* (as he does certain other motifs adumbrated in the *Antigone*) and establishes it as central to his own very different play.[23] Like Sophocles, Euripides draws together the themes of *technē* and *tychē*, medicine and mortality.

Apollo opens the *Alcestis* by apostrophizing the palace of Admetus and recounting the chain of circumstances that brought him to Thessaly (lines 1–9 of the Greek):

> O house of Admetus, in which I submitted, god though I
> was, to lead a servant's life. Zeus is the cause, for he
> killed my son Asclepius by hurling a thunderbolt at his
> breast. Angered at this, I killed the Cyclopes, who
> manufacture Zeus' fire. And he compelled me in recompense
> to be a servant in the house of a mortal. Coming to this
> land, I acted as herdsman for my host, and I have kept
> this household safe until this hour.

Why did Zeus kill Asclepius? Apollo does not say, but the audience would have known the answer from tradition.[24] The members of the chorus, moreover, provide an explanation later in the play: "[Asclepius] raised the dead to life, until the bolt of lightning sent by Zeus destroyed him" (127–29). By this action Zeus came to the aid of Fate or Necessity, whose authority had been challenged by Asclepius' all too efficacious interventions.

Asclepius' death set in motion a series of acts of requital: Apollo killed the Cyclopes, and was then compelled by Zeus to put in a term as Admetus' servant. The juxtaposition of Asclepius' story with Admetus', and Apollo's involvement in both, gives a hint that the action of the *Alcestis* will represent one more stage in the continuing vendetta of Zeus and Apollo.[25] By "tricking the Fates" (12) into offering Admetus an escape from death, Apollo is once more challenging the power of Necessity. The prologue suggests that the play will investigate the place of death in the mortal scheme of things—a problem left unresolved by Asclepius' abruptly terminated career.

As Apollo explains his bargain with the Fates in the play's opening lines, the audience is given to understand that the conventional attributes of death have been suspended. The narrative offers no inducement to the audience to dwell on the precise details of Apollo's arrangement; it is not explained, for example, whether Admetus has received his wife's allotted span of days in exchange for his old term or whether he has been granted a new, revised life expectancy all his own. What is made clear, however, is that the Thanatos of the *Alcestis*

is no longer inevitable, unpredictable and irreversible. For the duration of the play Death will be subject to variation: both predictable and
avoidable for Admetus, predictable but unavoidable for Alcestis, yet
ultimately reversible for her. Different characters have been permitted
to choose different deaths, and the question of eligibility has become
a subject of intense negotiation and debate. Apollo has maneuvered
the normally impartial Death into the role of arbiter.

This alteration in the ways of death has unforeseen but rigorously
logical results for the characters' continuing lives. We have noted that
death is by intuition and common understanding the opposite of life.
As soon, therefore, as death becomes subject to variation, life as if by
reflex begins to lose its distinguishing characteristics. Normal categories are thrown into confusion; motives, judgments, circumstances,
conditions become mingled with their opposites, or blurred with intermediate positions. It is no longer possible to differentiate friends from
enemies, sickness from sacrifice, heroism from cowardice, favor from
betrayal. The result of this breakdown of the normal order is finally to
render life not worth living; it becomes, in fact, indistinguishable from
death itself. Such is the process that the action illustrates—a process
set in motion as Alcestis lies dying, and gathering momentum in the
aftermath of her loss.[26]

When Apollo informs the audience that he has won Admetus a reprieve from imminent death and persuaded the Fates to accept a substitute victim, it appears that death has been civilized, becoming a matter of prearrangement and consent. Contrivance or *Technē* can go no
further. And having won this much, Apollo is half-hopeful of repeat-
ing his success. As he attempts to convince Thanatos to yield up Alcestis, he addresses him in the language of polished social intercourse. He
mentions exchange, persuasion, delay, money, and an interchange of
favors (46, 48, 50, 56, 60).

Thanatos, however, proves intransigent. He is suspicious of Apollo
from the outset. What is he doing hovering around the palace, he
wonders; was it not enough for him to "trip up the Fates with deceitful
contrivance" (33–34) that he now intends to deprive Death of a second
victim (43)? He accuses Apollo of aristocratic sympathies.[27] "You lay
down the law in favor of the wealthy," he remarks, after Apollo has
suggested that Alcestis will receive a more lavish burial if permitted to
live to old age. He rudely refuses to grant any further favors and

speaks, in contrast to Apollo, the categorical language of necessity (49, 53, 61, 63). Trick or bargain, whichever it was, Admetus' escape from death is an exception that Thanatos is determined not to repeat.[28]

By the end of their dialogue Apollo has lost patience with his gloomy interlocutor. Abandoning his gracious and cajoling manner, he angrily predicts that Thanatos will eventually be compelled to yield up Alcestis to a guest-friend of Admetus. Thanatos will thus lose Alcestis and gain Apollo's enmity into the bargain, when he could have earned his gratitude by yielding to his persuasion (64–71). Apollo's references to Eurystheus and Thracian horses point unmistakably to Heracles, but it is unclear from his tone whether he is indulging in angry bluster or unerring prophecy.[29] In any case Thanatos remains unruffled, and it is he who has the last word — a fact whose significance should be kept in mind for the end of the play.[30]

The Status of Alcestis

Apollo has clearly done his utmost for his favorite Admetus. Yet his initial intervention with the Fates sets in train the loss of distinctions that will transform Admetus' life, and shape the play. The effects are immediately apparent as the members of the chorus, entering on the heels of Apollo and Thanatos, express confusion as to whether Alcestis is alive or dead. They cannot interpret the silence around the palace (77–78). If Alcestis were dead they would expect sounds of lamentation, but they hear nothing (86–88, 103–4). Nor have the ritual bowl of water and lock of hair been set on the threshold to signify that death has taken place (98–103). Despite these omissions, the members of the chorus still suspect that Alcestis is dead, for this is the "appointed day" (*kyrion ēmar*, 105).

The chorus' initial questions and their subsequent dialogue with the maid follow up on the previous conversation of Apollo and Thanatos. Both gods and mortals are uncertain of the exact terms of Alcestis' sacrifice. In the first blurring of categories that this extraordinary event will induce, the customary dividing line between life and death has been put into question. Alcestis may indeed be alive, but can one call a person alive when there is no hope (130–31, 135) of her continued existence? "You could say," remarks the maid, "that she is both alive and dead" (141). What in another context would be merely an emphatic way of expressing the seriousness of Alcestis' condition becomes something more in this context, where the point at issue is the relationship between life and death. The maid seems to be hinting that events normally successive have become simultaneous.

Her paradox will be repeated with more conscious obfuscation by Admetus. In order to convince Heracles to accept his hospitality he needs to mislead him about Alcestis' status; accordingly he returns evasive answers to Heracles' inquiries. Alcestis, he asserts, is "alive, yet also no more" (521). When Heracles expresses bewilderment Admetus reminds him of Alcestis' offer to sacrifice herself. "How can she be still alive," he demands (525), "when she has agreed to this course?" Finally he instructs Heracles that "the one about to die is already dead, the one who has perished is no more" (527).

What Admetus is saying is not merely deceptive and not merely nonsensical. His formulations and the maid's represent an attempt to wrench language into conveying an elusive insight. When the future has become as certain as the present it casts its shadow over the present and even begins to merge with it. The fundamental distinction between the present as known, the future as unknown, is effaced; and with that development the boundaries between life (which is, after all, everybody's present) and death (which is everybody's future) also start to blur. Such an alteration in the conditions of human existence points to a real difficulty in Apollo's arrangement. What was formerly a simple matter ("Life and death are generally held separate," says Heracles, 528) has become problematic.

Alcestis is the first to suffer from the loss of distinctions, as the nature of her act is obscured even before she has carried it to a conclusion. Alcestis' self-devotion was, above all, an act of free choice; the voluntary nature of her death constitutes her unique glory. Apollo reports that Admetus canvased all his *philoi*, his friends and relatives; all refused to take his place except Alcestis, who was willing (17). Her voluntary sacrifice proves her the best of women, says the maid; how could anyone show one's husband more honor than by being willing to die for him (154–55)? Alcestis herself emphasizes the free nature of her choice: "I am dying, when it is possible for me not to die" (284). Admetus points out to Heracles that Alcestis "assented" to her fate (525).

Yet this act of free will is simultaneously spoken of as ineluctable necessity. It is not simply that sacrifice was a choice in the past which, the decision once made, is one no longer. That explanation would ac-

count for the references made by Apollo, the chorus, and the servant
to the "destined day" of her death.[31] But it does not account for the
insistent juxtaposition of the motifs of free choice and necessity. Alcestis sounds like a heroine dying an involuntary death when she reflects
that "some god made this come about" (298), insists that she "has to
die" (320), laments to her children that she is "dying, when I ought to
live" (379), and says her last farewell to them "quite against my will"
(389).

The contradiction between free choice and necessity has not gone
unnoticed by those critics who interpret the *Alcestis* as a psychological
drama. Alcestis, they explain, was willing to sacrifice herself when the
opportunity first arose—at that time she was still a bride, deeply in
love with Admetus. By now, however, her love has cooled, and she
regrets her original choice.[32]

The difficulty with explanations of this sort is that they treat the dramatic characters as if they were real people with a history and a whole
range of emotions lying outside the text that can be invoked to account
for their conduct within it. In fact, if we wish to speculate about the
past or future of the mortal characters of tragedy we must limit our-
selves to the most rudimentary assumptions—that they have been
born, that they are destined to die. Otherwise we are entitled to draw
only on the information conveyed by the words, gestures, and actions
of the play.[33]

The juxtaposition of free choice and necessity, applied to one and
the same circumstance, is not unique to the *Alcestis*. It is a device used
by all the dramatists to draw attention to some ethical complexity un-
perceived by the protagonists, something opaque or problematical in
the situation at hand.[34] In the *Alcestis* the motif points to another intolerable consequence of Apollo's arrangement. Just as Alcestis is perceived simultaneously as alive and dead, so her act is adjudged simultaneously voluntary and involuntary, and this double vision has the
effect of robbing Alcestis of her unique glory. If making a virtue of
necessity enhances many a sacrificial heroine (Polyxena in the *Hecuba*,
for instance), making a necessity of virtue can only have the opposite
effect.

Related to the blurring of free choice and necessity is the play's
presentation of Alcestis' mode of death. Repeatedly the point is made
that Alcestis is dying on behalf of her husband, that she is, in short,
a substitute or sacrificial victim.[35] As Thanatos comes into view,

Apollo identifies him as "the priest of the dead" (25), and Thanatos later explains that he has journeyed to the palace to attend to the ritual dedication of his victim (75–76): "A person is sacred to the gods below, when once this sword has consecrated the hair of his head."

But even as Alcestis' death is recognized as sacrificial it is described in ways that carry entirely different connotations. Her condition is also likened to bodily illness. The verb *psychorragein*, "lie at the last gasp," is used first by Apollo and then by the maid (20, 143) to describe the queen; it conveys a sense of her extremity without indicating what might have brought her to that pass. But the maid and the members of the chorus also emphasize that Alcestis is "fading away in illness" (203, 236), and Alcestis herself complains of her weakness and of darkness before her eyes (267, 269, 385). The extraordinary nature of her act is lost sight of in such descriptions; she might be any invalid dying of a commonplace disease. The difficulty in description is partly linguistic: because there are no terms available to depict Alcestis' unique status, it can only be assimilated to other more familiar conditions. But if Alcestis' act is so difficult to describe, it may be also because there is no place for it in the human scheme of things.

Passing references to Alcestis, now as sacrificial victim and now as invalid, are scattered throughout the text and do not obtrude on the audience's attention. But the two motifs are placed in sharp and unmistakable juxtaposition in Alcestis' notorious dual death scene. Alcestis first appears on stage weak and fainting; she has emerged from the house, "still breathing, though barely," because she wants to see the sun one last time before she dies (205–6). Speaking in broken phrases and emotional lyric rhythms (Admetus, in contrast, answers her in ordinary iambic trimeter), she salutes the sun and the sky, the land and the palace before her as well as her childhood home in Iolcus, present to her mind's eye—everything that stands for the life she loves and is reluctant to leave. Suddenly more ominous sights encroach upon her vision. She sees the river of Acheron and Charon in his boat; he has come to fetch her and is angry at the delay (252–57). She sees the winged figure of Thanatos, blackbrowed and lowering (259–62). These are terrifying apparitions, and Alcestis has to contend with them alone. Admetus sees nothing of what she reports; he can only stand helplessly by, clutching his wife and imploring her not to leave him.

Alcestis says farewell to her children and announces her own demise, drawing a last despairing protest from her husband. But then her whole aspect changes. Seemingly on the verge of dying, she abruptly abandons lyric for trimeter and the visionary for the analytic mode. In a lengthy, tightly reasoned speech she sets forth her reasons for offering herself as a sacrifice and makes a request of Admetus in return: not to take another wife who might abuse her two children (300–308). Admetus answers as collectedly, addressing her concerns point by point. Alcestis then says her farewells a second time, and this time dies in good earnest.

A. M. Dale explains the discontinuities of this episode by appealing to the different conventions of lyric and dialogue:

> The thread of action does not necessarily run continuously through both [stage-lyric and dialogue] in a strict sequence of time. There are many scenes where a situation is realized first in its lyric, then in its iambic aspect—that is to say, first emotionally, then in its reasoned form.[36]

This explanation offers an important insight into Greek tragic usage, which Dale reinforces with references to other Euripidean characters: Cassandra in *Trojan Women*, Phaedra in *Hippolytus*. But in no other surviving play is the incongruity between lyric and dialogue so glaring. Unlike the other heroines cited by Dale, Alcestis is on the very threshold of death when she so abruptly regains logic and composure. Her change of mood violates at once emotional and chronological probability, and the discontinuity cannot be entirely attributed to the antinaturalistic conventions of Greek theater. The dual death scene reinforces the play's thematic motifs: by juxtaposing a lyric evocation of terrified delirium with an analytical account of freely chosen sacrifice, Euripides is once again drawing attention to the confusion of categories that follows upon Apollo's bargain with the Fates.

Alcestis' death is envisaged in yet another way: as suicide. The maid describes the preparations Alcestis made once she realized that her last day was at hand (157–95). She washed and clothed herself with elaborate care, addressed a prayer to Hestia, and then made the rounds of the household altars, wreathing each with myrtle. All this she accomplished "unweeping, unlamenting" (173), but broke down when she reached her bedroom. After sobbing out an emotional farewell to the marriage bed, she took leave of all the members of her household.

That the audience might associate this sequence of actions with suicide can be inferred from a similar description in Sophocles' *Trachiniae* (900–922). Just before she stabs herself Deianira wanders through the palace, lamenting to the servants and weeping before the altars. She enters the bedchamber and sinks down on the bed, which she apostrophizes in heartbroken tones. Deianira is far more distraught than Alcestis — understandably enough, since she is committing suicide in the conviction that she has betrayed her husband, whereas Alcestis is dying precisely because she has refused to do so (180). Nevertheless, the two scenes are remarkably similar in content and tone. Both heroines make careful preparations for a self-chosen death. Both mime rather than express in words the conjugal love that has brought them to this pass.

Other elements associated with Alcestis' death are reminiscent of the suicide of another Sophoclean hero. When Admetus begs Alcestis not to "abandon" himself and the children (*prodounai*, 202, 250, 275, cf. 388), and when in an effort to rally her energies he reminds her of how much she means to him (277–79), we are reminded of Tecmessa in the *Ajax*. Like Admetus, Tecmessa reminds Ajax of his familial responsibilities (*Ajax* 496–513). Like Admetus she affirms her dependence on her spouse (*Ajax* 514–19). Later in the scene she begs Ajax not to "abandon" her.[37]

It is understandable that Tecmessa should make these pleas to Ajax, but scarcely reasonable for Admetus to accuse his wife, who is after all dying on his behalf, of abandoning him.[38] Some critics have read childishness, selfishness, and neurosis into Admetus' failure to appreciate his wife's sacrifice. This scene is crucial to their interpretation of his character.[39]

Yet such a view of Admetus fails to take into account Greek tragedy's priorities and its conventions of characterization. Aristotle maintains, and the texts themselves confirm, that the focus of tragedy was primarily on the event.[40] The fact, moreover, that the tragic actors wore masks suggests that where the playwright did concern himself with character, it was less with individual personality than with representative types.[41] That is not to say that the personages of tragedy are without expressive characteristics: every tragedy will display a greater or lesser "elaborating and overlaying . . . in the cause of verisimilitude."[42] But we should not expect tragedy to specialize in the minute exploration of individual psychology; nor should we be content to find in some psychological aperçu the significance of a given scene.

Applying these considerations to the *Alcestis* means that Admetus' pleas to his dying wife should be examined not for the light they shed on his nature, but for their contribution to the play's overall design. Admetus' failure to recognize the nature of his wife's sacrifice coincides with the pattern of loss of distinctions. If Admetus can entertain the idea that Alcestis' death is a kind of suicide, it is because the meaning of her act is becoming progressively obscured. His implication to Heracles that Alcestis is not dead at all is the climax of a process of devaluation that began before her death.

Admetus' Mourning

Admetus as well as Alcestis falls victim to the erosion of distinctions attendant on Apollo's favor. The king meets his impending loss with a variety of reactions. On the one hand he begs his wife to hold out against death; on the other he tries to emulate her extraordinary sacrifice with an extravagant program of renunciation.[43] In a series of measures designed to keep Alcestis' memory alive he commits himself to an atmosphere at his court that rivals Hades itself for gloominess.

To start with, Admetus deprives himself now and for all future time of the sexual pleasure that was, for the Greeks, synonymous with life itself. "What is life, what is joy without golden Aphrodite?" wrote the poet Mimnermus. "May I die when such matters no longer count for me!"[44] Although Alcestis had asked Admetus not to remarry, she had not intended to rule out all sexual gratification, for she was able to imagine another woman, "surely no more virtuous, but perhaps more fortunate," occupying her place (181–82). Admetus, however, pledges himself to an empty bed with only a statue of Alcestis for company—"a cold pleasure," as he himself admits (353–54). He will do his utmost to abide by this promise, persistently refusing Heracles' offer of a beautiful young woman to share his house and bed.

Admetus also unduly extends the period of mourning. His arrangements are disproportionate by any measure. In the *Iliad* the funeral rites for Hector last eleven days; in fifth-century Athens the normal period of mourning was one month.[45] Admetus, however, banishes feasting and music from Pherae for a year (430–31), and he declares that he himself will never touch the lyre or sing to the flute (345–47). His grief will last, in fact, his entire life (336–37).

Such extravagance works at cross purposes to the normal function of funerary rites, which was to "keep the world of the living rigidly apart from that of the dead."[46] Ordinarily the dead were the objects of exclusive attention for a fixed period of time; afterwards the survivors put aside their mourning and got on with their lives. When Priam describes his plans for burying Hector, he is quite specific about this program (*Il.* 24.664–67):

> Nine days we would keep him in our palace and mourn him,
> and bury him on the tenth day, and the people feast by him,
> and on the eleventh day we would make the grave-barrow for
>   him,
> and on the twelfth day fight again; if so we must do.

By prolonging his mourning Admetus breaks down the distinction between living and dead, between city and cemetery, which funerary rites are normally designed to reinforce.

Admetus also suffers in his human associations. The confrontation between the king and his father suggests that he has lost not only his wife but also, effectively, his parents. Both Admetus and Alcestis had earlier blamed them for failing to volunteer in Admetus' place, and Admetus had assured his wife that he would live "hating my mother, detesting my father" (338–39). These are shocking words in a culture that placed a high premium on filial respect.[47] The subsequent quarrel between father and son shows that Admetus means what he says.

When Pheres appears to share his son's misfortune (as he puts it, 614), Admetus rounds on him with violent abuse. He points out that Pheres was not invited to this funeral and is not welcome now that he has come. It strikes him as the sheerest hypocrisy that Pheres should now be mourning the woman he could have saved, if only he had been willing to die himself. Pheres has shown himself so deficient in a father's feelings as to cast doubt on his paternity (636). His cowardice inspires Admetus to disown him (641): Admetus will neither bury his father nor care for him in old age. "I am dead as far as you are concerned," he announces (666). He ends by complaining bitterly of the inconsistency of the old (669–72):

> Vainly the old implore the gods to die, grumbling at
> old age and their long lifetimes. But when death
> draws near, not one of them wants to die—old age is
> no longer a burden to them.

Pheres also flares into anger, denouncing his son in crude and telling terms. He points out that there is no local or national tradition that requires fathers to die for their sons; to the contrary, each person is responsible for his own destiny (681–86). He notes that he has done everything for his son that custom demands, and asks Admetus to consider that life is also precious to the old. Pheres then proceeds to revile his son for his cowardice. As he ends the scene by stalking furiously off the stage, he threatens his son with punishment for the murder of his wife. Alcestis' death will not go unavenged, he says; surely her brother will demand satisfaction from Admetus (731–33).

The scene is in shocking violation of decorum. Parents and children do not generally talk this way on the tragic stage. Fathers have the license to abuse their sons—Oedipus in the *Oedipus Coloneus* is one example, Theseus in the *Hippolytus* another—but the sons do not reply in kind, much less initiate the quarrel. Pheres and Admetus behave as if they were not kin at all, not *philoi* but *echthroi*, enemies. In fact, when Admetus subsequently imagines the reproaches an enemy might cast in his face (955–59), he reiterates the substance of Pheres' speech. Yet we should not assume that the scene is designed to reveal the wickedness or even the weakness of the two men. Each is capable of better conduct: the audience has seen a nobler Admetus, a more gracious Pheres.[48] There is no reason to believe that their ignoble behavior is somehow more authentic than their good. It is the logic of the situation that prompts their disintegration in this episode. Apollo's offer created the intolerable expectation that a father should sacrifice himself for his son. In the context of that crisis Pheres and Admetus deteriorate from gentlemen to brutes.

Admetus' reputation also suffers as a consequence of Apollo's favor. At first it is merely eclipsed by his wife's. This situation is unusual in itself, for it was usually the male's prerogative to garner fame, *kleos*, on the basis of his noble deeds, while the height of womanly glory was to remain anonymous—"to be least talked of," as Thucydides' Pericles put it, "either for good or for ill."[49] Alcestis, however, achieves notoriety by her sacrificial act. The members of the chorus note that she is dying *euklees*, "enjoying good fame," as "the best woman of those alive, by far" (150–51). They predict that her tomb will become a sacred spot where travellers will pause to say a prayer; she will be honored as a "blessed spirit" (995–1005).

Admetus makes a desperate effort to enhance his reputation by inducing Heracles to accept his hospitality. Initially the attempt seems to miscarry; the members of the chorus are shocked at the deception he has practiced on his friend and reproach him bluntly for his folly (552). Admetus then explains that his chief motive was to avoid blame (553–58):

> If I had driven him from home and city when he came as
> my guest-friend, would you have praised me more? Of
> course not; my misfortune would have been no less, and
> I would have been the more inhospitable. It would have been
> one more trouble to add to my other troubles, if my
> house were said to be unwelcoming.

The members of the chorus seem won over by this argument; they respond dutifully with a stasimon in celebration of Admetus' noble hospitality (569–605). Admetus recognizes, however, that his reception of Heracles remains controversial: not everyone will praise his decision (565–66).

A single act of hospitality is not in any case sufficient to reverse the loss of reputation set in motion by Apollo's favor. During the quarrel with Pheres it emerges that Admetus' standing has been seriously damaged; no longer is any distinction drawn between the well-born, prosperous, hospitable Admetus and a bastard (636–39), an orphan (666–68), a coward (702), even a murderer (730). When Admetus arrives at a full insight of how much he has lost, he couches his realization in terms of the reputation Alcestis has gained and he has forfeited. His wife has died "with good fame," (*euklees*, 938). As for himself (954–61):

> Anyone who is hostile to me will say: "Look at that
> man, so shamefully alive, who lacked the heart to die
> but escaped Hades, coward that he was, by offering his
> wife in his place. Is this what you call a man? He
> resents his parents, when he was unwilling to die
> himself." Such, in addition to my other troubles, will

be my reputation. What profit is there for me in
living, my friends, with bad repute and miserable
fortune?

Even time itself, as experienced by Admetus, is affected by Apollo's
bargain. When Apollo "rescued Admetus from death" (11), what he
obtained for him was time extending beyond the date initially fixed by
the Fates for his demise. There was never any question of immortality;
Pheres is merely sarcastic when he suggests that Admetus has "cun-
ningly" (sophōs) found a way to live forever by convincing an endless
series of wives to die in his place (699–701). As Alcestis lies dying
Admetus asks her to make ready a home in the underworld (363–64),
and at the funeral he tries to leap into the grave so as to join his wife
sooner rather than later (897–99).

Although extra time is all that Apollo offered, even that counts for
a great deal. Time is held in enormous esteem in this play: all but one
of the principal characters assume that quality is of no significance,
that sheer duration is equivalent to life itself. Extra time is what Apollo
tries to obtain for Alcestis when he asks Thanatos to "delay" her death
so that she can "come to old age".[50] Alcestis notes bitterly that if one
of Admetus' parents had been willing to die for him, she and her husband could have lived on together "for the duration" (295). Alcestis,
the chorus and Admetus all blame the parents for wishing to prolong
their lives (290–94, 466–70, 648–50); they assume that because the old
have less time remaining they should also have a diminished zeal for
life. Pheres offers an old man's view, which unabashedly stresses
quantity over quality. He does not care what kind of a reputation he
earns by clinging to life (726). For him the crucial distinction is not between youth and age but between time spent above ground and time
spent below. Time below is endless (that is, undifferentiated); time
above is short but sweet (692–93). That sounds like traditional wisdom,
and it is.[51]

The time that Apollo has gained for Admetus is of a peculiar quality.
It has the unchangingness normally associated with death, not life.
Time is ordinarily supposed to bring forgetfulness, and both Alcestis
and Heracles assure Admetus that "time will soften" his grief (381,
1085). But the maid remarks that Admetus will never forget his pain.[52]
Admetus himself assures his wife that he will grieve not for a year, but
for his entire lifetime (336–37), and he subsequently tells Heracles that

never again will he enjoy life (1084). His time above ground will have the same monotonous quality that is associated with time below. He will live, says the chorus in a striking oxymoron, "a life that is not like life for the rest of his time."[53]

Near the close of the play, when Heracles says consolingly that time will soften Admetus' pain, Admetus replies, "You can say that, if time means dying" (1086). Lifetime has become indistinguishable from deathtime. That is perhaps the essence of Admetus' recognition (935–36) that his wife is better off than he. By that point in the play it has been demonstrated beyond any doubt that Apollo's gift was carelessly given. A life filled with mourning instead of joy, with hatred instead of love, with contempt instead of esteem is worse than death for mortals.

The Intervention of Heracles

The developments outlined to this point all have their origin in a single event, Apollo's bargain with the Fates. All illustrate a single tendency: the loss of those qualitative distinctions that make life worth living. Their cumulative effect, in a final blurring of distinctions, is to render *charis*, favor, indistinguishable from *prodounai*, betrayal. Out of gratitude to Admetus, Apollo wins him a stay from death, but at a cost he could not anticipate. As a return on her favor Alcestis extracts from her husband a promise that Admetus, in his eagerness to match her heroism, enlarges into a pledge of lifelong deprivation. No enemy could have done Admetus so much harm as the benevolent Apollo and the devoted Alcestis.

One action of the play, however, differs markedly from the rest. On his way to Thrace Heracles breaks his journey at Pherae, and in receiving him Admetus sees a chance to break the pattern of misery, to avoid piling "pain on pain" (1039, cf. 557) by departing from his program of mourning. Euripides ensures the plausibility of this development by establishing hospitality or *xenia* as a prior virtue of Admetus: it was his gracious reception of Apollo, we remember, that initially earned him the god's gratitude. It is less important, however, that Admetus breaks his pattern by an act of hospitality than that he breaks it all.

To be sure, he is singularly fortunate in his choice of guest, for Heracles is the restorer of differences and the champion of Necessity. He endures without complaint his strange and arbitrary destiny of service to Eurystheus: when the members of the chorus express alarm at his latest assignment (capturing the man-eating horses of King Diomedes of Thrace), he answers simply, "It is not possible for me to refuse [my] labors" (487). In conversation with Admetus Heracles maintains that life and death are two separate conditions (528), rather than the identity proposed by his host.

Admetus induces Heracles to accept his hospitality by deceiving him about Alcestis' status. He then orders the servants to open up the guest-rooms, which lie "apart" (543) from the main quarters, and to close the doors communicating with the courtyard and the rest of the palace (546–49). Presently, as the servant reports, two distinct strains are heard: one of mourning, as the domestics continue to express their grief for Alcestis, and one of feasting, as Heracles wreathes his head with myrtle, eats and drinks to his heart's content, and bawls out drinking songs (755–64). Thanks to the presence of this guest, the distinctions banished from the kingdom begin to reassert themselves.

Is Heracles merely a grotesque and laughable figure—a character more at home in satyr play than tragedy? The second "hypothesis" or ancient summary of the play notes that it was produced in 438 B.C. as the last of a tetralogy—that is, in the position usually occupied by a satyr play—and adds that its ending is "on the comic side."[54] Some scholars have theorized that the play represents a hybrid form, a "pro-satyric" drama incorporating elements from both tragedy and satyr play.[55] The figure of Heracles, riotous in his conduct and simplistic in his philosophy, is adduced as the principal evidence in support of this interpretation.

Inventing a new genre to account for Heracles is a drastic solution for a phenomenon that can be explained far more economically. Heracles is not an intrusive figure in the play; both his actions and his philosophy are crucial to its outcome. The carousing that so offends the servant has the effect of setting a limit to the pervasive mourning initiated by Admetus. Heracles' speech to the servant, though based on a temporary misunderstanding of Admetus' situation, nevertheless offers an important corrective to some of Admetus' (and Apollo's) assumptions. It gives full value to the role of Necessity in human affairs (782–89):

All mortals are bound to die, and there is no one who
knows for sure if he will be alive on the coming day.

The outcome of Fortune is not clear, and it cannot be
imparted by instruction or seized through ingenuity. Now
that you have understood my words, enjoy yourself,
drink, claim as *yours* whatever takes place each day;
the rest belongs to Fortune.

No one can predict when he will die, says Heracles; *tychē* (785, 789)
cannot be affected by *technē* (786). He may speak simply and naïvely,
but what he has to say is a truth ignored by everyone in the play. The
scheme by which Apollo had tried to save Admetus was an attempt
to outmaneuver *tychē* by means of *technē*. Heracles seems to be warning that such efforts cannot succeed.

Heracles' conclusion is straightforward; human beings should pay
attention not to the span of their days, which lies outside their control,
but to how they spend the time allotted them. It is qualitative distinctions that have been disappearing from the play, and it is to the quality
of life that Heracles redirects attention. The jovial interpretation he
puts on his words ("Enjoy yourself, drink!") does not affect the seriousness of his basic perception, any more than the erroneous assumptions that inspire the speech undermine its broad validity. Alone of all
the characters Heracles understands that life is not to be measured in
terms of time but defined by attitudes and state of mind.

The freshness of Heracles' speech depends on its context, not its
content. His themes and even his language can be closely paralleled
in the victory odes of Pindar and Bacchylides; in particular, there is a
strong echo of Bacchylides' third poem.[56] The situation, however, imparts a distinctive tinge to Heracles' epinician commonplaces. Bacchylides' ode was commissioned by Hiero, tyrant of Syracuse, and his
internal addressee is a man of wealth (cf. *bathyplouton*, Bacchylides
3.82), who serves as a surrogate for Hiero himself. Heracles, however,
is speaking to Admetus' servant, whom in a spontaneous egalitarian
gesture (795) he invites to join the feast. Directed to an Olympian victor, Bacchylides' reminder of mortality serves as a check on pride and
arrogance. Directed to a slave, the same reminder carries a different
and more heartening message. With this speech Heracles aligns himself with the Thanatos of the prologue. Both characters strike a
democratic note, for they affirm the equality of all mankind in the face
of death.

At the moment he speaks, Heracles' account of "the nature of mortal affairs" (780) seems singularly inapplicable to Admetus. Admetus had, after all, received the privilege of foreseeing his own death and the additional opportunity of circumventing it. Thanks to this extraordinary favor, he now faces a life of misery. But Heracles himself will change all that. When he discovers Admetus' noble deception he determines to repay his host's favor (*hypourgēsai charin*, 842) by rescuing Alcestis. He asks for directions to Alcestis' grave and proclaims his intention of lying in wait for Death and wrestling Alcestis from his grasp. He is even prepared to descend to the Underworld, if necessary, to fetch her back (850–53).

Heracles is as good as his word. He is not only the spokesman of Necessity but also the catalyst of the action, restoring wife to husband and turning grief to joy. The last episode, which produces these happy transformations, carries obvious references to preceding scenes. Heracles has arrived as a second guest-friend; Apollo had been the first. In rescuing Alcestis from the Underworld, Heracles serves as a stand-in for Admetus, who had expressed the desire to descend to Hades to fetch back his wife (357–62). In deceiving his host as to the identity of the woman he has brought with him, Heracles echoes Admetus' own earlier deception of himself. In offering Admetus a favor that involves a betrayal – the extended loan or gift of a concubine – Heracles recalls both Admetus, whose hospitality to himself was an ambiguous, troubling gift, and Apollo, whose favor to Admetus has had such unwelcome consequences.[57]

Yet symmetry alone does not guarantee a clear or satisfactory conclusion. The final episode raises questions that have been resolved very differently by the critics. Does Admetus remain loyal to his wife, or does he seize the first opportunity to betray her? Is Alcestis' return a reward for his good behavior or an ironic recompense for his inadequacies?[58] What, in short, does the ending contribute to the play?

To address these questions we must look once more at the stasimon immediately preceding the last episode. We may remember that Necessity is there equated with Death. The strophe mentions the medical remedies of Asclepius, who has elsewhere in the play (3–4, 122–29) served as a reminder that death is not to be circumvented despite Apollo's best efforts. The antistrophe asserts that Necessity has no altars and heeds no sacrifices – that is to say, it accepts no substitutions, such as the replacement of Admetus by Alcestis. Then the members of the chorus turn to Admetus. Still speaking of the goddess *Anankē*, they tell him: "You also the goddess holds imprisoned in her ineluctable grasp" (984). They proceed to warn him that he cannot bring his wife back by mourning, but their words seem to harbor an additional implication. Are they not also reminding Admetus of his own mortality?

The *Alcestis* begins with a favor that places Admetus in a unique relationship with death. It ends with a favor that restores the order challenged by Apollo. If we bear in mind that Alcestis dies as a substitute for her husband, then it is worth considering whether her return does not constitute a silent corrective of Apollo's initial intervention. Heracles undoes what Apollo accomplished.[59] He restores Alcestis to life, thereby canceling the earlier arrangement. But if the substitute is withdrawn, the original will have to go instead. So much would seem implicit both in Death's dour character and in the original bargain struck with the Fates.

It is easy for both spectators and the characters themselves to forget, in the astonishment and joy of the reunion, the consequences for Admetus of Alcestis' return. Yet the connection between Admetus' death and Alcestis' formed the premise of the play. Unless the author states that this link has been dissolved, we must assume that it still holds strong. Euripides offers no such assurance. At the place where we might expect an explanation of any provisions governing Alcestis' return there is only a bare, laconic summary of the wrestling match between Heracles and Thanatos (1140–42). It may be that Alcestis' restoration, combined with Admetus' earlier reprieve, adds up not to a double defeat for Thanatos but a single victory.

That Alcestis' return is no second suspension of the rules of death, but an exception that cancels the earlier one and restores the status quo, seems the more probable if we consider the increasing emphasis placed on the inevitability of death as the play moves toward its close. Heracles' speech and the last stasimon both reassert death's ineluctable nature. Both would be very puzzling indeed if the action that followed them did not in some sense confirm their lesson.[60]

We need not imagine that Admetus will die instantaneously, any more than Alcestis had to die immediately upon Admetus' acceptance of her sacrifice; both the beginning and end of the play are purposefully vague about such details.[61] We need imagine only that Admetus will die at his appointed moment, and this time without reprieve. Euripides gives the audience, to be sure, no statement either of the fact or the timing of Admetus' impending death. But as noted earlier, the certainty of death—a death that will come without warning—is one of the very few extradramatic assumptions that can be made about any mortal character in any play. Euripides' very silence is instructive, for it was Admetus' foreknowledge of his own death that caused all the misery in the first place. If Admetus and Alcestis are to live out their lives in happiness, it must be in ignorance of the circumstances of their own deaths. They will live, in short, as other mortals do, free of the dubious privileges procured for them by Apollo.

The end of the play takes on a fresh significance if Admetus' death forms the unspoken corollary to Alcestis' return. Admetus was freed from Necessity by Apollo, with the results that the play illustrates. By the end of the play he is back where he stood before the god's intervention—bound by Necessity, as all mortals are, but only intermittently aware of it. The events of the play have taught both Admetus and the audience to contemplate this situation with a certain cheerfulness. If (as Heracles remarks, at 799) mortals should think mortal thoughts, then they should not know when they are destined to die, for such awareness encourages attitudes that are the death of life. At the end Admetus is looking ahead to life rather than death (1153–58). Regardless of when he is destined to die, that change of focus in itself constitutes "a better life" (1157).

The Democratic Context

The *Alcestis* emerges, on this view, as Euripides' defense of death—a position not without relevance to the political climate of democratic Athens. We have seen that Apollo is portrayed as an elitist catering to the interests of the privileged. His proposed modifications in the ways of death would result, as Thanatos caustically points out (57), in special favors for the wealthy. In contrast Thanatos is by inclination evenhanded; left to himself, he treats all mortals alike.

The conflict between Apollo and Thanatos reflects, at a mythical remove, certain tensions inherent in Athenian society. A salient feature of Athenian government was its emphasis on equality. This principle expressed itself judicially in equality for all citizens before the law, politically as equal opportunity for all citizens to influence public policy.[62] The egalitarian principle extended to social institutions as well—to nomenclature, for example. At the end of the sixth century

Cleisthenes, an early architect of democracy, organized the Athenians into ten tribes subdivided into smaller units known as demes. As part of the same reform Cleisthenes replaced traditional patronymics with a new system of demotics. Henceforth an Athenian citizen would be identified in life and in death not with his father but with his deme or tribe — an innovation that tended to de-emphasize social differences and foster civic over familial identity.[63]

Death itself is a fact of nature, but the treatment of the dead responds to cultural imperatives, and Athens' egalitarian ethos was reflected in its funerary practices. Repeated attempts at legislation from the time of Solon to the fourth century testify to a desire to place limits on conspicuous displays by wealthy families.[64] By the period of the Peloponnesian War, if not earlier, it had become the custom for the Athenians to bury their war dead in public graves.[65] While these two developments are in no way related, they testify to a common impulse to avoid preferential treatment in death for any Athenian.

Even as it cleaves to its own mythical plane, the *Alcestis* develops a political perspective on death. Under the terms set forth at the beginning of the play mortality becomes a matter of culture, not nature; but by the close it has emerged that Apollo's attempt to win special privileges for Admetus was misguided, and that Admetus will be much happier if he is allowed to live — and die — under the same rules as everybody else. The audience is thereby implicitly encouraged to recognize that death's egalitarian dispositions are not only preferable to any alternative arrangement, but actually essential to a meaningful life.

The politics of death constitutes one strand in the play's web of associations, but the story as a whole retains all its ties to fairy tale.[66] One critic has detected a contrast, deliberately sought, between the realm of the myth and the harsher world of real life — the two planes between which the action has constantly moved.[67] In the interpretation presented here, myth and reality do not reflect adversely on one another; instead they combine in an action that moves on both planes toward consolation and assent. In a process that mirrors the subtraction and restoration of Alcestis, Euripides first removes death from its accustomed place in the lives of his characters and ultimately brings it back. The pattern of the action is didactic, reminding the audience that if the balance of life and death is altered, the distinctions that shape human existence are quickly obscured. Apollo granted his guest-friend the fulfillment of a widespread fantasy: to escape from death. But this extraordinary favor is shown by the play to be no privilege at all, and Heracles' truest proof of friendship is not that he rescues Alcestis from the underworld but that he restores Admetus to ignorance—Prometheus' gift to mankind.

NOTES

1. Fr. r833 N^2 and 361 N^2.

2. For psychological approaches to the play cf. van Lennep 1949, Smith 1960A, von Fritz 1962, and Lesky 1966. These studies assume that there must be something wrong with a man who would accept his wife's offer to die in his place; but as Lloyd 1985, 120–21, points out, the structure of the play encourages the audience to accept this state of affairs without blaming Admetus. Dale 1954, xxvii (henceforth "Dale"), in contrast, affirms the primacy of action over character:

> So far from considering the *Alcestis* a full-length study of *naïveté*, weakness, hysteria, egotism, character development, and so forth, I do not believe that . . . Euripides had any particular interest in the sort of person Admetus was. The situations in which the plot involves him are too diverse for much personality to appear, or to be intended.

Steidle 1968, 132–51, establishes Admetus' good faith through an analysis of text and stage action. Nielson 1976 approaches my own view in seeing death as a crucial theme in the play. Seeck 1985 analyzes the *Alcestis* in terms of the motifs of exchange, death, parting, and lament.

3. See above, p. 40.

4. Cf. Vickers 1973, 101: "Since Greek tragedy drew the majority of its plots from myth or from epic of the heroic age, [and] was constantly involved in the process of *re*-presenting the past for the present, then the values and attitudes of the past must also be relevant." For a detailed study of tragic allusions to epic and lyric, see Garner 1990.

5. For discussion of the differences among gods, mortals, and heroes see Vermeule 1979, 118–22.

6. Inevitable: *Od.* 16.447; *Il.* 6.487–89; Simonides 19 (Page); Solon 24.9–10 (Page). See further Stobaeus 4.51. Irreversible: *Il.* 9.408–9; Hes. *Theog.* 765–66; Alcaeus B6a (Page), Ibycus 32 (Page), Anacreon 50 (Page). For Aeschylean references see Fraenkel *ad Agamemnon* 1018. Unpredictable: Callinus 1.14 f.; Semonides 1.4–5 (West). For an attempt to trace a shift in Greek attitudes toward death between 800 and 500 B.C. on the basis of both literary and archaeological evidence see Sourvinou-Inwood 1981, with the critique of Morris 1989.

7. At *Il.* 9.318–20. All translations from the *Iliad* are by Lattimore (1951). *Pace* Claus 1975 (18, n. 7), Achilles does not here seem to be punning on two different senses of *moira* in reference to his mistreatment by Agamemnon, but rather

making the same point about death, with increasing emphasis, three times in succession.

8. For the familiarity of the passage cf. *Crito* 44b2, where Socrates adapts *Il.* 9.363 in recounting his dream, and Crito immediately catches the allusion.

9. For this motif see Garland 1985, 77–88.

10. Semonides 1.4–5. For the concept of *ephēmeros* see Fraenkel 1946, 131–45; see also 1975, 133–35.

11. *Prometheus Bound* 248; cf. Plat. *Gorgias* 523d. The debate over the authenticity of the *Prometheus Bound* continues: cf. Griffith 1977, arguing against Aeschylean authorship, and Conacher 1980 and Saïd 1985, arguing in favor. The authorship is not important for my purposes; but since the ascription to Aeschylus was never challenged in antiquity, as long as there is room for doubt I shall continue to refer to Aeschylus as the author of the *Prometheus Bound*.

12. Rosenmeyer 1963, 211, gives a similar list.

13. For discussion of the concept see Nagy 1979, 175–88.

14. *Il.* 9.158–59; cf. Hes. *Theog.* 766.

15. Solon 27.17–18 (West), but cf. also 20 (West).

16. Cf. Mimnermus 2.10; Aes. fr. 255 N^2; Eur. *Hipp.* 1373.

17. I do not agree with Claus 1975 that Achilles' point of view is compatible with Sarpedon's. Sarpedon is willing to fight, even though he can imagine not fighting if men were not subject to death, because he is content with the balance between the risks the hero takes and the honors he receives. Achilles refuses to fight because he is deeply dissatisfied with the heroic value system not only as he has experienced it, but even in theory, because it does not give death its proper weight. (Claus' critique of Parry 1956, however, is telling. For a review of the whole "language of Achilles" controversy see Martin 1990, 150–59.)

18. Cf. Vermeule 1979, 26: "Everyone dies, but the wittier at least die twice."

19. *W.&D.* 106–201. Although the age of heroes interrupts the pattern of degeneration, the improvement is only temporary.

20. Cf. Plat. *Prot.* 320–23, Diodorus 1.8.1–7. Other passages are collected in Lovejoy and Boas 1935. Of the large literature on the idea of progress, one of the best short discussions is Dodds 1973. De Romilly 1966 is also excellent.

21. See Edmunds 1975, 1–3, with bibliography there listed.

22. At *Ant.* 365–75, translation by Wyckoff 1954.

23. Cf. also *Ant.* 850 ff. and Blumenthal 1974. Other possible thematic echoes are *Ant.* 519, where Antigone speaks of Death's impartial laws, and 580, where Creon notes that even the bold flee Death when they see it close at hand (cf. *Alc.* 668–72). While the parallels are not exact, there are enough of them to suggest that Euripides saw and remembered the earlier play.

24. Cf. Aes. *Ag.* 1022–24 and Pind. *Pyth.* 3.54–58.

25. Cf. Burnett 1965, 242: "Viewed from heaven, this whole affair is merely an incident in a series of repayments, transgression for transgression, made between Zeus and Apollo."

26. My discussion of the pattern of loss of distinctions is much influenced by Girard 1977, 77 ff. and passim. Girard defines cultural differentiation as the

essential ordering mechanism in society, whose loss leads to violence and chaos.

27. Noted by Wolff 1982, 236. Smith 1960A, 129, remarks that Death is "democratic."

28. Trickery is implied by 33–34 and 12. But in the same line the verb *aineō* implies conscious acquiescence (cf. 525). These contradictory views of the attitude of the *Moirai* toward the substitution might be considered an initial "loss of distinctions."

29. On false leads in Euripidean prologues, see Dodds 1960 *ad Bacch.* 52; also Hamilton 1978.

30. On last words, cf. Taplin 1977, p. 205. I owe this reference to Lloyd 1985, n. 39., 131.

31. At 27, 105, and 158. See Dale xvi and Rivier 1972, 128.

32. This theory has its origins in the discussion by Wilamowitz 1904–6, vol. 3, 87. It is further elaborated by von Fritz 1962 and Schwinge 1962 and 1970.

33. Cf. Gould 1978, 44:
We may follow an everyday person home, but not a dramatic person. It is clearly not an *accident* that dramatic persons are only visible to us while on stage. . . . The spatial "framing" of dramatic action is not a question of what is accessible, but of what exists. . . .

34. For this motif in Aeschylus see Nussbaum 1986, 32–41; in all three dramatists, Gill 1990, 22–29.

35. At 18, 155, 284, 340, 433–34, 524, and 620. For discussion of the *Alcestis* in the context of other Euripidean sacrifice dramas, see Burnett 1971, 26–28.

36. Dale *ad* 280 ff. Di Benedetto 1971, 23 ff., sees a development in rational understanding between the lyric and iambic passage.

37. *Ajax* 588; cf. also Eur. *Hipp.* 1456. On the sense of *prodounai* see Rivier 1968B; for the paradoxes associated with the motif see Scodel 1979, 55–56.

38. Cf. Seeck 1985, 75.

39. Cf. Smith 1960, 130–31, and Schwinge 1962, 48–49.

40. Arist. *Poetics* 1450a16–17. Garton 1957, 250, discusses "the tendency of the action to control the main lines of the project, the characterisation" and the fact that "the character tends to be an upshot of the thing done."

41. J. Jones 1962, 29–46. For discussion of the ancient preoccupation with "character" versus the modern interest in "personality" and the distinction between these two concepts, see Gill 1990 (summarizing and refining his own earlier discussions).

42. Garton 1957, 251.

43. Noted by Dale *ad* 365–66.

44. Mimnermus 1.1–2. For Mimnermus Aphrodite is identified with the *terpnon* of life. Admetus mourns that Alcestis has "taken away the *terpsis* of life" (347) by dying.

45. Garland 1985, 40.

46. Garland 1985, 121.

47. Cf. Socrates' surprise at Euthyphro's prosecution of his father (*Euth.* 4a) and his remarks in the *Crito* (51a–b) about the implicit obedience owed by chil-

dren to parents. Aristotle discusses filial inequality and obligation at *Nich. Eth.* 1158b11–24 and 1163b18–21. Aristophanes uses an inversion of the norm for comic effect when Pheidippides beats his father (*Clouds* 1321 ff.).

48. Pheres' opening words should not be taken as hypocritical (as does Burnett 1965, 248). By the very nature of the situation his gratitude to Alcestis must be genuine, and his counsel of endurance (616–17) is just as sincere as the chorus' similar advice at 416. Cf. Seeck 1985, 110, for a complementary interpretation.

49. Thuc. 2.46. For discussion see Loraux 1986, 147.

50. Reading Bursian's *ambalein* at 1.50 (justified by Dale *ad loc.*).

51. Cf. Anacreon 50 (Page) for the shortness and sweetness of life, and Semonides 3 (West) for the opposition of short life and long death; also Soph. fr. 518 N^2.

52. At 198, reading Nauck's *oupoth' hou.*

53. At 242–43. On Euripides' use of oxymoron, see Synodinou 1978.

54. For a discussion of the hypothesis and its appended second paragraph, see Dale xxxviii–xl and Sutton 1980, 191–92.

55. The pro-satyric aspect is discussed cautiously by Dale xviii–xxii and vigorously affirmed by Sutton 1980, 180–84. When Sutton argues that the *Alcestis* contains narrative elements that could (if the play were organized differently) figure in a satyr play, he does not persuade me that the play *as it stands* is satyric, or even pro-satyric.

56. Bacchylides 3.78–84. For the relationship of the passage to the *Alcestis*, see Burnett 1965, 253, and Garner 1990, 76–77.

57. For additional parallels with preceding scenes see Smith 1960A, 143, Burnett 1965, 247–49, and Lloyd 1986, 128.

58. Reward: Burnett 1965, 252. Ironic recompense: Smith 1960A, 145.

59. So Lesky 1966, 293: "So ist dann Herakles in gewissem Sinne der Gegenspieler Apollos, der wahre Retter, der das gute Ende schafft."

60. The contradictions are well brought out by Kullmann 1967, 145 ff. When Smith 1960A, 145, claims that "the incredible happens" and "Death is defeated" he ignores the thematic emphasis of the close.

61. Cf. Burnett 1965, 241: "The death that was offered and accepted was not an immediate death but one set vaguely in the future. . . ."

62. The formulation is that of A. H. M. Jones 1957, 45.

63. For Cleisthenes' reforms see Arist., *Ath. Pol.* 21.4. For the listing of the Athenian war dead according to tribal divisions, see Bradeen 1969, 147.

64. Cic. *de Leg.* 2.26.64 speaks of three attempts at funerary legislation: under Solon, under Demetrius of Phalerum, and at some period in between. Plutarch (*Solon* 21.5) describes the sumptuary laws of Solon. Discussion of archaeological evidence in Kurtz and Boardman 1971, 121–24.

65. Thuc. 2.34; for the ideological implications see Loraux 1986, 15–76.

66. For the folktale origins of the myth, see Lesky 1925.

67. Von Fritz 1962, 312.

2

Hippolytus

It is a boon to scholarship that Euripides' first version of the *Hippolytus* did not find favor with the Athenian public, so that he rewrote the play for presentation at the City Dionysia in 428 B.C. Although only a few fragments of the original version are extant, they allow for a limited comparison of the two versions and the identification of one element—the theme of moderation—that seems to have been fundamental to Euripides' concept of the legend from the outset.[1]

Plot and characterization, to be sure, underwent considerable alteration. Initially the playwright seems to have juxtaposed an impudent and brazen Phaedra to the austerely virtuous Hippolytus. The first Phaedra boldly made sexual advances to her stepson, who rejected them with horror.[2] The two characters thus offered extreme and contrasting responses to the onslaught of Aphrodite, and the lesson suggested by their fates may well have been the familiar and quintessentially Greek counsel of moderation. "Human beings who shun Aphrodite overmuch," according to a surviving fragment (fr. F [Barrett]), "suffer just as surely as those who pursue her overmuch." Other fragments (H, U) extoll *aidōs* and *sōphrosynē* and speculate on the sources of *hybris* (L, M). These qualities were so intimately associated in traditional Greek thought that mention of one could be counted on to evoke the others. *Aidōs* and *sōphrosynē*, roughly "respect" and "rectitude," were the two virtues most commonly associated with moderation, while *hybris*, "outrage," was moderation's dangerous antithesis.[3]

This constellation of motifs—moderation, *aidōs*, *sōphrosynē*, *hybris*—survived the revision, although its components were distributed differently among the characters. In Euripides' second version the stark polarity between the principals has disappeared.[4] The queen is fully her stepson's match in virtue, for both aspire to *aidōs* and *sōphrosynē*. Far from making advances to Hippolytus, Phaedra is determined to die rather than reveal her passion; her secret is betrayed, however, by her old nurse. By emphasizing Phaedra's struggle for self-mastery, the second *Hippolytus* invites the audience to reflect not only on the dangers of extremism but on the complex and elusive nature of "the middle way."

In the revised version the nurse assumes the crucial role of go-between. In keeping with her new prominence, she makes an important programmatic statement. The nurse first appears in attendance on her mistress' sickbed, which has been moved outdoors to satisfy Phaedra's longing for sunlight and fresh air (178–80). The queen is restless, irritable, and very weak, for this is the third day of a self-imposed fast (135–38, 275). She tosses uneasily on her bed (203–4) and expresses a feverish longing to drink from a cool spring, to recline in a luxuriant meadow (208–11).

As the nurse performs her ministrations, she turns to the audience to deplore her own emotional engagement with her mistress—an attachment that has recently, because of the baffling nature of Phaedra's illness, become "a heavy burden" (259). People should observe moderation in their emotions, the nurse observes; they should not be affected "to the very marrow of their souls" (255). She goes on to offer an even more sweeping prescription for human behavior (264–66): "I praise excess less than 'nothing too much' [*to mēden agan*]. And the wise will agree with me."

This statement brings to a close the anapestic exchanges between Phaedra and her nurse. Although it gains in emphasis from its climactic position, it already commands gnomic authority. When the nurse claims that the wise will agree with her, she is practically footnoting her source: the wise, as the scholiast to the passage explains, are the seven sages of archaic Greece.

Mēden agan—attributed in ancient sources now to one, now to another of the seven wise men—was inscribed over the entrance of the Temple of Apollo at Delphi, sharing public prominence with the injunction *gnōthi seauton*: "Know Thyself."[5] The proverbs predate the sixth-century temple, however, and their fame was independent of Delphi. In the fourth century Plato refers to them as sayings "which everybody repeats" (*Prot.* 343b). Aristotle says that they "have become public property" (*Rhet.* 1395a). Evidently they formed part of a moralizing tradition whose origins are lost to view but whose early manifestations can be seen in Hesiod, Solon, and Theognis among others.

The counsel of moderation might be viewed as an alternative to the competitive, self-aggrandizing ethos that pervades the *Iliad*. In the *Il-*

iad the advice proffered a young warrior is "Always excel!" — an exhortation that seems to necessitate the taking of risks.[6] But in the *Works and Days* Hesiod warns against overloading either ships or wagons and concludes: "Observe moderation (*metra*); due measure (*kairos*) is best in everything" (694). The counsel of moderation represents, for Hesiod, a practical response to a world that has been found by experience to be hostile and perilous. His admonition is intended as advice to the inexperienced: to heed him is to avoid at least some of the potential hazards of life, and through the exercise of a cautious conservatism to reclaim some ground from Fate or Necessity.

It is not long before the counsel of moderation is found linked to a specific set of moral virtues, associated not just with common sense but with the ethical qualities of *aidōs* and *sōphrosynē*. Moderation is considered a sign of good character because it represents the opposite pole from the rashness and excess of *hybris*. At this stage the proverb *mēden agan* does more than enshrine practical advice. Elevated to the status of ideology, it has become normative rather than empirical.[7]

There are signs of this development a century after Hesiod in the poetry of Theognis and Solon — both of whom are aristocrats producing their hortatory verses against a background of class strife and political upheaval.[8] Theognis of Megara repeatedly warns his young friend Cyrnus against the pursuit of excess: *mēden agan speudein*.[9] For Theognis, "a class-conscious aristocrat if ever there was one," the admonition has a combined ethical and political coloration.[10] In his view moderation is the virtue particular to his own class; the commoners, in contrast, are volatile and uncontrolled.[11]

Solon of Athens translated the doctrine of moderation into a political agenda infused (by his own account) with a spirit of compromise. While taking the side of the *dēmos* or common people in some important respects, he was unwilling to indulge their full desires. He cancelled debts, for example, but stopped short of a reallocation of land. His division of the Athenians into four groups based on property rather than birth may have posed a challenge to the hereditary aristocracy, but it did nothing to extend political power to the masses, since public office remained the prerogative of the three upper groups.

Using the imagery of the middle way, Solon described himself as the mediator between the two classes: "I stood between them like a stone marker in no-man's land" (fr. 37.9–10 [West]). Yet his efforts seem to have been largely directed toward protecting the aristocrats and controlling the masses; his poems reflect the assumption (shared with Theognis) that the *dēmos* is undisciplined and greedy.[12] For Solon as for Theognis the counsel of moderation is linked to an elitist political perspective.

This association was to persist into the fifth century. The adjective *sōphrōn* became "part of an oligarch's standard political vocabulary, for oligarchs always claimed a monopoly of self-control and moderation."[13] Thucydides reflects the influence of this usage: he avoids applying the term *sōphrōn* to the Athenian democracy, preferring the less loaded *metrios*.[14] He recounts that in 427 B.C.—a year after the production of the second *Hippolytus*—the oligarchic faction on Corcyra adopted the "fair-sounding slogan" of *aristokratia sōphrōn*.[15] And he makes Peisander argue in favor of the oligarchic revolution of 411 by asserting that the Athenians cannot expect any help from Persia "unless we adopt a more moderate form of government" (*ei mē politeusomen . . . sōphronesteron*, 8.53.3).

By the time of Euripides the ideology of moderation—that constellation of motifs encompassing the virtues of *aidōs* and *sōphrosynē*—had ceased to be merely prudential and had acquired connotations both moral and political. So broad was its domain and so vague its application that it could and did conceal a nexus of elitist attitudes scarcely compatible with the egalitarian principles of democratic Athens. Yet it also enshrined directives well worth retaining, for the sober virtues associated with moderation could only benefit the democratic social order.

Through pointed and unmistakable references, Euripides invites the audience to consider the political implications of his play. Viewed from such a perspective, the *Hippolytus* becomes paradigmatic for a society that needed to purge the ideology of moderation of its oligarchic associations in order to adapt it to its own purposes. Of the four principal characters, three—the nurse, Hippolytus, and Phaedra—govern their lives according to the principles of moderation. (The fourth, Theseus, will receive scant attention here, since he comes late on the scene and can only react to the situation previously created.) They are by no means helpless victims of Aphrodite but contribute actively to their own ruin through their principles as well as their actions.[16]

Many critics have assumed that Euripides' main interest in the *Hippolytus* is psychological, for each of the protagonists displays a personality that is striking, consistent, and delineated in elaborate detail.[17]

Yet the protagonists are explicitly presented not as individuals, but as cautionary examples. "We must not imitate the young when they take such attitudes," says the servant as he disassociates himself from the reckless pronouncements of Hippolytus (114–15). In the same spirit, Phaedra implies that the upper classes have a responsibility to set an example for the lower (407–12). It was a common Greek assumption that the protagonists of epic and tragedy served as models for the audience, and this exemplary relationship is mirrored within the *Hippolytus* by the imagined influence of upper upon lower-class characters.[18] The text itself, in short, directs the audience to evaluate the protagonists in representative terms.

By attending to what Hippolytus, the nurse, and Phaedra have to say about the principles that govern their actions, it becomes possible to trace the process whereby Euripides reconfigures for the benefit of the democracy the traditional values clustering around the concept of moderation. By the fourth century *sōphrosynē*, along with other terms previously identified with the conservative point of view, would have shed its reactionary associations. Aeschines speaks of the restored democracy as "the return of sound government" (*palin de sōphronōs politeuthentes*, 2.176), and the concept of the sound democratic citizen, the *sōphrōn politēs*, recurs regularly in the orators.[19] The *Hippolytus* sheds light on one aspect of a quiet redefinition that allowed this shift to take place.

Gods and Men

Aphrodite appears in order to speak the prologue, and she wastes no time defining her position. For Aphrodite there is no middle ground. One is either for her or against her (5–6): "Those who respect my power I advance, but I trip up as many as are presumptuous toward me."

Despite her neatly antithetical formulation, Aphrodite is not even-handed in practice. If it becomes necessary for her to choose between favoring her votaries and punishing her enemies, vengeance takes priority: Aphrodite does not hesitate to sacrifice Phaedra in order to destroy Hippolytus (48–50). From the beginning of the play, accordingly, the audience is put on notice that Aphrodite is a force dangerous to resist but not necessarily safe to accommodate.

Having explained the terms on which she judges mortals, Aphrodite proceeds to specify the nature of Hippolytus' offense. As she does so she sets forth a dialectic of excess and deficiency that will operate throughout the play. She explains that she does not object to Hippolytus' intense relationship with Artemis. What angers her is his conduct toward herself (12–22):

> Alone among the citizens of this land of Troezen he says
> that I am the worst of goddesses. He renounces sexuality
> and will not touch marriage. But he honors the sister of
> Phoebus, Zeus' child, Artemis, considering her the
> greatest of goddesses. He spends all his time with the
> virgin goddess in the forest, hunting out the wild animals
> from the land with his swift dogs—having happened on an
> association more than mortal. For this I bear no grudge—
> why should I? But for Hippolytus' mistakes on my account I
> shall take revenge. . . .

Aphrodite notes that just as Hippolytus considers her "the worst of goddesses," *kakistēn daimonōn*, so he considers Artemis "the greatest of goddesses," *megistēn daimonōn*. Despite Aphrodite's disclaimer, her parallelism of expression suggests that she does indeed harbor a grudge against Hippolytus, for to her mind his worship of the virgin goddess is inseparable from his rejection of herself. Hippolytus' devotion to Artemis does not, cannot exist in isolation: it defines itself only in antithesis to his neglect of Aphrodite. Excess in one direction produces deficiency in the other.

Aphrodite is not, however, a deity to be worshipped or ignored at will, but one of the ineluctable forces of the universe. Like the Thanatos of the *Alcestis*, she is an aspect of Necessity. By her own report she is "of much account among mortals," (*pollē . . . en brotoisi*, 1) but her next words reveal that description as an understatement: in fact her domain knows no limits, for it extends to all who "look on the light of the sun" (4). As the nurse explains, she is "not a goddess, but something greater" in her ability to affect human beings even against their will (359–60). Aphrodite's universality manifested itself in a number of different spheres, as the Greeks implicitly acknowledged when they worshipped her (at Athens, Thebes, Megalopolis, and elsewhere) as Aphrodite Pandemos, "Aphrodite of all the people"—a cult title later explained as carrying both a political and a sexual reference.[20] Both these associations will be important to the play. Aphrodite is the most indiscriminate or, to put it another way, the most democratic of goddesses. From the goddess' vantage point distinctions of birth are ultimately of no account, since all can claim descent from her (447–50):

> Cypris roams the heavens, she is in the sea-wave, and
> everything was born from her. She it is who sows and
> bestows love, and all of us on earth are her descendants.

Aphrodite emphasizes from the outset that hers is the force that binds all human beings together. If Hippolytus is as she describes him, his choice of virginity seems more than a matter of private sexual fastidiousness. His preference for Artemis implies a refusal to acknowledge himself as a member of the human community.[21] Aphrodite is presently proved an accurate witness: her account of the young man's character is confirmed by Hippolytus himself.

Hippolytus' first action in the play is to present a wreath of flowers to the statue of Artemis—ignoring the image of Aphrodite, which also stands before the palace doors.[22] As he prays he, like Aphrodite earlier, alludes to his special relationship with Artemis (82–87):

> But now, o beloved mistress, accept this garland for your
> golden head, offered by a reverent hand. Alone among
> mortals I enjoy this honor. I am with you and exchange
> speech with you—hearing your voice, but not seeing your
> face. May I round the final goalpost of my life just as I
> began it.

Hippolytus' language echoes Aphrodite's in two instances; both remind us that his devotion to one goddess is inseparable from his rejection of the other. "Alone among mortals" he enjoys Artemis' company; Aphrodite had noted that "alone among mortals" he refused to worship her. The young man's choice places him in an isolated and dangerous position.[23] Furthermore, when Hippolytus speaks of "being with" Artemis, he uses the same verb as does Aphrodite when she notes, with sneering sexual innuendo, that Hippolytus "is with" Artemis continually in the forest.[24] Neither Aphrodite nor Hippolytus, of course, is suggesting an actual sexual relationship. Rather, the communion between the virgin goddess and her young votary takes the place of normal sexuality; therein lies its challenge to Aphrodite and its danger to Hippolytus.

Aphrodite's condemnation of Hippolytus receives reinforcement from a human source: Hippolytus' old servant. This man's evident loyalty and affection for his young master make his views all the more worth taking seriously. He has something of the function of the "tragic warners" who appear in Herodotus' *Histories*. These admonitory figures, "pessimistic, negative, unheeded and right," serve to alert the audience to the presence of danger and to predict trouble to come.[25]

We have seen that, although the stage is framed by statues of Artemis and Aphrodite, Hippolytus has offered a garland to Artemis alone, along with a prayer that the end of his life may match its beginning (87). The servant is alarmed by this conspicuous neglect of Aphrodite. Although determined to admonish his master, he approaches the task with elaborate circumspection. Hippolytus' prayer had emphasized the uniqueness of his association with Artemis, and the servant adverts to the topic of conformity when he asks Hippolytus if the young man is aware of "the custom [*nomos*] prevailing among men" (91). When queried, he explains that he has in mind the tendency to dislike "pride and exclusiveness" (93). Presently he suggests that approachability is a trait prized by gods and men alike. Hippolytus concurs, "if," as he notes carefully, "we mortals share the customs of the gods" (98). Finally the servant comes to the point, urging Hippolytus to pay his respects to Aphrodite, "the proud goddess" (99). But at this juncture Hippolytus parts company with the old man, warning him sternly against bringing Aphrodite into the discussion and proclaiming his independence from the goddess: "I salute her from a distance, in my purity."[26]

The dialogue has turned on the differences and similarities between gods and mortals. The servant began by asserting that human beings dislike pride (*to semnon*), only to add that Aphrodite, "the proud [*semnē*] goddess," deserves her due.[27] Is Euripides implying that gods and men share the same qualities and should accordingly be judged on the same terms?[28] That seems unlikely, since elsewhere in the play the term *semnos* is applied favorably to divinities but unfavorably to mortals.[29] More germane is the confused perception, implicit in the servant's usage, that the same quality that is to be rejected in mortals is to be revered in divinities. The servant's inexactitude may inspire the audience to ponder the implications of his words. They may thus be reminded of a circumstance both he and they know well but that Hippolytus seems in danger of forgetting: divinities and mortals may share certain qualities, but they are very differently placed. The servant's salute to Hippolytus had emphasized the difference: human beings may be addressed as "lord," the servant had declared (88), but only the gods may be called "master." The disparity between gods and mortals hinted at with these words will only widen in the course of the play. *To semnon* encompasses both an aspect of remoteness and an aspect of sheer power. Aphrodite is not *semnē* in the sense of being difficult of access: she invites the worship of all mortals. She is, however, *semnē* in the second sense: those who neglect her injure her pride and awaken her powerful anger. Hippolytus commands the first aspect but not the second; nor does he as yet understand the difference between the two.

Though the servant cannot analyze his intuition, he is conscious both of Aphrodite's power and Hippolytus' vulnerability. He brings the episode to a close by recommending that the gods depart from mortal practice in at least one critical respect. He entreats Aphrodite to overlook Hippolytus' youthful folly, since "gods should be wiser than human beings" (120). The end of the play will make it clear that this notion needs to be reversed. A differentiation will indeed be established, but it will be left to human beings to show themselves wiser than the gods.

Hamartia or Sōphrosynē?

The opening of the play has summoned a number of witnesses who have defined Hippolytus' way of life in terms of excess and deficiency. His exclusive regard for Artemis has as its corollary the neglect of Aphrodite. Yet the two goddesses have more in common than Hippolytus imagines. The poet repeatedly links them through imagery: the bee that traverses Artemis' meadow at 77 reappears as Aphrodite's emblem at 563–64, and the poet associates both goddesses with the sky, with destructive shafts, with cool water.[30] He makes them speak in similar language, and by the end of the play it will have become clear that the two goddesses share the same goals and methods.[31]

The key to these coincidences lies in the perception that together Aphrodite and Artemis define a continuum spanning virginity and experience. To deny Aphrodite is to deny the necessity for development along this continuum, and thereby to ignore another important difference between mortals and gods. For whereas the immortal gods are immune to change, mutability is the essence of the human condition. To cherish the hope that the end of life will match its beginning (87) is to ignore the terms of mortal existence. Here is another aspect of what Aphrodite terms Hippolytus' mistake or *hamartia* (cf. 21).

Yet Hippolytus himself does not recognize any shortcomings in his character or way of life; his self-evaluation is consistent and altogether approving. In his own judgment Hippolytus exemplifies chastity, moderation, and self-restraint—all the qualities implicit in the term *sōphrōn*.

Sōphrōn is Hippolytus' favorite self-description, as well as his highest commendation for others. On his first entrance he describes the meadow where he has gathered his flowers for Artemis: a sacred place, untainted by human cultivation, and reserved for a special class of individuals (72–81):

> For you, mistress, I bring this garland, gathered in a
> pure meadow, where neither the shepherd thinks it right to
> pasture flocks nor has iron ever come, but this pure
> meadow the bee passes through in the spring. Respect
> [*aidōs*] waters it, and for those to whom rectitude
> [*to sōphronein*] in everything without exception is part of
> their nature, not something taught—for those it is
> allowed to gather flowers, but for the wicked it is not
> allowed.

In describing the meadow Hippolytus is evoking an ideal landscape in some sense emblematic of his own way of life.[32] It is striking that he defines it in terms of impenetrability and exclusion. Neither animals nor the implements of human labor are permitted in the meadow, which is open only to the human beings of conspicuous rectitude. Yet Hippolytus himself enjoys unrivalled access to his meadow, for he is not only *sōphrōn* by nature but more *sōphrōn* than anyone else on earth. That is his own assessment, offered to Theseus in self-defense (993–95); he repeats the statement to his companions as he is about to depart for exile (1100–1101) and again as he lies dying (1365). If the audience is to evaluate him as an exemplar it must decide whether he is indeed the most righteous of men or whether his understanding is fatally mistaken. To assess his claims it becomes necessary to look more closely at the various components of his *sōphrosynē*.

A crucial element of *sōphrosynē*, as far as Hippolytus, is concerned, is chastity—a sense of the term commonly associated with women, but in fact applicable to both sexes.[33] For Hippolytus, anyone who is not *sōphrōn* is simply and sweepingly *kakos*—"wicked." He uses *kakos* so frequently as the opposite of *sōphrōn* that it seems clear that he believes Aphrodite to be "the worst of goddesses," *kakistēn daimonōn*, chiefly on account of her promiscuity.[34]

Hippolytus' description of the elect who are permitted entrance to his meadow reveals that he views *sōphrosynē* as an inherited rather than an acquired characteristic.[35] He apparently also considers its possession a talisman that will keep him from harm. Defending himself before Theseus, and again on the point of his departure from Troezen, he makes the following petitions (1028–30, 1191):

> Truly, may I die unknown and without a name, and may neither sea nor land receive my corpse, if I am by nature an unchaste man [*ei pephuk' kakos anēr*].

> Zeus, may I cease to live, if I am by nature an unchaste man [*ei pephuk' kakos anēr*].

Hippolytus utters prayers for his own destruction in the perfect confidence that they will go unfulfilled. After all, he knows that he is not *kakos*, but *sōphrōn* by nature. In this confidence in his invulnerability he is in error. He does not realize that his innocence offers him no protection; but that is scarcely the full extent of his miscalculation. He also fails to take into account the impression he makes on others—to understand, for example, when Theseus denounces him as a hypocrite, that his continual assertions of his chastity have aroused suspicion in the past and will only enrage Theseus further at this juncture. Even more fundamental is Hippolytus' inability to realize that he is not a free agent, but subject to the judgments and desires of other human beings—subject, that is, to Necessity in the form of Aphrodite. For Aphrodite represents the claims of others upon the self, the force that interdicts human beings from passing through life in purity and isolation.[36] Long before Phaedra fell in love with Hippolytus and the nurse conspired to entrap him, his father had already formed his own assessment of his son, and young girls had already dreamed of marrying him (cf. 952–54, 1140–41). Whether he likes it or not, Hippolytus has lived his whole life in relation to others.

Hippolytus is willing to stand or fall on his reputation for *sōphrosynē*. But the term does not, for him, connote chastity alone. As he defends himself before Theseus he uses the concept in a different sense, one that invites the audience to extend its understanding of his character.

Hippolytus attempts to forestall Theseus' accusations by reconstructing all the possible motives that Theseus might ascribe to him, then brusquely dismissing each.[37] Does Theseus believe, he demands, that he desired Phaedra on account of her exceptional beauty? Or because he hoped to usurp Theseus' property? Or will Theseus argue that power is attractive to "sensible people," *tois sophrosin* (1013)? This possibility is debated at far greater length than the others. He himself would prefer, says Hippolytus, to be first in the Panhellenic Games but second in the city, "enjoying uninterrupted good fortune with the nobility (*tois aristois*) as my friends" (1018). Such a status, he explains, opens a sphere for activity while keeping danger at bay (1019–20).

So discursive a statement at so critical a juncture arrests attention. When Hippolytus links his *sōphrosynē* to quietism it becomes necessary to consider the political aspects both of the term and of his way of life. It is not as if he uses the term here in a political sense and elsewhere with an unrelated sexual connotation.[38] For a Greek listener, both would be latent at each occurrence of the word. The content of Hippolytus' speech to Theseus focuses attention on the political implications of his entire way of life.

We have noted that at the time the *Hippolytus* was written the word *sōphrōn* carried unmistakable conservative overtones. Not coincidentally, Euripides has given his protagonist the habits and attitudes of a young oligarch, a member of the elite described by Aristophanes as "the well-born, the *sōphrones*, the upright, the fine gentlemen" (*Frogs* 727–28). Bastard though he is, Hippolytus considers himself an aristocrat: even as he is being dragged to his death by his runaway horses he will shout to his friends to come to the rescue of "the best of men" (*andr'ariston*, 1242). Hippolytus' very name is evocative of aristocratic hauteur; we may compare Pheidippides in Aristophanes' *Clouds*, whose upper-class mother "wanted a name with 'Hippos' in it: Xanthippos or Charippos or Callippides" (*Clouds* 63–64). The Panhellenic Games mentioned by Hippolytus were a favorite arena for young members of the aristocracy; for the entire period from the seventh to the fourth centuries the members of a few upper-class Athenian families dominated the chariot races.[39] Hunting, a favorite activity of Hippolytus, was another upper-class pursuit nostalgically associated by conservative thinkers with the way of life established by Lycurgus in Sparta and by "our ancestors" in Athens.[40] Hippolytus' faith in the primacy of heredity is typically aristocratic: Pindar, for one, repeatedly makes the point that natural characteristics are superior to acquired skills.[41] Finally, Hippolytus makes explicit his ideological preference for the nobility and his contempt for the common people. He is uncomfortable at the prospect of defending himself before "the rabble" (986, 989), and he feels more at ease in the company of "the few" (987).

Hippolytus' rejection of public life and his contempt for the masses mark him as a recognizable type, though he does not represent any specific Athenian living or dead. He is emblematic of those conservative upper-class citizens, out of sympathy with the direction of Athenian policy, who habitually avoided civic involvement; they could be described either as *apragmones*, "nonparticipants," or, more harshly, as *achreioi*, "useless."[42] The comportment of this group is consistent with other signs of a conservative presence in Athens in the last third of the fifth century. The reactionary viewpoint speaks forth loud and clear in the anonymous document that has been preserved among the works of Xenophon, a treatise on Athenian government so sourly antidemocratic in tone that its author has been nicknamed "the Old Oligarch."[43] The same viewpoint found political expression in the revolution of 411 B.C., whose proponents wrapped themselves in the mantle of *sōphrosynē* and who ultimately put in place a regime that Thucydides accounted the best he had ever known, featuring as it did a "moderate mixture" of democratic and oligarchic elements.[44]

If Euripides has chosen to endow Hippolytus with the outlook of a young oligarch, then the young man's *hamartia* extends far beyond the rejection of sexuality. Hippolytus' contempt for the goddess "from whom we all were born" (450) is only one aspect of a "haughtiness and exclusiveness" (93) that also manifests itself in the social and political spheres. Hippolytus lays claim to *sōphrosynē*, the virtue of moderation—and the virtue appropriated by the oligarchs. But his rectitude involves a rejection of ordinary experience, a lofty disdain for the common man. The refusal to worship Aphrodite is emblematic of a more pervasive and more dangerous desire to remove himself from the universal lot, to be "exceptional," as Theseus puts it (948), or to live life "on special terms" (459). In warning against such tendencies in the mythical person of Hippolytus, Euripides seems to suggest that sōphrosynē must be given a different construction if it is to become available as a democratic virtue.

A Crisis of Sōphrosynē

The aloof Hippolytus receives a violent shock when the nurse comes to him bearing the tale of Phaedra's illicit passion. His response is wholly in character for a young man who has refused to "touch" marriage (14), has defined his spiritual landscape in terms of exclusion, and has acknowledged Aphrodite only "from afar" (102). Hippolytus' immediate instinct is to dissociate himself from the nurse and Phaedra, to mark out the distance separating his purity from their vileness. He cries aloud to earth and sun (601) in an effort to dispel the pollution attached to the nurse's words. When the nurse, frightened by his vehemence, attempts a gesture of supplication he forbids her to touch him (606). When she reminds him of his oath of silence he retorts, "My tongue swore, but my heart was unsworn" (612).

These words will prove fatal for Hippolytus, for they make a profound impression on the listening Phaedra. She takes them as expressive of Hippolytus' fixed intent and proceeds on the assumption that the young man means to betray her to Theseus. In fact Hippolytus not only abides by his oath, but at the end of this scene explicitly assures the nurse of his intention. It is only in the first shock of revelation that he tries to deny any suggestion of complicity with the nurse, even the minimal complicity implied by the swearing of an oath. In the same mood of violent rejection, Hippolytus "spits out" (apeptus', 614) the suggestion that Phaedra is his philos: the term implies an intimacy that revolts him. At the end of his diatribe he announces his intention of purifying himself in running water; he feels polluted by the mere hearing of the nurse's proposals (653–55).

The nurse had not anticipated such a reaction. She entreats the young man to "grant pardon" (syngnōth', 615) on the grounds that "it is natural for human beings to make mistakes." The word for "pardon" implies comprehension, sympathy, and fellow feeling, but Hippolytus at this crisis is far from experiencing such emotions. He does not even reply to the nurse's plea, launching instead into a diatribe against women that contains a revealing fantasy on alternatives to sexual reproduction.

Hippolytus wonders why Zeus ever created woman, that "counterfeit evil" (616–17). If it was for the sake of propagation, then Zeus should have arranged matters so that men could go to the temples and lay down a certain amount of bronze, iron, or gold. Each could then purchase a child suited to his economic position, and men could enjoy their homes "in freedom, without women" (624).

Hippolytus' proposal would rid the world not only of sexual relationships but of the entire female sex. For contracting marriages, as he goes on to explain, is a troublesome and chancy business. Presumably the begetting of children is equally uncertain, since there is no guarantee that they will possess a good character—a consideration touched on later in the play by both Theseus (938–40) and Hippolytus (1455). For these variables Hippolytus would substitute, in a kind of Solonian reform, a fixed order of reproduction based on economic position. Men would thus be able to procure heirs with ease and security. Their domestic "freedom" (624) would be freedom from Necessity, from random external factors.

Hippolytus' denunciation of women exposes the extremism that underlies his self-proclaimed *sōphrosynē*. To be sure, his scheme is not without precedent. It had occurred to other Greeks before him that there ought to be some better means of obtaining heirs: the philosopher Democritus (Diels-Kranz B277) proposes adopting the children of friends, while another Euripidean protagonist, Jason, wishes for some alternative to begetting children through women; his wishes, indeed, that women did not exist (*Medea* 573–75). But Democritus is concerned only to ensure compatibility between parents and children; he does not propose suspending female reproduction. As for Jason, he is an experienced roué who has married before and "is about to marry again."[45] It is only Hippolytus who not only preaches but practices a wholesale rejection of the female sex.

The misogyny that informs Hippolytus' speech is also not unusual for Greek culture. Phaedra acknowledges her society's low estimation of her sex: "I know," she says, "that I am a woman, an object of dislike for all" (406–7). But it is instructive to compare Hippolytus' diatribe with another misogynist text, the poem on women by Semonides of

Amorgos. Semonides cruelly and wittily links various types of women to beasts and other natural phenomena. One woman, he explains, is descended from a sow, because she is fat and dirty; another from a vixen, because she is volatile; another from a bitch, because of her avid curiosity; another from mud; another from the sea. Semonides names ten different types in all. But they are not uniformly wicked. The last wife is compared to the virtuous and industrious bee:

> One from a bee. The man is lucky who gets her.
> She is the only one no blame can settle on.
> A man's life grows and blossoms underneath her touch.
> She loves her husband, he loves her, and they grow old
> together, while their glorious children rise to fame.
> Among the throngs of other women this one shines
> as an example. Heavenly grace surrounds her . . . [46]

Two aspects of this passage are relevant to the *Hippolytus*. Semonides' choice of the bee as emblem of mature female sexuality confirms the incursion of Aphrodite (in the form of a bee, 77) into the meadow sacred to Artemis, and confirms the futility of Hippolytus' attempt to banish *erōs* from his life.[47] Secondly, Semonides describes the bee wife as a shining exception who can serve as a model to all wives.[48] Hippolytus in his extremism rejects all women — an attitude which itself, according to a fragment of Euripides, bespeaks a lack of wisdom.[49]

Hippolytus brings his diatribe to an end with the assertion that he will never (*oupot'*) tire of denouncing women, even if he is accused of always (*aei*) harping on the same theme, because women are invariably (*aei*) unchaste. "Let someone teach them to have sound sense," he concludes (667–68), "or else grant me license to rail on forever (*aei*)." Hippolytus is in fact convinced that *sōphrosynē* is innate (cf. 79–80). He is therefore framing an impossibility when he proposes that someone should teach women rectitude, and claiming for himself the privilege of endless denunciation. This is not moderation but dangerous excess.

It is not Hippolytus' rejection of the nurse's proposals so much as his vehement and contemptuous tone that awakens an answering anger in Phaedra. For no one, Phaedra least of all, could have expected Hippolytus to respond to the nurse with enthusiasm. Phaedra was herself so horrified by her illicit passion that she initially resolved to commit suicide rather than reveal it. Even after she was induced to confess her secret, she remained firm in her resolution to die (400 ff.). Her response to Hippolytus' diatribe—which she overhears, though he largely ignores her presence—permits the audience to identify one further deficiency in Hippolytus' *sōphrosynē*.[50] It is a lack that will, however, be remedied by the end of the play.

What enrages Phaedra is precisely that attitude of remoteness and dissociation that Hippolytus has been so desperate to establish. She is determined that he shall learn not to be "arrogant toward [her] troubles" (729–30)—he shall learn that he cannot hold himself apart, but is implicated in her situation despite himself. At the same time she is desperate to take steps to preserve her own reputation, for she has been persuaded that Hippolytus means to denounce her (690–92). By a sudden inspiration she realizes that a letter to Theseus can serve a dual purpose. It will both protect her good name and compromise Hippolytus (716–18): "I have found a means . . . to pass on a reputable life to my children, and get some profit myself from what has happened."

Like Aphrodite, whose votary she is, Phaedra lays her principal emphasis on vengeance (730–31): "When he has a share with me in this malaise, he will learn rectitude." As far as Phaedra is concerned, Hippolytus' much-vaunted chastity has nothing to do with true *sōphrosynē*; that is a virtue he has yet to acquire. And it is not some painful yet ultimately salutary experience that Phaedra has in mind, but "learning through suffering" in its oldest and starkest form.[51] Phaedra intends that Hippolytus will recognize his vulnerability and come to share with her the helpless sense of being at Aphrodite's mercy only at the cost of his life.

Aphrodite, the huntsman, Phaedra, and Hippolytus himself combine to demonstrate that the young man's *sōphrosynē* has more to do with excess and deficiency than with temperance. Where then is moderation to be found? Who in the play provides an example worth imitating?

The Rhetoric of *Sōphrosynē*

The nurse appears a promising exemplar, since she draws lavishly on the vocabulary of moderation.[52] Early on, as we have seen, she takes her stance with the seven wise men and the counsel of *mēden agan*

(265). She opposes extremism in any form, declaring: "It is not right for human beings to labor overmuch at life" (467). It is she who diagnoses the elitist intransigence of both Hippolytus and Phaedra, their "unyielding standards in life" (261), their desire to live "on fixed terms, with other gods for masters" (459).

In all respects the nurse is Hippolytus' polar opposite. Whereas Hippolytus' political sympathies are oligarchic, she is clearly democratic by birth, class, and inclination.[53] Whereas Hippolytus believes that inborn qualities are crucial to human character, the nurse trusts in the value of learning and experience. "Many things," she declares, "my long life has taught me" (252), chief of which (in marked contrast to Hippolytus) is to acknowledge the power of external forces. She has developed a policy of ready acquiescence in the face of necessity, which serves her well in minor crises. Characteristically, she urges Phaedra not to struggle in her sickness but to rest "quietly" (205). But when the nurse discovers that Phaedra's illness is much graver than she had imagined, that the queen is sick with desire for Hippolytus, her counsel of acquiescence remains the same (443–46):

> Cypris is not to be endured when she arrives in full
> force; if one yields to her she comes on quietly, but when
> she finds someone who is exceptional and arrogant, she
> seizes him and does him untold violence.

In contrast to Hippolytus' ethical rigor, the nurse is characterized by a fluctuating moral sense. When her mistress confesses her love for Hippolytus she is initially overcome with horror, but quickly recovers herself and amends her attitude. Declaring that "among mortals, second thoughts are somehow wiser" (436), she redirects her energies to arguing her mistress out of any sense of wrongdoing. To this end she adopts methods that owe more to the sophists than to the seven wise men.

The nurse deploys an array of rhetorical techniques to place Phaedra's situation in the best possible light. First she advances the "argument from human nature."[54] "You are in love? What wonder? So are many people" (439). Since it is eminently natural for human beings to fall in love, she implies, there is nothing culpable about Phaedra's passion. Certainly it is not a matter worth dying over (440–42). In any case, Aphrodite punishes only those who resist her—and at this point the nurse passes over to the argument of superior force.[55] Aphrodite, who is everywhere and in every living creature, is clearly far more powerful than a single weak human being; there is no sense, the nurse suggests, in provoking her anger by resistance (443–50). The very gods fall in love, and manage to endure the embarrassment of their position; should not Phaedra (an argument by analogy, 451–60) do likewise? Reverting to the argument from human nature, the nurse reminds Phaedra that it is normal practice for people to wink at moral frailty (462–67). Boldly experimenting with language, she defines Phaedra's surrender to her passion as "endurance" (*anechein*, 459), whereas resistance would constitute *hybris* (474–75).[56] The nurse closes with the assurance that some "charms and magic incantations"—devices dear to the sophistic spirit—can be found to help Phaedra in her need.[57]

The members of the chorus adjudicate between the nurse's point of view and Phaedra's, and they decide in Phaedra's favor. The nurse's arguments are expedient, they note, but Phaedra's worthy of praise (482–85). Yet the nurse's rhetoric is so seductive that Phaedra must implore her to stop talking, lest she be persuaded to yield (503–6).

If Hippolytus' rigorous *sōphrosynē* reveals itself as excess and deficiency, the nurse's policy of infinite accommodation amounts finally to little more than deception or fraud. "It is the way of human beings to conceal what is not pretty," she assures Phaedra (466), and adds an analogy from architecture: there is no need to be punctilious about the parts of a house that will not be seen (468).

The nurse resorts to subterfuge even against the mistress she loves and has raised from childhood (cf. 698). Finding herself thwarted by Phaedra's obstinate silence, she pretends to abandon the effort to wrest information from her (289–93). In fact she is not giving up, but merely varying her approach: instead of questioning Phaedra directly she launches into a long, discursive monologue in the hope of stumbling upon the cause of Phaedra's wretchedness. She is unexpectedly successful as Phaedra reacts violently to the mention of Hippolytus. A few more questions and the story is out.

After Phaedra has revealed her secret, the nurse again has recourse to a strategic deception. She assures her mistress that she knows of remedies that will be "a drug (*pharmakon*) for your disease" (478–79). The ambiguous word *pharmakon* can refer to drugs that help or drugs that harm, either medicine or poison.[58] When the nurse finally reveals that the drug she has in mind is a tryst with Hippolytus (490–91), Phaedra begs her to proceed no further with her skillful but corrupt proposals. At this juncture the nurse pretends to have changed her mind and to have bethought herself of some *other* drugs that will help Phaedra—but honorably (508–12). Just as on the earlier occasion, she has not varied her intention in the least. And Phaedra, though suspicious (520), does not pursue her intuition but allows the nurse to reassure her. Her credulousness will have disastrous results.

When her plan goes awry the nurse is flustered but unapologetic. It is only because she has failed that she admits to a lack of *sōphrosynē* (704); if she had succeeded, she claims, the end would have justified the means and she would have been adjudged "one of the clever ones" (700). Even at this crisis her faith in her own ingenuity is undiminished, and she believes that some further strategem can yet be devised (705). This time, however, Phaedra will have none of her help.

The nurse's misuse of the counsel of moderation is simpler to diagnose than Hippolytus'. Because she was "zealous to do favors in an evil cause" (694), she became the effectual "betrayer" (591, 595) of her mistress. She subverts the principles of *mēden agan* when she twists the traditional warning against *hybris* into a justification for moral laxity (474–75). Her eloquence consists of "making shameful proposals in an attractive form" (505). She is in her own way as extreme as Hippolytus: her words are "all too fine" (487) and she herself "all too cunning" (518). She is finally, we might conclude, all too cynical and debased: for Phaedra's noble scruples she has nothing but contempt (cf.490–91). She constitutes another of the play's cautionary examples, for her "amoral realism" suggests the kind of value system that might take hold if the new relativism popularized by the sophists were not tempered with old-fashioned ethics, if there were no transmission of aristocratic ideals into the modern context.[59] The nurse proves finally as inadequate a representative of moderation as does Hippolytus.

Intelligence and Failure

When we come to consider Phaedra, it can only be with relief. She seems to strike a mean between Hippolytus and the nurse, uniting realism and experience with unshakable moral standards. Unlike Hippolytus, she does not proceed by exclusion: she avoids simplistic dualities and indulges in no fantasies about expelling or abolishing whatever she finds morally ambiguous. Almost every statement Phaedra makes includes a specific acknowledgment of complexity. She knows that one human being can ruin another without intent (319). She appreciates the difference between origins and outcomes, and is determined to "contrive good out of shamefulness" (331). She is aware that speech can sound fair but have ruinous effects (487, 503). She has come to dislike women who are "righteous in speech, but in secret possess evil daring" (413–14). She has reflected long and hard on the gap between inclination and action (373–81). She knows that the reputation of their parents can affect even sturdy, self-confident children (424). And she is aware that *aidōs* or "respect," a quality she holds in high esteem, is double-edged (385).

On the other hand Phaedra, in contrast to the nurse, declines to make her experience in life and her knowledge of Necessity's power a pretext for abandoning ethical strictures. Her sense of *noblesse oblige* exemplifies the attractive side of the aristocratic ethos: she reflects that the practice of adultery had its origins among the aristocracy, and "when shameful practices are countenanced by the nobility, they will also be approved by the low-born" (411–12). In keeping with this aristocratic perspective, Phaedra's principal concern is for her reputation. She hopes to preserve her *eukleia*, good name and good fame, intact for herself and her children (423, 489, 687, 717), and she dedicates her sophisticated awareness of complexity to this very end. She may not be able to conquer her private feelings, but she can at least control the way she is perceived by her society. It is, in fact, the motive of *eukleia* that has governed all her actions since she first fell in love with Hippolytus.

As Aphrodite recounts in the prologue, Phaedra has struggled against her passion from the outset. Her first step was to dedicate a temple to Aphrodite in an elaborate bid to propitiate the goddess. Phaedra herself fills in the rest of the story. She explains that she resolved on a policy of silence and concealment, while trying to master her passion by self-control (*tōi sōphronein*, 399). When these strategies proved futile, she resolved on suicide (401–2). That solution, she believes, will ensure her good name and permit her children to grow up "in freedom . . . enjoying a good reputation on their mother's account" (421–23).

At the moment she speaks to the chorus, Phaedra believes that she has been successful in her struggle.[60] She has heard it said that it is through "a noble and upright consciousness" (*gnōmē dikaia kagathē,* 427) that human beings can stay in contention.[61] It is in an attempt to bring such a consciousness to bear on her own situation that she offers the chorus a description of her reasoning (375–81):

> Even before now, at different times, in the long hours of
> the night I have considered in what way human life comes
> to ruin. And it seems to me that it is not because of the
> nature of their intellect [*kata gnōmēs phusin*] that men do
> wrong, for many have the ability to reason well. We should
> rather look at it this way. We know and recognize the
> right course, but fail to follow it through.

This is not the first time Phaedra has considered these problems. Her train of thought is not contrived to fit the occasion (which is what we should expect of the nurse), but represents an attitude of long standing.[62] Phaedra takes *gnōmē* or consciousness to be hereditary: she speaks of the *gnōmēs physin,* the nature of the intellect. Evidently she shares Hippolytus' aristocratic faith in *physis,* inborn nature. When she notes that human beings fail to "follow through" the right course, she uses in a positive sense the same verb, *ekponein,* that the nurse had earlier employed pejoratively (467). Phaedra thus seems to range herself on Hippolytus' side rather than the nurse's when it comes to consistency, trust in innate qualities of character, and moral resolve.

Phaedra differs from Hippolytus, however, in recognizing that human beings may fail to "follow through" not out of wickedness but from other factors, including an ambiguity in the very moral standard they have taken as their guide. Phaedra names as distractions the pleasures of conversation and leisure. Finally she speaks of *aidōs* (385–87):

> Respect [*aidōs*] is twofold: the one not evil, the other a burden
> on
> families [*achthos oikōn*]. If the *kairos* were clear, the
> two would not be spelled with the same letters.

Phaedra's whole speech has been elliptical, but her discussion of *aidōs* is particularly puzzling.[63] She does not bother to explain what she means by "respect," how it can be both "not bad," and "a burden on families," or the sense in which she is using the term *kairos*.

Aidōs can be roughly described as a concept spanning respect for oneself, for others, and for the normative standards of society.[64] We have seen that *aidōs* early on was linked to *sōphrosynē* as part of the constellation of moderation; in the spirit of this association, Hippolytus personifies *aidōs* as the gardener in his untouched meadow (77). When Phaedra speaks of a double *aidōs* she is making a distinction that goes back to Hesiod and is also to be found in a fragment of Euripides.[65] As for telling the good *aidōs* from the bad, Phaedra states unambiguously that the one factor that distinguishes them—or that *would* distinguish them, if only it were clear—is the *kairos*.

Kairos has been here variously translated as "the right occasion" or "what is appropriate to the situation."[66] But such a temporal meaning is not relevant to the play. *Aidōs* is not, in Phaedra's austere understanding, a standard to be invoked on some occasions and ignored on others. There is, for instance, no such thing as a right occasion for Phaedra to yield to her passion or for the nurse to approach Hippolytus.[67] As the play's most authoritative editor points out, *kairos* is not originally temporal in meaning: "The noun itself first appears (in proverbial expressions) as the right degree or amount, in opposition (expressed or implied) to *agan*."[68] In support he cites Hesiod (who, we may remember, concluded his warning against overloading ships and wagons with the adjuration, "Observe moderation; due measure [*kairos*] is best in everything"), as well as Theognis and Critias.

In default of any thematic emphasis on "the right time," and in view of the prominence in the play of the ideology of *mēden agan*, it is arguable that Phaedra is using the term *kairos* to differentiate between degrees of *aidōs*. Too much respect, she will then be saying, is a burden on families, while the right amount, the appropriate amount, is no bad thing. Such a statement is applicable both to Hippolytus' situation and to her own. Hippolytus, as we have seen, cultivated the related virtue of *sōphrosynē* to excess and with disastrous consequences. But the disaster would not have occurred without Phaedra's active participation. Her conduct too can be seen as a miscalculation—but in her case of *aidōs* rather than *sōphrosynē*.

Phaedra defines *aidōs* in terms of her own good name. Her aristocratic concern with reputation is consistent with the norms of her society, but she goes too far when she resolves to ruin Hippolytus in order to safeguard her own position. Her vengeful impulse would be appropriate if Hippolytus were her enemy, but he has stated explicitly that he will not denounce her, that he intends to abide by his oath of silence.[69] Phaedra's excessive concern for her own reputation translates into a reckless disregard of Hippolytus'. Phaedra's mistake or *hamartia*, like her stepson's, is that of disproportion.

Phaedra also resembles Hippolytus in her excessive self-assurance.[70] At the moment that she makes her speech to the chorus she is confident that she has negotiated all the dangers of her situation. But when she describes the obstacles to discovering the right amount of *aidōs* she is offering a self-diagnosis, and when she comments on the difficulty of "following through" on the right course of action she is predicting her own destiny. Despite her deep understanding of human nature, Phaedra is unable to maintain her clarity of purpose. She allows herself to be deceived by the nurse—a misjudgment that will indeed (as she remarks, 386) prove grievous for the *oikos*.

The right and the wrong amount of *aidōs* should not, according to Phaedra, be called by the same name. How, then should her own conduct be described? That question puzzles even Artemis, who offers two alternative assessments: "either lustful frenzy, or a kind of nobility" (1300–1301). Even though Phaedra carries her pursuit of *aidōs* to excess, Artemis acknowledges the element of idealism in her effort. In making this measured and even compassionate judgment the goddess points the way, at once for Hippolytus and for the audience, toward the revised form of moderation displayed in the closing scene of the tragedy.

The Reallocation of Virtues

Even as it displays the inexorable working out of Aphrodite's revenge, the end of the play brings forth a revised paradigm of moderation. Euripides had already changed his allocation of moderation's constituent qualities between the first and the second versions of the play, transferring Phaedra's hubristic audacity to the nurse and abolishing the stark polarity of Hippolytus and Phaedra. At the end of the extant tragedy, as if to emphasize their migratory and protean quality, he makes a broader distribution of the virtues so single-mindedly pursued by the protagonists. He also introduces into the constellation of moderation an element hitherto unrepresented.

Hippolytus had initially pronounced himself the epitome of *sōphrosynē*, while condemning Phaedra's wantonness. Artemis takes care to reaffirm his first claim (cf. 1402); but Phaedra's *sōphrosynē* is also commended, and that by no less a judge than Hippolytus himself. As he stands beside her corpse Hippolytus acknowledges that Phaedra, "though not possessing temperance, found a way to manifest it; whereas I, who possessed it, did not use it well" (1034–35). He cannot speak openly for fear of breaking his oath of silence, but clearly he is referring to Phaedra's suicide and contrasting her hard-won victory over her passion with his inability to turn his virtuous qualities to good purpose. Beyond its immediate context, the statement suggests that Hippolytus has been led by harsh experience to revise his previous definition of *sōphrosynē*. He here seems to acknowledge that rectitude is not purely innate and cannot be achieved simply through renunciation.

Hippolytus' words suggest a new sense of the limitations of quietism and a new appreciation for a more active and dynamic mode. Although he is thinking in purely individual terms, his recognition also has implications in the public sphere. From the outset Euripides has invited the audience to evaluate the protagonists as exemplars, and in Greek thought the additional step of drawing an analogy between the exemplary individual and the state was one easily made.[71] Hippolytus' words suggest that *sōphrosynē* is no longer to be envisaged as a static virtue, no longer defined in terms of aristocratic quietism and renunciation. It has thus been made compatible with the vital, energetic temper of imperial Athens—the spirit that differentiated Athens so sharply from Sparta and which was condemned as "interference" (*polypragmosynē*) by its opponents but commended as "dynamism" (*to drastērion*) by its advocates.[72] With such a shift in connotation, *sōphrosynē*, along with its constellation of associated qualities, becomes available as a democratic quality. Euripides has achieved a revised image of moderation by fusing its mythical and its contemporary, its private and public, its sexual and political manifestations.

Sōphrosynē is not the only quality to be reallocated at the close of the play. The good name that had been Phaedra's particular concern is bestowed on her victim. When Artemis appears and tells Theseus the truth about Phaedra and Hippolytus, it is with the primary aim of redeeming Hippolytus' reputation (*eukleia*, 1299). The story does not damage Phaedra, since Artemis is careful not to pass judgment on her

(1300–1301), but it does not precisely enhance her reputation either. Artemis prophesies, to be sure, that Phaedra's name will also endure (1429–30), but in connection with the cult of Hippolytus to be established at Troezen. Ironically, Phaedra will be remembered for the passion that she had perceived as fatal to her reputation and had done her utmost to suppress.

The action of the play does not constitute an attack on the aristocratic ideals cultivated so ardently and so disastrously by Hippolytus and Phaedra; to the contrary, they are commended as well worth honoring. The protagonists' solipsistic pursuit of these ideals, however, is shown to have been based on a miscalculation, for moderation cannot be defined merely in terms of personal rectitude. At Artemis' instigation and in the last moments of his life, Hippolytus succeeds in modeling an attitude that has been absent from previous representations of the middle way: *syngnōmē*, comprehension or forgiveness. It is this quality that makes it possible to bridge the gap separating each individual from his fellows and ensures that individual integrity will not be achieved at the expense of other human beings.

Tolerance, compassion, and forgiveness are manifested in Greek literature as early as the *Iliad*, but only under the most extraordinary circumstances.[73] It is only possible, after all, to pardon those who have first done wrong to oneself, and forgiveness runs counter to the traditional Greek adjuration to help one's friends and harm one's enemies. As is so often the case Achilles, with his generous reception of his enemy Priam at the end of the *Iliad*, is the exception who proves the rule and who also furnishes a point of departure for the subsequent literary tradition. For the rest, *syngnōmē* is not a familiar concept before the fifth century. The term comes into use primarily in judicial contexts, as acquittal, punishment, or pardon begin to be based on careful determinations of personal responsibility. Only gradually does it establish itself outside such contexts as a positive virtue.[74]

The term is used by the humbler characters in the *Hippolytus* in connection with the ignoring or glossing over of faults.[75] Thus the servant prays to Aphrodite on Hippolytus' behalf (117–19):

You must grant pardon [*syngnōmē*]. If someone speaks
follies . . . on account of his youthfulness, seem not to
hear it.

The nurse invokes *syngnōmē* to the same end when she begs Hippolytus to keep Phaedra's passion a secret (615). Artemis, in contrast, uses the term in its judicial sense. She promises Theseus exculpation (1326) on technical grounds: he was ignorant of all the facts, and Phaedra's letter positively misled him (1334–37). But she sounds anything but forgiving as she berates Theseus and expresses her own bitterness over Hippolytus' death. She supplies Theseus with the legal grounds for his self-defense, but there is no compassion in her words.

Hippolytus takes his cue from Artemis, but he goes far beyond legal technicalities when he absolves his father of responsibility for his death.[76] His decision is based on a clear understanding of everything his father has said and done. There is no glossing over of Theseus' conduct: Hippolytus knows that his father cursed him in addition to banishing him (1411), thus punishing him twice over. He also points out that Theseus would have killed him even without the curse, so furious was he (1413). But he feels pity for his father: he mourns for Theseus more than for himself (cf. 1405, 1407, 1409). He asks his father to hold him close at the moment of dying (1444–45). Most important of all from Theseus' point of view, by freeing him from accountability Hippolytus saves the man who has ruined him twice over from twofold punishment. Hippolytus exempts Theseus not only from the exile that would otherwise be the penalty for involuntary manslaughter, but also from the uncleanness of pollution (cf. 1448).

As he grants pardon to his father, Hippolytus sets limits to anger and vengeance—a course of action that Artemis recommends to both parties (1431–36) but does not herself put into practice. Artemis' own anger, as befits an immortal, is never-ending. She announces that she intends to destroy Aphrodite's next favorite in retaliation for the death of Hippolytus (1420–22). Aphrodite, we may imagine, will respond in kind, and so the divine vendetta will continue.

Hippolytus' forgiveness does not extend to the gods. He dies unrepentant toward the divinity who destroyed him, wishing (1415) that it were possible for human beings to become a curse on the gods. But the form of his complaint (grammatically it is an "impossible wish") shows that he has finally grasped the vast distance that separates mortals from gods—an insight underscored by his rueful observation that Artemis can "easily" abandon their long association (1441).

Hippolytus' recognition of the gods' imperviousness makes him more responsive to the human suffering of his father, and to what it means, in fact, to be human himself. The ability to let go of anger is a characteristic closely bound up with the recognition of mortality and the possession of *sōphrosynē*. Those connections are only implicit here, but Euripides makes them explicit in a fragment from another play (799 N²):

> Since we have mortal frames, it is fitting for anyone who understands the meaning of rectitude not to harbor immortal anger.

Moderation truly understood must include an acknowledgment not only of our distance from the gods but also of our connection to other human beings—of certain universals of human experience, above all the fact that we are all subject to Necessity. Such is the lesson Phaedra had wanted Hippolytus to learn (667). He shows that he has done so when he links himself, his father, and Phaedra as triple victims of Aphrodite (1403), and he acts on this understanding to forgive his father.

Hippolytus has travelled a long way since the beginning of the play. Initially he had personified the limitations of a traditional, elitist *sōphrosynē*. The nurse proved a false representative of moderation, which served her merely as a pretext for abandonment of principle. While Phaedra appreciated the obstacles standing in the way of a principled life, she was unable to translate her insights into practice. It is left for Artemis to recommend and the dying Hippolytus to adopt an attitude that springs from fellow feeling and whose salient characteristic is tolerance. In absolving Theseus Hippolytus the bastard shows himself truly noble, *gennaios* (1452). He offers a model not only for Theseus' legitimate children (1455), but for all who watch or read his story.

Will such an attitude keep its practitioner safe from harm? Such had been the original impulse behind the counsel of moderation. In this play the members of the chorus express the hopeful prayer that a spirit of accommodation may go hand in hand with prosperity and happiness (1108-19):

> Change comes now from one direction, now from another;
> life for human beings is always restless, always shifting.
> If only, I pray, may fate grant me this from

the gods: a destiny that is prosperous and a spirit
untouched by grief. May my judgment be neither rigid nor
falsely stamped, but by changing my ways to adapt
to the passage of time, may I live my whole life in good
fortune.

To avoid Hippolytus and Phaedra's rigidity and the speciousness of
the nurse is indeed to find the middle way. But it is naïve to expect that
such a policy will result in good fortune. The power of Necessity, represented in this play by Aphrodite, is too vast for human beings to appease it by accommodation. It is in any case (Euripides seems to intimate) not for safety's sake that we should practice moderation; the
play acclaims *sōphrosynē* as an ethical virtue independent of its utilitar-
ian value. In recognizing the instability of life, in attempting a
balanced existence with no guarantee of success or reward, in forgiving themselves and others for inevitable failures, mortals acknowledge
and confirm that which in themselves is most characteristically
human.

NOTES

1. Evidence for the first *Hippolytus* is discussed in Barrett 1964 (henceforth "Barrett"), 11–12.

2. The best evidence for the first Phaedra's character is fr. C (Barrett), in which she announces that Eros is her "instructor in boldness and reck-lessness."

3. See North 1966, 6–10, for the connection between *sōphrosynē* and *aidōs*, and 16–18 for *hybris* as the antonym of *sōphrosynē*.

4. For polarity and complementarity among the divine and human charac-ters, see Frischer 1970, 85–87.

5. Critias credits the gnome to Chilon, as does Aristotle; Demetrius of Phalerum attributes it to Solon, Plato to "the seven wise men." References in Mette 1933, 8–9, n. 3. For the inscriptions on the temple see Wilkins 1917, 1–7; see also Parke and Wormell 1956, vol. 1, 386–87.

6. At *Il.* 6.208. The exhortation is associated with aristocratic values by Greenhalgh 1972, 190.

7. For discussion of normative and empirical *gnōmai* see Solmsen 1975, 149.

8. For the political context of Theognis, see Figueira 1985, 128–46; of Solon, Murray 1980, 173–91.

9. *Theog.* 335, 401. *Mēden agan* occurs also at 219 and 657. Discussion in Wilkins 1926, 135.

10. De Ste Croix 1981, 278. Nagy 1985, in contrast, interprets the corpus of Theognis as poetic accretion not attributable to a single author.

11. Cf. Theog. 441–46.

12. Cf. frr. 5, 6, 34, and 37 (West). For the aristocratic assumptions behind Solon's reforms, see Greenhalgh 1972, 194–95.

13. Graham and Forsythe 1984, 34. On political *sōphrosynē* see also Grossman 1950, 126–45.

14. North 1966, 137.

15. Thuc. 3.82.8. Graham and Forsythe 1984 take *protimēsei* with *aristokratias sōphronos*, producing a three-word formula. Although they make a good case for their interpretation, *aristokratia sōphrōn* still sounds more effective as a slogan.

16. Kovacs 1987 maintains (71) that the characters' "faults—such as Hippolytus' intolerance and extremity and Phaedra's willingness to sacrifice her stepson's life for her own honor and revenge—are without real relevance to their fate, a fate for which Aphrodite must bear full responsibility." But this statement is at odds with his argument (30–31) that both protagonists are cast in the mold of the Sophoclean hero who makes his choice and pays the penalty. If Hippolytus and Phaedra were not responsible for the tragic outcome, they could not attain the heroic status Kovacs assigns them.

17. Devereux 1985 offers an extreme example of the psychological approach. For a good discussion of ethos in the play see Michelini 1987, 290–94. For possible reasons for the unusual psychological elaboration of the *Hippolytus*, see Griffin 1990, 134–39.

18. Cf. Aristoph. *Frogs* 1050–51 and 1063–66; Plat. *Prot.* 325e–326a; Lycurgus, *Against Leocrates* 100–104. For discussion see Verdenius 1970, especially p. 4, n. 3, and p. 7, n. 20.

19. For discussion of this development, with references, see North 1966, 135–42.

20. Apollodorus is cited by Harpocration as deriving the epithet from the fact that the Athenian temple was built close to the agora, the place of assembly for *panta ton dēmon FGH* (244 F113). Nicander of Colophon's explanation, also cited by Harpocration, is that the temple was built from the profits of prostitutes. For a whimsical derivation of the name see Plat. *Sym.* 180d. Discussion and references under "Pandemos," Pauly/Wissowa, *Real-Encyclopädie* 18.3, cols. 507–10.

21. This point is made by Goldhill 1986, 120, who further associates Hippolytus' hunting with a rejection of society.

22. For the statue of Aphrodite see 101. Barrett notes (p. 154) that there is no explicit mention of a symmetrical statue of Artemis, but that the action at 58 ff. and again at 1092 ff. supports its existence.

23. Cf. the use of *monos* with the same connotations of vulnerability at *Bacch.* 962 and 963.

24. Barrett *ad* 17. The same verb, with the same implication, recurs at 949.

25. Lattimore 1939, 24. The analogy between the servant and Herodotean advisers is also noted, but rejected, by Kovacs 1987, 36. Kovacs believes that Hip-

polytus manifests his (Sophoclean) heroism by rejecting "prudential advice from a sensible underling." But a more typical pattern for Euripides is to portray underlings (for example, the messenger later in this play who believes in Hippolytus' innocence, or the messenger in the *Bacchae* who advises Pentheus to acknowledge Dionysus, or the old man in the *Iphigenia in Aulis*) who are morally correct in their advice and show themselves more perceptive than their masters. Euripides also portrays underlings, like the old man in the *Ion*, or the nurse in this play, who are both rash and morally obtuse, but Hippolytus' old servant obviously does not fall into this category.

26. At 103. Dimock 1979, 246, argues that l. 100 is evidence of Hippolytus' piety: "Hippolytus is properly and naturally shocked at what he takes to be the Huntsman's inadvertent impropriety." But (as Dimock himself acknowledges) *semnos* is so commonly used of divinities in a favorable sense that this interpretation seems unlikely.

27. "Pride" is Barrett's translation; he is attempting (*ad* 93), to find a single word with both positive and negative connotations to match the Greek.

28. So Barrett *ad* 97, but he does not pursue the implications of his statement. Frischer 1970, 97, takes up the suggestion and argues that the whole play serves to confirm the "hypothesis" of l. 98, namely that "gods observe the same laws as men." This position leads him to a very forced reading of the close of the play, where most scholars have seen a definitive parting of the ways between gods and men. Like Frischer, Kovacs (1980B, 133; cf. 1987, 37) argues that "the whole of the prologue blurs the contrast between humanity and divinity by the statements that are made about the gods and men." He adduces lines 7–8, where Aphrodite explains that divinities, like mortals, delight in honor. But as Barrett points out *ad loc.*, this statement is something of a commonplace, recurring in both *Bacchae* and *Alcestis*. The realm of pride and honor is one of the few areas of coincidence between gods and mortals. Otherwise, Greek observers seldom lose sight of the basic discrepancies in power and hence in situation.

29. Cf. 25, 61, 103, 143, 886, and 1130 for *semnos* in a religious context or used of divinities; 957 and 1064 for *semnos* used unfavorably with reference to Hippolytus by Theseus; 1364 for *semnos* used favorably by Hippolytus *of himself*—an exceptional usage that suggests that at that point he still does not acknowledge the discrepancy of situation between mortals and divinities.

30. See Segal 1965, 158–59, and Frischer 1970, 88–90, for these coincidences of imagery.

31. Knox 1952, 28 ff.

32. Segal 1965, 122. Hippolytus' fatal ignorance of his own nature is suggested by the fact that even his chosen landscape carries reminders of Aphrodite. From the *Iliad* on, the image of a grassy meadow has powerful sacroerotic associations (Motte 1973, 1–37 and 207–13; see also Bremer 1975). For the bee see below, n. 47.

33. North 1966, p. 76, n. 105, and p. 99.

34. For *kakos* in this sense cf. 81, 651, 666, 949 (where Theseus is quoting Hippolytus' own words back at him), 1031, 1071, 1075, 1191. Ann Michelini reminds

me that the sense of "base" or "lowborn" is also latent in the aristocratic Hippolytus' use of *kakos*.

35. For the play's debate over the origins of *sōphrosynē*, cf. Winnington-Ingram 1960, 183–84.

36. Cf. Zeitlin 1985, 56: "Broadly speaking, Hippolytus' refusal of eros can be summarized as the self's radical refusal of the Other."

37. For the technique of argumentation involved, see Solmsen 1975, 14–15.

38. As suggested by North 1966, p. 79, n. 120. Adkins 1972, 3–4, has a good discussion of the difficulties involved in matching the connotations of Greek to English.

39. Davies 1981, 100–102.

40. Cf. Xen. *Const. Laced.* 4.7 and *On Hunting* 12.6–19.

41. *Oly.* 2.80 ff.; *Oly.* 9.100 ff.; *Nem.* 3.40 ff.

42. Cf. Thuc. 2.40.2. Euripides' Ion resembles Hippolytus in his aristocratic fastidiousness and quietism (cf. Walsh 1978, 305–6). Connor 1972, 184–85, and Carter 1986, 52–56, both discuss Hippolytus as representative of the "noble youths" who declined to participate in public life; neither, however, relates this aspect to other features of his character.

43. For the character and date of the treatise see Will 1978.

44. *Sōphrosynē*: Thuc. 8.53.3, 8.64.5. "Moderate mixture": 8.97.2. For discussion of the intellectual climate leading up to the revolution, see Forrest 1975.

45. Page 1964⁵, *ad* 573.

46. Semonides 7.83–89, translated by Lattimore 1955.

47. For the cultural associations of bees see Detienne 1974.

48. For an alternative interpretation of the poem see Loraux 1978, 64, who argues that because the praise of the bee-wife is followed by a sweeping condemnation of all women she is "un mirage." But Semonides makes it clear that he is excepting the bee-woman from the others with the adjective *alla* (94). To expect him to mark the exemption any more clearly is to apply an unreasonable standard of rigor.

49. Fr. 657 N²: "The man who lumps all women together and reviles them in a single phrase is foolish and unwise. For among many women you will find this one bad, that one . . . possessed of a noble character."

50. The staging of this scene has been much debated. Kovacs 1987, p. 134, n. 80, revives the suggestion of Smith 1960B that lines 669–79 are sung by the nurse, Phaedra having left the stage at l. 600. The proposal is attractive because it explains why Phaedra does not take into account Hippolytus' reaffirmation of his oath (she cannot do so if she heard nothing about the oath in the first place), but it is unacceptable on other grounds. Kovacs himself admits that it would be irregular to have a lower-class figure sing a monody. Further, the content of the song is much more suitable to Phaedra than to the nurse. It would be out of character for the nurse to reflect that she had received her just deserts (672) or refer to her *erga* as *adika* (677), for she has no use for that kind of morally evaluative language (cf. 500). The monody is suitable for Phaedra because, as Barrett notes, it echoes her previous identification of herself with the lot of all women. The reference to *technai* and *logoi* prepares for

her ingenious letter. And when she calls on earth and light she echoes Hippolytus (cf. 601), as she has earlier been wont to do. For additional objections to the suggestion see Michelini 1987, 289, n. 57.

That Phaedra seems to discount Hippolytus' final assurance in fact poses no great difficulty. His promise, coming after his statement at l. 612, is phrased so reluctantly and with so much hostility that she has no reason to believe him *unless* she understands the sort of scrupulous person he is, which she does not. Theseus too does not appreciate this quality in his son, and Artemis stresses the point for his instruction (1307-9).

51. Cf. Aes. *Ag.* 176-81, where it is again *sōphrosynē* that is to be learned through suffering.

52. Cf. Smith 1960B, 175: "The nurse is an authority on moderation." He views her as an essentially comic figure (171), but the fact that she divides the theme of moderation with Phaedra and Hippolytus, coupled with the very serious consequences of her intervention, tells against such an interpretation.

53. Knox 1952, 18.

54. For a description of this ploy see Finley 1942, 54-55.

55. Cf. Saïd 1978, 178-98, for a discussion of this and other sophistic contributions to fifth-century discussions of personal responsibility.

56. For sophistic experimentation with language, cf. Solmsen 1975, 83-125.

57. At 478. For the connection between magic spells and the sophists cf. de Romilly 1975, 3-10.

58. Cf. de Romilly 1975, 34-35.

59. The term "amoral realism" is Kovacs' (1987, 52).

60. Kovacs 1980, 291.

61. She is evidently expressing a traditional aristocratic belief: for the same faith in *gnōmē*, cf. Theog. 1171-76.

62. Phaedra addresses the issue of consistency at 388-90.

63. For detailed analysis of the speech see Willink 1968, Claus 1972, and Kovacs 1980.

64. Cf. Barrett *ad* 78 with further references. For a survey of usages see von Erffa 1937.

65. At *W.&D.* 317-19; Eur. fr. 365 N^2 (references in Barrett *ad* 385-86). These parallels, as well as the word order of the Greek, make it likely (*pace* Willink 1968, 15, followed by Claus 1972 and Kovacs 1980) that Phaedra is referring to "two kinds of *aidōs*," rather than "two kinds of pleasure"—also a syntactical possibility.

66. "Right occasion": Dodds 1929, 103. "Appropriate to the situation": Segal 1970, 286. Goldhill 1986, 135, however, translates "right measure."

67. Dodds 1925, 103, interprets Phaedra's words with reference to the other occurrences of *aideisthai* in the play, and he argues that Phaedra honors *aidōs* appositely at l. 244, when she refuses to take refuge in delirium and madness, and inappositely at l. 335, when she honors the nurse's "conventional claim" of suppliancy. In addition to the obscurity of these references (noted by Kovacs 1980, 289), Dodds' notion of "conventional" suppliancy tells against this interpretation. The Greeks viewed suppliancy as a powerful religious

claim. Blame might be attached to the nurse, who misused suppliancy for trivial purposes, but not to Phaedra who honored it.

Segal 1970, 283–85, focuses on the same lines and explains the double *aidōs* as an "externalized" respect for the opinion of society (manifested at 335), and an "inward" sense of individual standards (manifested at 244). But Phaedra's "shame" at 244 is surely at having expressed her fantasies *aloud*, risking the censure of her audience. Phaedra is primarily outer-directed in her overwhelming concern for her reputation, as Segal seems to acknowledge when he refers to her "tendency to give too much weight to public opinion and *eukleia*" (285). She does not articulate any inward "conscience," distinct from her fear of public exposure.

68. Barrett *ad* 386–87. Cf. also Wilson 1980 and Race 1981.

69. I owe this point to George Dimock.

70. For additional similarities between the two, see Frischer 1970, 92–93.

71. Cf. Plato's statement (*Rep.* 368d–e) that the state is simply the individual "written in larger letters."

72. For the contrast between Athenian activity and Spartan inactivity, see Thuc. 1.70. For *to drastērion* see Thuc. 2.63.3. For discussion of the *polypragmosynē-apragmosynē* complex as applied to both individuals and states, see Ehrenburg 1947, Kleve 1964, Adkins 1976, Allison 1979, and Carter 1986.

73. See de Romilly 1979 for a survey of the vocabulary, contexts, and development of the qualities that she groups under the rubric of "la douceur." She shows (97–126) that in the fourth century the claim of tolerance and compassion was closely linked to Athenian democracy. This association may be latent in the *Hippolytus* but is certainly no more than that.

74. For differentiations of responsibility in Attic homicide law, see Barrett *ad* 1431–36. For the development of *syngnōmē*, see de Romilly 1979, 66–67.

75. As de Romilly 1979, 66, points out, these are the associations proper to the Latin *ignoscere* rather than to Greek *syngignōskein*.

76. At 1449–51. De Romilly 1979, 89, notes both the legal basis of the pardon and Hippolytus' tenderness for his father.

3

Hecuba

The *Hecuba*, out of critical favor for many years, has recently become the object of renewed interest. Studies by Reckford (1985) and Nussbaum (1986) both take as their point of departure Hecuba's soliloquy (592–602) on the consistency of human nature. Hecuba reflects that human beings are innately either good or bad (although she acknowledges that teaching and example also have a role to play) and behave in character throughout their lives. Both critics maintain that Hecuba constitutes the exception to her own rule — a character who degenerates under vicissitude until she resembles a beast more than a human being, the moral equivalent of the howling dog she will actually become in the metamorphosis foretold by Polymestor at the end of the play.

Michelini (1987) concurs with this assessment, assimilating Hecuba's characterization to the other aesthetic anomalies she perceives in the play. Kovacs (1987) departs from the other treatments in viewing the play in political terms: "One of the most important contrasts in the play is between Greek and barbarian. . . . It is the contrast between the newer democratic world of the Greek army and the older dynastic world of the barbarian nations."[1]

Kovacs has drawn attention to an important dimension of the play, for political oppositions inform the action and are underscored by repeated allusions to Athenian scenes and institutions: the popular assembly with its noisy tumult, its speakers and demagogues; the Athenian "enactment formula"; the cherished democratic principle of *isonomia*.[2] But his formulation tells only half the story. It is quite true that Euripides makes critical reference to some internal features of Athenian democracy in his account of the Greek assembly and his portrait of the soldiery, whose volatile nature is denounced by Hecuba and exploited by Odysseus the demagogue.[3] In the interpretation advanced here, however, the play's main political thrust lies elsewhere: Athenian imperialism is the reference point for the unequal relationship between the Greek commanders and the Trojan captives, between the powerful and the powerless. If we take the Trojan queen as representative of the second group and trace her interchanges with her captors through the play, we shall arrive at a different account of Hecuba's development from that offered by critics of her moral degeneration. We shall also find that the play warns against the imperialist mentality that would (if we can believe Thucydides) emerge a decade later as part of the official discourse of Athens.

Hecuba and Trojan Women

Two surviving plays of Euripides, *Hecuba* and *Trojan Women*, take place in the immediate aftermath of the Trojan War. The postwar setting seems to have crystallized for Euripides the moral questions associated with disparities in power—questions that remained in abeyance so long as the outcome of the conflict was undecided.

Although *Trojan Women* was written some nine years later than the *Hecuba*, its action is chronologically earlier, and the two plays' respective points of departure suggest different stages of the readjustment that follows upon war. At the start of *Trojan Women* the war has just ended. Troy is still standing, the Greek fleet is still drawn up on the Trojan shore, and the captives have yet to be allotted to their Greek masters. Of the two groups the victors remain in the background, for the most part transmitting their orders through the herald Talthybius. Their primary function in the play is to torment the Trojan women—a role that is at any rate unequivocal and allows their victims to view them without illusions. Throughout the Greeks are treated as an undifferentiated group—all equally guilty of sacrilege in Athena's eyes, of folly in Cassandra's.[4]

The focus of *Trojan Women* centers on the royal captives, who in contrast to the Greeks are highly individualized. Each of the women interprets her situation distinctively, in accordance with her own history and ethos, and these differences testify to the persistence of individual character even in circumstances that might be expected to mute or suppress it. The women still function as a community, and Hecuba draws sustenance from her encounters with the other royal women: Cassandra, Andromache, even Helen.

The opening of the *Hecuba* gives notice of a different state of affairs. After burning Troy to the ground the Greeks have crossed over to the

Thracian Chersonese. As the play begins, the fleet has been in Thrace for three days (32–36). Departure has been delayed by the appearance of the shade of Achilles, holding the fleet in check and demanding some honor (*geras*).[5]

The unspecified amount of time that has elapsed since the taking of Troy has brought about important changes, both breaking down the division between the two communities of Greeks and Trojans and altering relationships within the two groups. The community of royal captives has been broken up and distributed among the Greek commanders. They are not in close contact with one another, as we realize when Hecuba, in need of a dream-interpreter, wonders "where on earth" (*pou pote*, 87) she might find Helenus or Cassandra. She is by no means certain which members of her family are still alive; she fears for Polydorus, yet when his draped corpse is first brought before her she wonders whether it is Cassandra's (676–77). The only member of her family whose presence Hecuba can rely on is Polyxena—as becomes clear when Polyxena too is about to be wrested from her (280–81): "She, in place of many, is my consolation, my city, my nurse, my staff, my escort of the road."

To be sure, Hecuba still counts on support from her fellow captives. Their coalescence into a group characterized only as "the excellent Trojan women" (1052) serves the needs of the plot—both Euripides' and Hecuba's. In their choral capacity the Trojan women lament the past and voice their anxieties for the future, conveying a sense of the general fate of which Hecuba is the representative. It is also by functioning as a group that the captive women can most effectively come to the aid of their former queen. They overpower Polymestor by consummate deception and sheer numbers. As Hecuba observes, "A multitude is formidable—and hard to resist when it brings cunning into play" (884).

If the Trojan women have merged into a collective, then the conquerors have lost, with the advent of peace, whatever unanimity they may have once possessed. The conflicts among the leaders, only partially subordinated to the common goal of taking Troy, have reemerged with the coming of peace. Engrained character traits, familiar to the contemporary audience from the *Iliad*, have reasserted themselves: once more Achilles shows himself wrathful and exigent, Agamemnon an indecisive womanizer, Odysseus crafty and manipulative.[6]

In reporting the decision to sacrifice Polyxena (220), Odysseus adopts the stylized language of an Athenian decree: "The Greeks have resolved . . . " His phraseology glosses over the heated debate that preceded the vote and his own role in its outcome. Because of his intimacy with Cassandra, Agamemnon made an attempt to shield Polyxena, but the two sons of Theseus accused him of letting private motives outweigh the public interest (127–29): "They said that they would not let Cassandra's bed take precedence over Achilles' lance."

Such an implication might be expected to hit home with the army, recalling as it does both Agamemnon's dilemma at Aulis over the sacrifice of Iphigenia, and his confrontation with Achilles at Troy over the return of Chryseis. The argument does not, however, prove decisive with the soldiers, who remain divided over the necessity for a sacrifice. Solidarity is only achieved through Odysseus' rhetorical intervention.

If the dynamics within the two communities have shifted, the relationship between them has undergone an even more striking change. The Trojan captives, formerly considered by the Greeks as enemies but also as equals, have now become their slaves—personal property placed in their care and keeping. It is an intimate yet ambiguous relationship. The Trojan women are not certain whether the Greeks are kindly or "ill disposed" (*dysmenēs*, 300, 745–46); that is, they do not know whether the Greeks are prepared to assume responsibility for their well-being. If they are not, then nothing can save Polyxena. In the Greek scheme of values the death of a captive slave is a matter of no consequence; what signifies (as Odysseus puts it, 134) is paying honor to "the best of all the Greeks." If they are well disposed, then (as Hecuba argues, 291–92) Polyxena should be spared, since Greek homicide law "applies equally to the shedding of slave and free blood."

Hecuba makes a desperate effort to define the new relationship in terms that will ensure the captives certain basic rights. What she is seeking is justice—a quest of common concern (as Agamemnon admits, 902–4) to individuals and communities. Her pleas to Odysseus and Agamemnon are couched in personal terms, but they simultaneously raise questions of urgent import for the imperial city of Athens. What standards should prevail in the interchanges of strong and weak? Do the victors have a right to behave exactly as they please, or are they subject to universal standards equally applicable to strong and weak? What are the recourses of the conquered? Should they submit to their masters' will or should they do their utmost to resist?

Since those currently weak were only recently strong, and since those now prosperous may well, according to traditional Greek wisdom, suffer reverses in the future, these questions are closely bound up with the theme of change. One of the play's final images is that of transformation (*metastasis*, 1266): of Hecuba changed into a "bitch with fiery eyes," whose watery grave will bear the name of Cynossema, "The Bitch's Tomb" (1265, 1271–73). The backdrop of the tragedy is the war that has turned a queen into a slave, a mother rich in offspring into a crone "childless, cityless, abandoned, the most wretched of human beings" (810–11), and a city into ashes. The transfiguration of the city is an image to which the women of the chorus constantly return, even specifying the very instant when it occurred: the midnight hour when the men had retired to sleep, the women were preparing for bed, and the streets were suddenly filled with the shouts of enemy soldiers (905–32).

Framed by the transformation of Troy into ashes (already part of history at the opening of the play) and by Hecuba's metamorphosis into a bitch (still to come as the play draws to an end) comes a methodical investigation of the alterations brought about by war. Euripides takes note of the effect of power on human conduct, catalogs the resources available to strong and weak, and finally affirms the tenacity of the human quest for justice.

The Resources of the Powerful: *Anankē*

War is an event so complex in its origins and far-reaching in its consequences that it seems natural to trace its advent to the gods or impersonal fate. Such is the pattern of attribution set by the *Iliad*, whose action is traced to "the will of Zeus" as early as its fifth line; it is a pattern frequently echoed in this play. When the ghost of Polydorus predicts his sister's sacrifice, he speaks of the "fixed destiny" that is bringing her to her death (43). He also suggests that Hecuba's enslavement is the work of "one of the gods" and represents a balancing of past prosperity with present hardship (57–58).

The Trojan women themselves ascribe their situation to *anankē* or necessity. "Toils, and necessity stronger than toils, circle round," they lament (639–40). Polyxena decides to die "as a matter of necessity" (346) as well as of her own free will. According to the play's closing anapests, "harsh necessity" compels the women's departure to Greece. Yet the term *ananke* also appears in the play in contexts that challenge this fatalistic interpretation and encourage the audience to look more closely at the responsibility of the conquerors for the suffering of the conquered.

Ananke figures in Greek literature from Homer on, but with connotations that vary over time. In its first appearances it has an essentially concrete and pictorial value, suggesting something like "yoke" or "chain."[7] It is regularly used of the constraint exercised by the strong over the weak: so in the *Iliad* the "day of freedom," *eleutheron emar*, is contrasted to the "day of slavery," *emar anankaion* (*Il.* 16.831, 836).

By the fifth century *ananke* becomes more abstract in connotation. It is now commonly associated with fate, instinct, and need, with the impersonal laws that exercise their sway over all human beings.[8] So Hecuba in *Trojan Women* (886) speculates on whether Zeus represents the mind of man or the necessity of nature. Aristophanes refers jocularly to sexual appetites as "needs of nature" (*tes physeos anankai*, *Clouds* 1075). On the subject of power and domination, Thucydides' Athenians remark to the Melians that "our opinion of the gods and our knowledge of men lead us to conclude that it is a general and necessary rule of nature to rule wherever one can."[9]

The *Hecuba* offers several examples of *ananke* used "impersonally" both with respect to construction and to underlying idea. Hecuba informs Odysseus that "it is urgently necessary" (*polle g'ananke*, 396) that she die along with her daughter. Agamemnon acknowledges the necessity of remaining in Thrace, because the winds have failed to rise (901), and the necessity of adjudicating Polymestor's case (1241). Polymestor observes that "it is necessary"—that is, predestined—that Cassandra die by violence (1275). In each of these cases the necessity lies outside the speaker and inheres in the situation.

These instances are in contrast to a use of *ananke* that entails a return to the Homeric sense (but with a critical overtone unknown to Homer) and suggests not the impersonal power of fate but the compulsion exercised by privileged human beings over those weaker than themselves. That connotation is brought to the audience's notice by a pointed rejoinder of Odysseus to Hecuba. When she claims that "it is urgently necessary" for her to die together with Polyxena, Odysseus replies, "How so? I am not aware that I have any masters" (397). It is up to him, he is reminding her, to decide what is "necessary," for he is the one in power.[10]

Odysseus' response to Hecuba is unusual in its frankness. More commonly the conquerors attempt to obscure the fact that *ananke* is essentially identical with their own will, and they are at some pains to present their own decisions as constrained or involuntary. Even as he refuses to authorize Hecuba to die with Polyxena, Odysseus disingenuously expresses regret that the Greeks should be obliged to sacrifice the young girl: "The death of your daughter is quite sufficient. Another must not be added to it. If only we did not have to [put her to death]."[11] Yet as the audience knows from the earlier account of the Greek assembly, there was nothing inevitable about the decision; Odysseus, in fact, was its principal architect. Achilles' ghost had demanded only "honor"; it was Odysseus who won the soldiers over to the sacrifice of Polyxena.[12] His refusal to allow Hecuba to die appears as arbitrary as his insistence on killing her daughter. Neither his cruelty nor his apparent kindness is responsive to any necessity but his own whim.

Throughout the play, arbitrary behavior is the prerogative of the powerful. In the case of Agamemnon also, what sounds like kindness is simply an expression of impulse. When Hecuba approaches him in supplication, he tries to guess her request (754–55): "What is it you are seeking? To be set free? That is an easy matter for you."

As he speaks these careless words the condition of enslavement that has operated as the very foundation of Hecuba's existence is abruptly revealed as conditional on Agamemnon's whim—a circumstance that can "easily" be changed if she so requests and he is so inclined. Since Hecuba's experience epitomizes that of the other Trojan captives, their miserable condition suddenly appears in a different light. Far from inevitable, it is merely the consequence of their conquerors' will.

Although the word *ananke* does not occur in either connection, two other passages convey the same flavor of false constraint. When Hecuba begs Agamemnon to avenge the murder of Polydorus he replies that he "wants" to help her (*boulomai*, 852), if only he could avoid giving the army the impression that he "planned this murder of the king of Thrace for Cassandra's sake" (855–56). His mixed conditional structure implies personal willingness on the one hand and compelling strategic considerations on the other. Agamemnon has some grounds for his uneasiness, since the two sons of Theseus had already accused him at the assembly (127–29) of acting on Cassandra's behalf. Still, the issue of Cassandra's influence had not on that previous occasion swayed the soldiers against Agamemnon, so the audience might be inclined to question his good faith in invoking it as an obstacle now. Hecuba, at any rate, seems to doubt his claim that he is not at liberty to act as he pleases, for she answers in exasperation that no one is "free," that everyone is a "slave" to external forces, but in this instance she can "set him free" from his fear (864–69).

By reversing the categories that actually apply and portraying Agamemnon as a frightened slave and herself as the one in power, Hecuba exposes the incongruousness of his claim. She has realized that he is taking refuge in a specious plea of constraint when in reality he is motivated by self-interest. The mixture of factors contributing to Agamemnon's reluctance to intervene is reminiscent of the Athenians' argument in Thucydides (1.75.3) that three considerations—fear, honor, and advantage—"compel" them to retain their empire. The Athenians are more straightforward than Agamemnon, however, in acknowledging the dubious motives that drive them.

The murder of Polydorus serves as a final demonstration of the bad faith of the powerful. Two different interpretations of the deed are advanced in the course of the play. Polymestor, the perpetrator, defends his crime as judicious if not inevitable, the product of wisdom and foresight (*sophē promēthia*, 1137). He killed Polydorus, he explains, out of fear that he might grow up to spark another Trojan war, with another return of the Greeks and attendant damage to Thracian crops (1138–44).

Polymestor implies that the murder was actuated by concern both for the Greeks and for his own people. Yet his real motives have been known to the audience as early as the prologue. There the ghost of Polydorus explained that his host had murdered him "for the sake of gold," subsequent to the fall of Troy (25). At their first glimpse of Polydorus' corpse, the women of the chorus divine that avarice was the inspiration for the crime (712); so, later on, does Agamemnon (775). Polymestor himself confirms that greed is the driving force of his character by his response to Hecuba's offer to reveal the hiding place of the Trojan treasure. So eager is he for this information that he jumps ahead of the pace of the dialogue, impulsively countering her initial question with two more:

Hecuba: Do you know the temple of Athena Ilias?
Polymestor: Is that where the gold is? What sort of a sign is there?[13]

The final exposition of Polymestor's motives comes in the last episode, as Hecuba offers her own reconstruction of the crime. She points out the significance of its timing: if Polymestor had truly wished to help the Greeks, as he claims, he would not have awaited the fall of Troy to murder his charge (1208–13). Agamemnon concurs with Hecuba's analysis, telling Polymestor (1243–46):

> To me, frankly, it doesn't look as if you killed your
> guest-friend for my sake or the Greeks', but so that you
> could have the gold laid up in your palace. Because you
> are in difficulties, you are saying what is to your own
> advantage.

Polymestor has been convicted of murdering Polydorus for the most selfish, the most frivolous, the least justifiable of motives. He cannot even claim to have acted out of panic when confronted by an unexpected situation, for Priam had dispatched his son to him precisely in anticipation that Troy might fall, and sent along the gold to sustain the surviving royal children (10–12). In murdering the boy and stealing the gold Polymestor has betrayed not merely the faith implicit in all guest-friendship, but an explicit arrangement concluded between himself and Priam.

The bad faith of Odysseus and Polydorus encourages the audience to trace the deaths of Hecuba's youngest children to an *anankē* that has little to do with fate and everything to do with arbitrary violence. Such a finding tends to connect two events that had initially been presented as unrelated.[14] The death of Polyxena is debated in open assembly, then formally announced to Hecuba. The execution takes place in public and is justified on religious grounds; the corpse is treated with care and respect. In contrast, Polydorus' death takes place in secret and is concealed as long as possible. The boy is clumsily butchered and his corpse tossed into the sea (698, 716–17, 782).

The role of *anankē*, certain suggestive details, and Hecuba's own responses link the two deaths in a single pattern. Hecuba envisages each child as her last support: Polydorus is "the sole remaining anchor" of the *oikos* (80–81), Polyxena her "one consolation" (280). Hecuba's dream of a fawn torn from her lap by a bloodstained wolf awakens in her anxiety for both her children (74–75), and in fact the portent applies equally to both. The preparations for the burial of Polyxena lead to the discovery of Polydorus' body: it is while fetching lustral water from the sea that Hecuba's attendant comes upon the corpse. When Hecuba conceives of punishing her false guest-friend she describes the plan as her only means of avenging "my children" (750): a single act of retaliation will requite them both. Despite the difference in their fates, Hecuba sees her children as threatened by an equal danger, avenged by a single act, to be buried in a common tomb (895–97) — victims not of impartial necessity but of the compulsion exercised by the powerful.

It is not finally impersonal necessity that is harsh (*sterra ananke*, 1295) so much as human nature that is proven to be harsh (*sterros anthrōpou physis*, 296). Against this pressure the weak deploy every strategy at their command. They avail themselves, in fact, of a far greater variety of responses than do the conquerors, who rely on the single fact of their power to enforce their will. By showing how the captives first exhaust all other avenues, Euripides renders morally intelligible Hecuba's final act of revenge.

The Recourses of the Weak: Assent

Polyxena is the only Trojan captive besides Hecuba to be individualized. It is she who first frames a coherent answer to the *ananke* of the powerful, and it is in light of her choice that Hecuba's behavior has been described as unworthy, bestial, and grotesque.[15] An assessment of her sacrifice is therefore crucial to an interpretation of the play as a whole.

When the news comes that Polyxena is to be sacrificed, her mother pleads with Odysseus to spare her and then, failing in her appeal, urges the girl to speak on her own behalf. Polyxena informs both Hecuba and the embarrassed Odysseus, who is physically shrinking away to avoid her anticipated supplication, that she has no intention of pleading for her life. In fact, she actively desires death (349–50, 354–61):

Why should I keep on living? My father was king of all
the Trojans; such was my start in life. . . . And I—the pity

of it—was mistress of the women of Troy,
and conspicuous among the young girls—equal to the gods, except only for
being mortal. Now I am a slave. First off, the very name
makes me wish to die, so strange is it. Then I might
happen on a hard-hearted master, who would buy me
for silver—me, the sister of Hector and many other
[heroes]. . . .

Polyxena will not attempt to dissuade Odysseus or to resist her fate.
Odysseus had earlier urged Hecuba to realize the hopelessness of her
position and refrain from resistance (225–28). Polyxena has assimilated
this point of view: "Don't fight the powerful!" she advises Hecuba.[16]
She accepts her sacrifice as necessary, and even welcomes it, for it
offers her an escape from the other "compulsions" that would otherwise be her lot: the enforced making of bread, for instance (*anankē sito-
poios*, 362), which a cruel master would compel her to perform
(*anankazein*, 364). To die now, Polyxena reasons, will ensure that she
departs with honor and status intact, and spared the humiliations that
the life of a slave would entail.[17]

Polyxena sustains her courage to the end. Talthybius gives an
affecting description of how she insisted on kneeling unbound before
her executioner; how she affirmed that she was dying "voluntarily"
(*hekousa*, 548); how she offered Neoptolemus a choice of slitting her
throat or stabbing her in the breast (563–65).[18] The entire Greek army,
Talthybius reports, was struck with admiration, and the soldiers—as
ever susceptible to good influences as well as bad—vied with one another to collect offerings for her pyre (571–80).

Polyxena tries to undercut the compulsory quality of her death by
embracing it as her personal desire. She can claim to be dying as a free
woman not only because she has avoided the humiliations of slavery,
but because she has affirmed the sacrifice itself as a matter of free
choice. Although she has gone far beyond what her conquerors required of her, she views her assent as a victory rather than a capitu-
lation.

Polyxena's courage wins praise for her even from the Greeks. As for
the Trojans, first the chorus and then Hecuba reflect, in connection
with her death, on the excellence of noble character combined with
high birth (379–81, 592–602). If we view her in isolation—as a figure not

unlike the marble statue to which Talthybius compares her (560) – her gesture is morally praiseworthy and esthetically attractive. But the context invites a more critical perspective. We need to consider the value system to which she makes appeal and the judgments returned on it in the play; we need also to take into account the anomalies of her situation, the atmosphere prevailing at her death, and the ultimate inefficacy of her sacrifice.

In her brief autobiography (349–58) Polyxena explains the motives actuating her decision, and these are the same principles that are set forth at greater length by such women as Megara in *Heracles* or Andromache in *Trojan Women*. Theirs is the traditional aristocratic ethos, in these instances articulated by women but no different from the standards of a male hero such as Sophocles' Ajax.[19] For such aristocratic types the sense of self is vested in ancestry and position. Death is deemed preferable to any diminution in happiness or – what is almost equivalent – any reduction in status. In none of these plays does Euripides make a direct attack on these traditional assumptions, but in each he obliquely puts them into question.

In *Trojan Women* Andromache takes a stance similar to Polyxena's in *Hecuba*. Assessing Polyxena's death in retrospect, Andromache concludes that Polyxena is more fortunate than any of the surviving captives because "it is better to die than to live a life in grief" (*Trojan Women*, 637). But Hecuba finds fault with Andromache's reasoning and urges her to adapt herself to circumstances, to look ahead rather than behind. In the *Heracles* (95 ff.), Amphitryon similarly defends hopefulness in the face of Megara's fatalism.

Although the confrontation between Hecuba and Polyxena is less openly expressed, it proceeds along similar lines. When Polyxena declines to plead for her life, Hecuba is torn between admiration and anguish: she acknowledges the nobility of her daughter's words, but emphasizes the grief they bring with them (382–83). By no means won over to Polyxena's view of the situation, Hecuba then redoubles her pleas to Odysseus to spare Polyxena's life; she does not subside until Polyxena herself, adopting the perspective of the conquerors, reminds her mother that resistance will be met with physical force (405–8).

After Polyxena's death Hecuba's ambivalence persists. While praising her daughter, she also reflects on the illusory quality of the old, vanished way of life, the fine luxuries and high pretensions of the house of Priam (619–28). Her words seem to make critical reference to Polyxena, who took that way of life as her standard and preferred to die a sacrifice to her enemies rather than to endure even the "name" of slave.[20]

It is not primarily the response of Hecuba, however, but the incongruities of Polyxena's situation that call her act into question. At first glance she appears a standard Euripidean type, one of those youthful heroes and heroines—like Menoeceus in *Phoenician Women*, or Iphigenia in *Iphigenia in Aulis*—who voluntarily sacrifice themselves for the good of their community. Scholarly analysis has determined that two ingredients are required to create the typical sacrificial configuration: a "divine request" and a "communal purpose."[21] But both, in Polyxena's case, are problematic. As we have already seen, it is Odysseus rather than some higher power who is the prime mover of the sacrifice. And it is not the remnants of the Trojans whose interests are served by Polyxena's death, but the community of the Greeks. These anomalous circumstances cast a shadow of doubt on Polyxena's act.

Polyxena plays into the hands of her enemies not only by the fact of her sacrifice but by her willing participation. She is, as Hecuba points out, a human offering in a situation where "it [would be] more suitable to kill an animal" (261). Studies of ancient animal sacrifice have revealed that the victim's consent was felt to be a crucial element in the success of the ritual.[22] Polyxena's readiness to die makes her the ideal sacrificial victim; although such is scarcely her intention, she effectively becomes the Greeks' collaborator.

Precisely because Polyxena is not an animal but a woman, her youthful beauty adds to the strangeness of the occasion. To judge by Talthybius' account, a pronounced erotic atmosphere prevailed at the sacrifice. Once freed from her bonds, Polyxena tore open her robe down to the waist (560–65):

> She revealed her breasts and her torso, lovely as a
> statue, and as she sank to her knees she spoke the most
> courageous words of all: "See, young man, if you wish to
> strike my breast, strike; if you prefer my neck,
> here is my throat."

The eroticism is far from abstract: necrophilia is a possibility envisioned by both Polyxena and Hecuba.[23] As debased emotions impinge on the sacrifice, it becomes more difficult to assess Polyxena's act with wholehearted approbation.

To be sure, candidates for human sacrifice are invariably young and beautiful as well as immaculate. The reasons may well have been as much aesthetic as ritual, for the spectacle of an aged body collapsing in the dust would inspire very different emotions in the spectators: grief, shame, disgust.[24] That the old are ineligible for a sacrificial death is made brutally clear to Hecuba when she volunteers to die first in place of, then along with her daughter, and Odysseus rejects both suggestions (385–95). Sacrifice is not a choice open to Hecuba or any other of the captives. As a response to the compulsion exercised by the conquerors, Polyxena's gesture has only a limited applicability.

The final comment on Polyxena's sacrifice lies in its absence of effect. The ritual was intended to appease Achilles' shade; in a broader sense, it was expected to heal the cosmic disorder signified by the failure of the winds.[25] But Polyxena's death does not start the winds blowing. Soon after she has been killed, Agamemnon notes that there is still time for Hecuba to attempt vengeance on Polymestor (898–901):

> If we could start our voyage, I would not be able to grant you
> this favor. But as things stand—for the god has not sent us
> favoring winds—it is necessary for us to wait quietly,
> watching for our chance to sail.

When it came to religious ritual, the Greeks expected results commensurate to the effort involved.[26] Here the gods do not appear mollified by Polyxena's sacrifice, although the winds will in fact rise at the end of the play—a fact whose significance will be considered in due course. For the present, we may conclude that Polyxena's self-devotion is first called into question by the anomalous context, then undercut by the futility of her sacrifice. If the weak are to maintain themselves against the powerful, they must find some other means than assent.

The Recourses of the Weak: *Nomos*

Hecuba takes a different approach. Far from acquiescing to the violence done her, she protests every step of the way. She appeals first to Odysseus and then more explicitly to Agamemnon on the grounds of an *isos nomos* which, she argues, applies to slaves and free, weak and strong alike. Her entreaties have a contemporary dimension, for the scope of *nomos* was a controversial issue of the day. Furthermore, they carry a specifically local reference, for Hecuba invokes not just *nomos* but the celebrated Athenian principle of *isonomia*, "laws equal for all."[27]

The original sense of *nomos* is "usage" or "norm." The *nomoi* were "customary practices unquestioningly accepted as valid and correct."[28] *Nomos* incorporated and was early bound up with the notion of justice, and in time it came to embrace the concepts of regulation and law. With travel and increased sophistication came the realization that laws and customs varied from one society to another; that all *nomoi*, therefore, were relative. An anecdote of Herodotus (3.38) famously conveys this insight: King Darius of Persia asks some Greeks what sum of money would induce them to eat their dead, and some Indians what would induce them to cremate theirs; each group is appalled at the very suggestion. A fragment of Archelaus (Diels-Kranz 60A1) makes the same point more succinctly: "What is just and shameful exists not by nature, but by *nomos*."

Such observations led to speculation about the scope of the *nomoi*. Did at least some have universal validity, or did they apply only within one's own society? Within one's own society, were they construed differently for different social groups? In Athens, at least, every citizen had an equal claim to the protection of the law. *Isonomia*, a term closely associated with the reforms of Cleisthenes and the development of Athenian democracy, stood for a uniquely democratic impartiality. *Isonomia* guaranteed the legal rights of the citizenry; the weak, in particular, when injured by the powerful could look to the law for recourse.[29]

In the democratic context *nomos* was regarded as an improvement on one-man rule; law, in particular written law, was felt to offer a protection from the arbitrary whims of tyrant or oligarch.[30] In tragedy, however, where mythical and contemporary conditions have a tendency to fuse, the upholding of *nomos* is often presented as the particular responsibility of the ruler.[31] An enlightened leader might be expected to defend the *nomoi* even at some risk to himself, and even if the issue did not involve him personally. That is precisely what transpires in Euripides' *Suppliants*.[32] In that play Theseus, on his mother's urging, decides to intervene in the war between Thebes and Argos in order to assure the burial of the fallen Argive warriors. Theseus is not about to incur the reproach of having permitted "the ancient *nomos* of the gods" to perish; he is prepared to use force, if necessary, in its defense (*Suppl.* 563, 584 ff.). When once victory is attained, he emphasizes the importance of the cause by personally attending to the burial of the Argives. Such an outcome offers reassurance that the *nomoi* command universal respect.

In the *Hecuba* the appeal to *nomos* meets with no such success. Given two opportunities to come to its defense, the Greeks prove twice unresponsive. Hecuba initially raises the issue with Odysseus, when she argues that Polyxena should not be killed. She has already been spared once and, since it is now peacetime, the civilian law relating to homicide should obtain (291–92): "You have an equal law [*nomos . . . isos*] pertaining to the murder of both free and slaves."

In the kind of anachronism that is commonplace in tragedy, Hecuba is referring to a fifth-century Athenian statute.[33] But her collocation of *isos* and *nomos* also suggests that she is claiming the protection of *isonomia* for herself and her daughter.[34] Technically, of course, she has no right to do so, for any number of reasons: the two of them are non-Athenians, non-Greeks, barbarians, and slaves. But desperation, it was conceded, had its privileges: in the Melian Dialogue (5.90) Thucydides makes the Melians suggest that it would benefit everybody if those in danger could have access to persuasive arguments that are not rigorously accurate. If Hecuba's attempt to extend an Athenian norm into a universal principle does not convince Odysseus, it enlists the sympathy of the audience and may inspire them to question the double standard of justice prevailing in fifth-century Athens: within the polis, *isonomia*; outside the polis, the ruthless imposition of Athenian power.

Odysseus replies that he is willing to spare Hecuba's life but not her daughter's—a concession that is worse than useless to her. To Hecuba's invocation of the *nomos isos* he opposes the Greeks' obligation to honor one of their own heroes in death. The Greeks must be careful, he believes, about setting a precedent. For the sake of future recruitment, it is critical to pay honor to the dead Achilles (311–16):

Is it not shameful if we treat a man as a friend while he
is alive, but not when he is dead? What will people say if
there should be another mustering of troops and armed
conflict? Will we go forth to fight, or will we
protect our own lives, when we see that a man receives no
honor once he is dead?

The scope of *nomos* having obtruded itself into the debate, Odysseus proceeds to offer a convoluted acknowledgment of the universal validity of the convention of honoring the dead. The Trojans, he asserts, are welcome to assume that this particular *nomos* does not apply to them. The outcome will prove otherwise (326–31):

If this is a bad *nomos* of ours [*ei kakōs nomizomen*] to pay
honor to a noble man, we will [gladly] incur the charge of
folly. You barbarians continue not to treat friends as
friends or to revere dead heroes, so that Hellas may
prosper and you may receive just what you deserve!

Odysseus has countered Hecuba's appeal to *isonomia* by invoking a rival *nomos*: the solemn duty to honor the noble dead. Odysseus' interpretation prevails not so much because his is the stronger case as because his is the superior power.[35] The outcome of their exchange suggests that the *nomoi* do not really command independent authority, but rather that they depend on the willingness of the powerful to endorse them.

Hecuba, however, is not yet ready to concede defeat. To Agamemnon as to Odysseus, but even more urgently and more explicitly, she makes an appeal to *nomos* (798–805):

We, it may be, are both slaves and weak. But the gods are
strong, and so is the power that rules over them: *nomos*.
Through *nomos* we believe in the gods, and make
distinctions of justice and injustice in our lives. If
nomos, which [now] depends on you, is destroyed, and if
there is no punishment for those who kill guest-friends
or dare to plunder what is sacred to the gods
then there is no equality [*ouden ison*]
remaining among human beings.

Once more Hecuba draws together the two halves of *isonomia* in an effort to claim its protection for herself and her family. Hecuba acknowledges that she is situated at the very bottom of a hierarchy extending from the Trojan slaves through King Agamemnon to the gods. But *nomos*, she argues, applies impartially to all. Like Odysseus, Hecuba recognizes the importance of precedent. If Agamemnon neglects *nomos* now, the very principle will perish; the notion of "equality" (or, as we might put it, of human rights) will disappear.[36]

When Hecuba appeals to *nomos* she is referring, as her subsequent examples make clear, not to law but to custom or convention. She cites two specific abuses that demand punishment: violations of guest-friendship and the profanation of temples. These *nomoi* comprise two elements of the Greek "triple commandment": to honor the gods, parents, and guest-friends.[37] As such they have strong claims to universal validity — as Agamemnon, like Odysseus earlier, eventually acknowledges in backhanded fashion. Judging Polymestor guilty as charged, Agamemnon informs him (1247–48): "Maybe for you it is an easy matter to kill guest-friends, but to us Greeks it carries shame with it." Yet it quickly emerges that he has propounded this hypothesis of the merely local force of the *nomos* of guest-friendship only to reject it. His subsequent remarks imply that if Polymestor harbored such a notion, the outcome has proved him wrong. His blinding is condign punishment (1250–51): "Since you dared to commit an ugly crime, now pay an ugly penalty."

This judgment comes in hindsight, however, after Hecuba has taken justice into her own hands. At the moment when she asks for Agamemnon's assistance in bringing Polymestor to justice Agamemnon replies that he would like to help her, both out of pity and a desire to punish "the impious guest-friend for the sake of the gods and of justice" (851–53). But he adds that he is reluctant to render assistance out of fear for his own reputation. Hecuba's appeal to a *nomos* that takes precedence over all other considerations has failed. With Agamemnon, reverence and justice are subordinate to self-interest. He will give Hecuba only passive support, and that only if it does not interfere with his other plans (cf. 898–99). The combined lesson of the Odysseus and Agamemnon episodes is that *nomos* is not a reliable protection for the weak, since the powerful will either manipulate or ignore it in accordance with their own interests.

The Recourses of the Helpless: Pity

Hecuba reasons that if an argument from *nomos* has failed to influence the Greeks, perhaps they can yet be moved by pity. Her gambit carries no promise of success, for pity is a volatile emotion originating in a sudden, unpredictable surge of empathy.

One of the clearest and most memorable examples of the workings of pity is to be found in the last book of the *Iliad*. After Achilles has killed Hector, the gods prompt Hector's father to seek out Achilles and request the body of his son. With the help of Hermes, old King Priam makes his way unnoticed through the Greek camp. Taking Achilles by surprise, he entreats him:

> Achilleus like the gods, remember your father, one who
> is of years like mine, and on the door-sill of sorrowful old age.
> And they who dwell nearby encompass him and afflict him,
> nor is there any to defend him against the wrath, the de-
>   struction.
> Yet surely he, when he hears of you and that you are still living,
> is gladdened within his heart. . . .
> But for me, my destiny was evil. . . .
> Honour then the gods, Achilleus, and take pity upon me,
> remembering your father, yet I am still more pitiful;
> I have gone through what no other mortal on earth has gone
>   through;
> I put my lips to the hands of the man who has killed my
>   children.[38]

The appeal is effective because Priam induces Achilles to shift his focus and identify him not with the enemy but with his father Peleus, and to associate both with the whole tribe of wretched old men. Pity involves taking a long view, detaching oneself from identification with one's group, and recognizing the qualities that all humanity holds in common.[39]

It is in the hope of convincing Agamemnon to adopt such a perspective, to take the long view, that Hecuba implores him (807–08): "Take pity on us, and standing away, like a painter, observe me and behold all my troubles."

The attitude least conducive to pity and most likely to encourage anger is to dwell closely on the situation at hand, concentrating on it so closely that vision becomes distorted. A passage from Thucydides illustrates this mechanism. He reports that during the debate held in the

Athenian assembly over the appropriate punishment for Mytilene, Cleon urged the Athenians not to yield to pity for the rebels, but rather to fuel their rage by "getting as close as possible to the state of mind of being injured" (Thuc. 3.40.7).

Hecuba's plea for pity has no more effect than did her appeal to *nomos*. Agamemnon's response is to turn away from her, edging backwards in a gesture that visually replicates Odysseus' embarrassed retreat from Polyxena.[40] She eventually draws from Agamemnon the careless acknowledgment that he does indeed pity her (851). But he will act on his pity, as on behalf of *nomos*, only if he can do so at no personal cost. This easy pity, entailing no consequences, is not what Hecuba was seeking.

It should come as no surprise to the audience that Hecuba cannot move her Greek master to pity, for she has already failed in a similar attempt in an earlier episode. Hecuba's dialogue with Odysseus prefigures her confrontation with Agamemnon: the same elements recur in reversed order. To Agamemnon, as noted, Hecuba appeals first to *nomos*, then to pity; when these arguments have no effect, she reminds him of the gratitude or *charis* he owes her on account of his sexual relations with Cassandra.[41] In her speech to Odysseus, Hecuba's initial appeal is to the *charis* Odysseus owes her for having at one time saved his life. There follows an appeal to pity. Assuming a suppliant posture, Hecuba speaks eloquently of her own wretched condition and her reliance on Polyxena, and she begs Odysseus (286–87) to "have regard for me, have pity!" Her final argument depends on *nomos*, as she reminds Odysseus of the *isos nomos* that she hopes will save Polyxena.

Odysseus refutes Hecuba in the fashion already noted, by exalting the *nomos* of honoring the dead over any other obligation. As for pity, he has this to say (322–26):

> If you lay claim to sufferings deserving of pity, hear
> this from me in return. There are at home in Greece old
> women no less miserable than you. . . . Bear up.

Odysseus has already made the connection implicit in Hecuba's appeal, perceiving that Hecuba has much in common with Greek women of her age and situation. But his identification is purely intellectual and engenders harshness rather than compassion.[42] Hecuba succeeds in raising the issue of pity with her masters, but does not succeed in mitigating their indifference.

The Recourses of the Helpless: *Peithō*

After Hecuba has appealed in vain to *nomos* and pity, she reflects bitterly on her failure to convince (814–19):

> Why do we mortals toil and search after all other kinds of
> learning, as required, but persuasion, the only tyrant over
> men, we don't pursue to the utmost, paying money to learn
> it—for if we did, we could be persuasive whenever we
> wished, and gain our wishes too?

In a celebrated phrase Pindar had acclaimed *nomos* as "king of all."[43] Having failed in her argument from *nomos*, "which rules over the gods" (799), Hecuba now revises both Pindar and herself to label *peithō* or persuasion "the only tyrant over men." Her words do not, however, signal any radical change of heart. The appeal to rhetoric is in itself rhetorical, for Hecuba has been employing persuasive techniques from the outset.[44] Her earlier arguments from *nomos* and pity were both intended to win over the conquerors; the only sense in which they did not constitute *peithō* was that they failed of their effect.

At this point, to be sure, Hecuba varies her approach. Whereas her earlier arguments were designed to move from the particular to the general (in the case of *nomos*, to a shared intellectual awareness of obligation; in the case of pity, to a shared emotional sense of situation), she attempts now to reverse direction. She forges a persuasive argument from reciprocity specifically tailored to her listener. But even this is not new, for Hecuba had earlier argued that Odysseus owed her a favor in return for her saving his life.[45] Her invocation of *peithō* at this point does not signify that she has been corrupted from her earlier ideals; what it does convey is her weariness, her frustration and near-despair.

Persuasiveness, as Hecuba well knows, depends not merely on eloquence but also on the status of the speaker.[46] Earlier she had assured Odysseus that he would have no difficulty convincing the army to spare Polyxena (293–95):

Your authority, even if you speak in a bad cause, will be
persuasive [*peisei*]. For a statement issuing from the
unregarded and the powerful does not carry the same
weight.

Hecuba reiterates her insight as she launches into her argument to
Agamemnon. She is pessimistic about the outcome (820–23):

How might anyone still anticipate a good issue? The children I
    had
are no more; I am undone, humiliated, a slave; now I see the
smoke rising above my city.

But Hecuba takes steps to augment her standing in the eyes of
Agamemnon. Although she can claim no family, city, or position, she
tries to minimize these lacks by means of a persuasive analogy.
Agamemnon had made Cassandra his mistress, but Hecuba speaks as
if he had taken her for his wife. She notes that Agamemnon owes Cassandra a favor (*charis*) in return for his sexual enjoyment – a favor that
should now be extended to Hecuba. In avenging Polydorus, she argues, he will be acting on behalf of a brother-in-law (827–35).

Commentators have regularly seen in Hecuba's appeal to Aphrodite a sign of the degeneration of her character. It is "demeaning" for
her to mention her daughter's relations with Agamemnon. "It is all ter-
ribly indecent."[47] These censorious responses do not take account of
fifth-century conventions. Hecuba is not launching upon a subject ta-
boo either to her culture or to the dramatic stage; her only anxiety is
that her appeal will be "perhaps useless."[48] It is worth remembering
that Danaus in Aeschylus' *Suppliants*, Heracles in *Trachiniae*, Creon in
Antigone, Menelaus in *Andromache*, and Hecuba in *Trojan Women* all
concern themselves openly and in detail with their children's sexual
lives.[49]

The notion that sexual relations constitute a *charis* has good dramatic precedent: Sophocles' Tecmessa makes the same point to Ajax.
Tecmessa is no more Ajax' wife than Cassandra is Agamemnon's; each
is a captive who has been chosen as her master's concubine. But Tecmessa, like Hecuba, makes a persuasive glide from concubinage to
legitimate marital status. She assimilates her situation to that of a
wife – in fact her arguments, as has been recognized since antiquity,

are closely modeled on those of Hector's wife, Andromache, in Book 6 of the *Iliad*.[50] Like Hecuba, Tecmessa argues that the relationship between man and woman involves *charis*. Discreetly but unmistakably she implies that it is sexual pleasure that creates the *charis* (*Ajax*, 520–22):

> Keep some memory of me. A man should keep the memory, if he has enjoyed some pleasure. For *charis* is something that always gives birth to *charis*.

This parallel suggests that a fifth-century audience would have seen nothing unusual or demeaning in Hecuba's concept of *charis* as a return on sexual favors. Nor would it have seemed irregular for Hecuba to claim the protection of a man whom she regards as her in-law.[51] The only element in Hecuba's appeal that involves an extension of normal assumptions is her blurring of Cassandra's status. Yet we have noticed a similar strategy on the part of Tecmessa, and Agamemnon himself is not unwilling to entertain the notion that Polydorus is his *philos*.[52]

Although Agamemnon readily admits the force of Hecuba's argument, she only partially persuades him. He tells her that he will not stand in her way if she wants to pursue vengeance; on the other hand, he will not actively assist her. Just as Hecuba had feared, *peithō* turns out to be intimately linked to status and prestige. The weak can expect only limited results even from their most eloquent speeches.

The Recourses of the Helpless: Revenge

From the outset Hecuba has taken a stand against the gratuitous violence directed against her family by the powerful. In each case she has demanded justice: protection for her innocent daughter Polyxena, and punishment for Polymestor, the false host.

We must beware of approving her first demand while condemning the second. For the Greeks, retribution, whether publicly or privately obtained, was an essential component of justice. Hecuba takes matters into her own hands only after she has appealed in vain to Agamemnon for the protection of *nomos*, appealed in vain for the external arbitration whose invention had been chronicled in an earlier drama of justice and revenge, Aeschylus' *Oresteia*.

In the last play of that trilogy Athena replaces the old system of vendetta, symbolized by the Furies, with a new system of justice based on law. But the Furies do not abandon the field. Their role may have been diminished by the new legal structures, but they have by no means been rendered obsolete. They remain in residence in Athens, their presence emblematic of the continued force of the ancient standard of vengeance. It is to the justice represented by the Furies that Hecuba finally has recourse. Revenge becomes her driving force after she has looked upon Polydorus' mutilated body—a new *nomos* for her, but a well-respected concept for her society.[53] Her story is a kind of *Oresteia* in reverse: private vendetta comes into play after an appeal to institutionalized justice has failed.[54]

Hecuba accomplishes her revenge by means of deception, traditionally the last weapon of the weak and helpless.[55] She sends a message to Polymestor inviting his attendance on a matter that concerns him "not less than" herself (892). In appealing to Polymestor's self-interest, Hecuba has accurately gauged his character. He arrives with dispatch, but before embarking on her plan Hecuba puts him to the test. Polymestor fails on every count. Not only has he previously respected "neither the gods below nor the gods above" (791) by violating guest-friendship and denying Polymestor burial; he now demonstrates—before the eyes of Hecuba and the audience—his disregard for all the conventions of *philia* (friendship).

That these conventions apply is never open to doubt. During the war Polymestor had not, to be sure, been a military ally of the Trojans, but neither could he be considered a political neutral. He proclaims himself an intimate friend of the Trojan royal family (cf. 953, 982). His present situation is not easy, since he must cope with the uninvited presence of the Greeks on Thracian soil. Nevertheless his decision to curry favor with the conquerors smacks of opportunism, for it runs counter to the principle that friends should share the same loyalties and enmities.[56]

Polymestor's betrayals do not end there. It is axiomatic that friends should not abandon one another in misfortune, but Polymestor reverses that norm.[57] So long as Troy was intact (16–20), the boy Polydorus was allowed to flourish; Polymestor chooses the Trojans' time of trial to betray his trust. When Hecuba arrives in Thrace, he avoids her until she lures him to her presence with the prospect of gain.

Another convention of friendship is that friends do not deceive. (So in the *Alcestis* [1008] Heracles reproaches Admetus: "One ought to speak freely to a friend.") But deception is the keynote—set by Polymestor—of the meeting of these old friends. Polymestor enters on a stream of sententious generalizations and fluent improvisations, and the dialogue soon evolves into a sequence of double entendres.[58] When Hecuba asks after her son and the treasure, Polymestor dismisses her enquiries with plausible evasions and then turns, with transparent eagerness, to the topic of the gold of Troy. The avarice that had inspired him to murder Polydorus appropriately proves his ruin.

In the course of the scene Polymestor reveals himself as a man who demands quick gratification and relies on improvised excuses and techniques.[59] He seems to have killed Polydorus and hastily disposed of the corpse without reflecting that the boy would be missed, that the body would float to shore, or that the crime would be easily traceable to himself. His nonchalant attitude to his crime goes far toward reconciling the audience to Hecuba's vengeance.

After she has thoroughly tested Polymestor, Hecuba lures him into the tent with the promise of further valuables. As described by the victim himself, the blinding of Polymestor and the murder of his two children is horrific—as repugnant aesthetically as Polyxena's self-sacrifice was aesthetically attractive. Yet in this case as in Polyxena's it is essential to consider the act in context. The trial scene that closes the play implicitly invites the audience to do just that, to weigh Polymestor's crime—the last in a series of gratuitous acts of violence—against Hecuba's revenge.

Certain indications point to a favorable assessment of Hecuba. It is noteworthy that the justice of the punishment is acknowledged by Agamemnon, the chorus, Hecuba, and even Polymestor himself.[60] Moreover, one intriguing detail suggests that Hecuba's act has been somehow instrumental in restoring cosmic order. Agamemnon closes the trial scene by urging Hecuba to make haste in burying her children: he has realized that the winds have at last begun to blow (1289–90). The timing may, of course, be sheer coincidence; but we must also consider the possibility that the gods who failed to acknowledge the sacrifice of Polyxena have responded favorably to the blinding of Polymestor.

Yet other considerations seem to point in the opposite direction, for with respect to methods and outcomes there seems little to choose between Hecuba and Polymestor. Polymestor killed an innocent child and subsequently lied to Hecuba. After he has been blinded he emerges from the tent on all fours, a frightening doglike creature. Hecuba deceived Polymestor and killed two innocent children. She, it is predicted, will actually metamorphose into a dog. Are not the two precisely alike—equally criminal and equally corrupt?[61]

Two circumstances are generally adduced to support the thesis of Hecuba's degeneration. The first is her readiness to claim a *charis* from Agamemnon on the basis of his sexual relations with Cassandra—but such a claim, as we have seen, lies well within the norms of her culture. The second is Hecuba's metamorphosis, which is often taken as a kind of moral judgment on her act of vengeance, or at least a commentary on the inhuman qualities manifest in it.[62]

The text posits a link, certainly, between the act of vengeance and Hecuba's transformation.[63] To understand the nature of the connection we need to consider some of the connotations of dogs in Greek literature. These are by no means so negative as critics have conventionally assumed.[64]

The most obvious link between Hecuba's act and her metamorphosis is found in the image of the Erinyes, doglike creatures whose province is blood-vengeance. Vengeance is further associated with dogs in a mysterious passage of Theognis (349–50):

I am a dog and I cross the black stream, intending to get
vengeance for everything. May I drink their black blood!

Even if we discount "intending to get vengeance" as an emendation, the association with retribution still stands.[65] A dog, or doglike Fury, has an implacable thirst for vengeance. But as both the *Oresteia* and Sophocles' *Oedipus at Colonus* make clear, the Furies commanded respect as well as fear—they were awesome forces certainly, but by no means simply savage and horrifying. By assimilating Hecuba to a Fury, the metamorphosis offers her an escape from her degraded status and endows her with a fierce grandeur.

Another characteristic of dogs is signaled by a simile in the *Odyssey* (20.14–16). Odysseus catches a glimpse of the maids of his household slipping off for assignations with the suitors. At this sight

his heart barked within him, just as a dog standing over
her feeble puppies barks at strangers and remembers to
fight. . . .

Dogs, this passage suggests, are savage in their maternal protectiveness. So indeed are all animals, and throughout the play Hecuba's
children are evoked through animal imagery—as fawn, colt, cub,
nightingale, calf—that encourages the audience to think of them as the
young of any species, and of Hecuba as universal mother.[66] The protective fury of mothers for their vulnerable offspring is a trait no less
human for being shared with animals.

After her young have perished, Hecuba turns on one of their de-
stroyers with a rage that has no practical value. It cannot repair the
damage or bring the children back to life, and we may reflect that
animals would not resort to such an act of vengeance. But the animal
world does not know anything like the wanton, careless destruction
of life perpetrated in this play by Hecuba's conquerors. Nor do animals
possess a concept of justice or the ability to perform symbolic acts.[67]
Seen from this perspective, Hecuba's act of vengeance is an affirmation not of her beastliness but of her humanity. Despite the symmetrical nature of her revenge, there is a crucial difference between her
crime and Polymestor's. Polymestor violated all the *nomoi*—of fellowship, guest-friendship, burial—that make human intercourse possible.
Hecuba's vengeance constituted a defense of these *nomoi*.[68]

A final trait of dogs that is also applicable to Hecuba is their noisy
barking. The sound can be interpreted as a cry for vengeance: in the
Iphigenia among the Taurians (293–94) Orestes mistakes the barking of
dogs for the howling of the Furies. In conversation with Agamemnon
Hecuba had expressed the wish to become a single speaking instrument: "voices in my arms, my hands, my hair, my feet"—all crying in
unison and demanding justice.[69] Her wish will be granted as she becomes, with her metamorphosis into a dog, a single, concentrated
howl for retribution. By the end of the play such an outcry may well
impress the audience as the only way for the weak to capture the attention of the powerful.

Hecuba as Exemplar

On hearing the account of Polyxena's death Hecuba was prompted to
reflect on the stability of human nature. The action of the play generally confirms her claim. Agamemnon and Odysseus behave with consistency throughout; they are also true to their characters as established by the tradition. Although we cannot measure Polyxena and

Polymestor against any earlier literary representations, they suggest natures inherently good and inherently evil, respectively. What should we conclude about Hecuba herself? Is she in fact, as some critics have suggested, the exception to her own rule? Or does she not rather furnish the standard or exemplar that will enable others to understand the difference between good and evil?

Hecuba twice adverts to the question of how human beings determine moral standards. She describes how upbringing inculcates ethics, how men judge what is shameful by the measuring rule of the good (600–602). It is through *nomos*, she informs Agamemnon, that we distinguish justice from its opposite (801). From the outset of the play Hecuba functions as a kind of measuring rod for sheer unhappiness, a standard against which to measure the plight of others.[70] By the end of the play she has herself provided a means for gauging not only the extremes of misery, but also the point at which victims can be expected to retaliate against their tormenters, asserting the claims of justice at whatever cost to themselves.

Polymestor prophesies that Hecuba's tomb will become "a beacon for sailors" (1273). It will serve as a warning for seafarers—for those who (like the Athenians) embark on imperialistic maritime expeditions—to venture no further. No one, Hecuba had earlier told Agamemnon, is truly free: even the powerful are subject to constraint (863–67). Hecuba's revenge serves notice to the mighty that it is dangerous for them to overreach themselves, for retribution may be forthcoming not from the gods but from the abused victims themselves. The beacon of Cynossema signals that the desire for justice is rooted deep in human nature and cannot be torn out by force.

Euripides' audience had good reason to hearken to such a warning. Hostilities between Athens and Sparta had broken out in 431, and in 425/4—the probable date of the *Hecuba*—Athens enjoyed its most notable military successes of the war. Cleon won an astonishing victory when he seized the island of Sphacteria and took its Spartan garrison alive. On Corcyra, after scenes of bloody conflict, the democratic, pro-Athenian faction prevailed. Athenian armies made successful forays into Corinthian territory. In response to these events Sparta made overtures culminating in the Peace of Nicias and a temporary lull in the war, while the Athenians tripled their cash assessments on their "subjects," (formerly their allies), their fellow members of the Delian League.[71]

Against this background of splendid military achievement Euripides wrote a play reflecting on power, powerlessness, and the stubborn fixity of human nature. It proffered lessons the Athenians did not choose to heed. In 426 they had invaded the neutral island of Melos with inconclusive results.[72] In 416 they tried again, issuing an ultimatum to Melos to become a tribute-paying member of the Athenian Empire. In reporting this incident Thucydides constructs a dialogue between the Athenians and the Melians whose themes, as we have already had occasion to notice, encapsulate many of the issues raised in the *Hecuba*. The parallels between the two texts do not, of course, suggest a direct relationship; rather, both Euripides and Thucydides reproduce intellectual positions that must have had widespread currency in Athens during the 430s and 420s.[73]

The Athenians open discussion by warning the Melians not to invoke the concept of justice, since justice can only be adjudged between equals (*apo isēs anankēs*). Under conditions of inequality "the powerful do what they can get away with, and the weak go along" (5.89.1). The Athenians thus make explicit the belief in the natural rights of the powerful that informs Odysseus' speech in the *Hecuba*.

The Melians counter with the suggestion that it would benefit everybody if those in danger could have access to arguments relating to justice as well as to persuasive arguments that are not rigorously accurate. They warn the Athenians that someday they will be defeated in turn and that their defeat will be the occasion for "the greatest vengeance" (5.90.1). We are reminded of Hecuba's persuasive efforts to apply *isonomia* to herself and Polyxena and to extend the range of *charis*. We may recall as well her warning to Odysseus that prosperity does not last forever (282–83).

The Athenians have little use for these arguments. Once more they appeal to *anankē*, remarking that "by a necessity of nature" (*hypo physeōs anankaias*) human beings take power wherever they can (5.105.2). They remind the Melians (5.107.1) that self-interest goes hand in hand with safety, whereas considerations of justice and honor involve one in danger—the same calculation that dictated Agamemnon's initial response to Hecuba. Much as Odysseus lectured Hecuba (299–300), the Athenians urge the Melians (5.111.4) to recognize their fundamental good will. Finally they affirm that survival depends on a system of assertiveness toward equals, circumspection toward the powerful, and moderation toward inferiors (5.111.4–5). Their assumption of a graduated standard of justice recalls the reasoning of the Greek commanders in the *Hecuba*.

Nevertheless the Melians, having exhausted all their arguments, take a final stand on justice and honor. They refuse to join the League and declare their intention of fighting for their independence. The Athenians retaliate by laying siege to Melos. The city once taken, they kill the male inhabitants and sell the women and children into slavery (5.116). Agamemnon himself would not have acted any differently.

NOTES

1. Kovacs 1987, 81 and 82.

2. The Greek army in assembly is described at 116 ff. For the soldiers' noisy tumult (*thorybos*) cf. 872, 1111; see Bers 1985 for the dicastic connotations of the term. The two sons of Theseus are called *rhētores* at 124; for the term in the sense of "politician" see Connor 1972, 116–17. Odysseus is described as a demagogue at 131–32 and 251–57. For the use of *dokein* to suggest the "enactment-formula," cf. 108, 220; for the different versions of this formula see Rhodes 1972, 64. For *isonomia* (paraphrased as *nomos isos*), cf. 291, 805.

3. I do not agree with Kovacs' contention (82 and passim) that the Greek army is "all-powerful." In my view Euripides portrays the army as a turbulent but directionless force — like fire or the sea, to which Hecuba and Talthybius liken it (608, 533) — which can be manipulated by Odysseus (131 ff.), reduced to silence by Talthybius (531–33), and is as open to good influences as to bad (cf. 575 ff.). That the real power and responsibility rests with the commanders emerges from the episodes, as I aim to demonstrate, and also accords with the chorus' and Hecuba's emphasis on the individual wrongdoing of Paris and Helen, which proved so disastrous for the collective (cf. 442–43, 641–42, 943–52).

I also disagree with the other half of Kovacs' thesis, namely that the Trojan royal family exemplifies "real authority" in the play (82). That may have been true in the past, but the play's action repeatedly emphasizes their present helplessness as compared to the power of the Greek commanders.

4. Sacrilege: 71; folly: 365–83. The Greeks are, to be sure, differentiated in two contexts involving distribution: when the Trojan women speculate on their possible destinations in Greece (197–229), and when Talthybius allots each Trojan captive to a different master (246–77).

5. Kovacs 1987, 145, argues that Achilles does not physically prevent the ships from sailing by stilling the winds; rather, Achilles' "*appearance . . . checked the Greeks while they were already sailing away*" (his emphasis). However, *katesch'* (38) and *esche* (111) imply physical intervention, and that remains the most economical interpretation for the Greeks' lingering in Thrace. Otherwise it becomes necessary to imagine an initial epiphany of Achilles and a subsequent, unrelated failure of the winds.

Euripides' indirectness of expression may reflect a certain tension between two available explanations of windlessness, the mythical and the naturalistic. Aeschylus' description of the failure of the winds at Aulis (*Ag.* 188 ff.) is similarly oblique.

6. For the play's relationship to the *Iliad*, see King 1985, who however overstates Euripides' literary, as opposed to his political, polemics.

7. Schreckenberg 1964, 2–6. On *ananke* see further the excellent discussion of Aeschylean usages by Rivier 1968 and of Thucydidean usages by Ostwald 1988.

8. Schreckenberg 1964, 50 ff.

9. Thuc. 5.105.2, trans. Warner 1954. The Athenians are actually conflating the two connotations of *ananke* when they say that by necessity (= fate), necessity (= force, will of the stronger) will always prevail. On the natural rights of the powerful cf. Democritus, Diels-Kranz 68B67.

10. The same point—that *anankazein* is the prerogative of the powerful—is made more plainly at Eur. *Suppl.* 519–20.

11. *Mēde tonde ōpheilomen*, 395: a different term is used to express the notion of necessity, but the implication of compulsion is the same. Odysseus is so clearly sadistic in denying Hecuba her desire to die along with her daughter that I do not see how Kovacs (1987, 94) can ascribe his words to "almost . . . a misplaced and ineffectual delicacy or scrupulosity."

12. Achilles' words are paraphrased four times and quoted once. Polydorus reports that the shade has demanded Polyxena as an offering and a *geras* (40–41). Hecuba says that the ghost of Achilles has demanded "one of the much-enduring Trojan women as *geras*" (94–95). The chorus quotes the ghost as having reproached the Greeks for leaving his tomb "without honor" (*ageraston*, 115). Odysseus reaffirms his commitment to sacrificing Polyxena to Achilles "since he demanded it" (*exaitoumenoi*, 305). He also tells Hecuba that the ghost asked for Polyxena, not her (389–90). The chorus' report on the Greek assembly (116–40) casts some light on these disparate versions. As the members of the chorus tell it, two different views were expressed: some were for sacrificing a victim, others were against it. Agamemnon advanced Hecuba's cause (that is, opposed the idea of a sacrifice in order to protect Polyxena), out of loyalty to Cassandra. The two sons of Theseus denounced Agamemnon's motives. Odysseus won the day by emphasizing the importance of giving Achilles his proper *charis*.

Meridier's interpretation (1927, vol. 2, 169, n. 2) seems to me correct: Achilles demanded a *geras* without specifying Polyxena, but Polyxena was the obvious choice since she was young, pure, and of royal blood. Polydorus telescopes the initial demand and its interpretation by the Greeks since he, being a ghost, has knowledge of the future. Odysseus, of course, is scarcely a reliable reporter; we may assume that in conversation with Hecuba he conflates Achilles' demand with the interpretation he himself puts on it.

13. At 1008–9. For a detailed analysis of this scene, see Schwinge 1968, 144–48.

14. The thematic linkage of the two actions via *ananke* addresses the vexed

question of the play's structural unity, for which see, e.g., Matthaei 1918, 120–24; Kirkwood 1947, 60–63; Steidle 1968, 44–49; and Michelini 1987, 132–33. The reversed symmetry of Hecuba's addresses to Odysseus and Agamemnon forms an additional connection between the two episodes.

15. Cf. Matthaei 1918, 155: "There is a contrast meant between the way in which Polyxena met injustice and the way in which Hecuba meets it"; see also Reckford 1985, 121, and Michelini 1987, 158.

16. At 404. Verbal and physical details point up how Polyxena "sides with Odysseus against her mother" (Daitz 1971, 219). She begins her speech with a vocative and an imperative (*mēter, pithou moi*, 402), just as Odysseus had begun his (*Hekabē, didaskou*, 299). There is a conflict between Polyxena's "voluntary" death (548) and Hecuba's refusal "voluntarily" to give her up (400). Hecuba clings physically to her daughter, and Polyxena urges her to let go.

17. She asserts her free status at 367–68 (reading Blomfield's *eleutherōn*) and again at 550.

18. See Loraux 1985, 92–97, for the symbolism of each mode of death.

19. The parallel between Polyxena and Ajax is noted by Kovacs 1987, 93.

20. Michelini 1987, 166, draws attention to the appearance-reality antinomy and concludes, "There seems to be here a faint implied criticism of the standards for which Polyxene died." For another view on slavery cf. *Ion* 854–56, where it is said that it is *only* the name of the slave that carries shame, and *Helen* 728–33. These and other passages challenging the traditional view of slavery are discussed by Daitz 1971, 222–24.

21. O'Conner-Visser 1987, 2. Her introduction offers a useful survey of previous scholarship on Euripidean sacrifice plays; she also devotes a chapter to the *Hecuba*.

22. Burkert 1966, 106–7 with n. 43. The connection is already made by Matthaei 1918, 135: "In Greek ritual the perfectly acceptable sacrifice presupposed a willing victim, and the willingness of Polyxena completes and perfects the religious propriety of the occasion."

23. Cf. 568–70, 604–6. Gellie 1980, 34–35, discusses the "sexual innuendo" of the scene. Loraux 1985, 94, points out that although Polyxena's gestures were not erotic in intention, they are in effect. For Michelini 1987, 158–68, the scene is one of the many dissonant effects contributing to the play's bizarre aesthetic. I do not believe that the audience would be as alert to differences in tone as is Michelini herself; they would be too much caught up in the action.

24. Cf. Tyrtaeus 10 (West), modeled on *Il.* 22.66–76, on the sorry spectacle of an old man's death in battle, along with the comments of Humphrey 1983, 145.

25. At the sacrifice of Polyxena Neoptolemus prays not only for good sailing at the start of the voyage, but also for a safe homecoming for all (534–41). Later Agamemnon notes that "god" (not "Achilles") has not yet given them favoring winds (900). This language suggests that the crisis transcends Achilles and extends beyond the start of the journey.

26. Cf. Gould 1985, 14–16, on the "assumption of reciprocity" underlying Greek prayer. For the motives behind sacrifice and votive offerings, see Van Straten 1981, 65–69.

27. The translation is Stinton's; his comments are quoted by Collard 1975A, vol. 2, 440–42. Vlastos in his classic article (1953, 350 ff.) devotes most of his attention to a second sense of *isonomia*, that of equal access for all to the political process, but it is surely Stinton's sense that is in question here: Hecuba is asking for the protection of the law, not the right to make policy. For the two senses of *isonomia* see also Collard 1975A, vol. 2, *ad Suppl.* 429–32.

28. Ostwald 1969, 37. Cf. also the discussion by Kerferd 1981, 112.

29. Cf. Eur. *Suppl.* 429–37.

30. Cf. Ostwald 1969, 101.

31. Cf. the democratically minded king in Aeschylus' *Suppliants* and the discussion by Podlecki 1986, 82–86.

32. The (slightly varying) resolution-figures arrived at by four different scholarly counts all confirm that *Suppliants* and *Hecuba* were written very close to one another (see Cropp-Fick 1985, table 2.1, p. 5). We cannot, therefore, speak of an evolution in Euripides' thinking about the responsibility of leaders to defend *nomos*, but rather of two contrasting treatments of the question in a pair of almost contemporary plays.

33. For the statute cf. Demosth. 21.159. For discussion of tragic anachronisms, see Easterling 1985.

34. The term was apparently susceptible to paraphrase: cf. Aesch. 1.5 (*Against Timarchus*), where *isēn kai ennomon politeian* is equivalent to *isonomia*, and Eur. *Suppl.* 430–31, on which Collard 1975A, vol. 2, points out that *nomoi koinoi* is "a paraphrase of prose *isonomia.*"

35. For a different interpretation, see Adkins 1966, 195–99. Adkins sees Achilles' claim on the Greeks as more powerful than Hecuba's, since he is an *agathos* and a member of the group, whereas Hecuba and Polyxena are foreigners and slaves. This formulation, however, also recognizes status as a factor in Hecuba's failure to persuade Odysseus.

36. For *isonomia* as "rights" see Ostwald 1969, 113, n. 1. Hecuba does not say here (although she has made the point previously at 282–83) that prosperity will not endure forever, but that is an additional reason why the upholding of *nomos* should matter to the powerful.

Kovacs 1987, 101, is surely correct in maintaining (against Heinimann, Reckford, and Nussbaum) that "the objective existence of the gods is not the issue here. That is taken for granted." The human beings in this play do not operate in a vacuum; the gods form the assumed background, and the careless agnosticism of Polymestor (958–60) is refuted by his own punishment.

37. For references see de Romilly 1971, 35.

38. At *Il.* 24.486–506, translated by Lattimore 1951.

39. Cf. Burkert 1955, 104 ff. That pity depends on empathy seems to be commonly assumed; cf. lines 339–41, where Hecuba expresses the hope that Odysseus will pity Polyxena because "he too has children."

40. At 812, cf. 342–44; the similarity is noted by Steidle 1968, 49.

41. Kirkwood 1947 analyzes Hecuba's speech to Agamemnon in terms of *nomos* and *peithō*, but he overlooks the appeal to pity. For *charis* as a theme of the play see Adkins 1966.

42. So at *Il.* 21.105–12 the raging Achilles rejects Lycaon's plea for mercy. He understands perfectly what he, Lycaon, and Patroclus have in common, but his sense of their common mortality only renders him the more savage.

43. Fr. 169. For discussion see Heinimann 1945, 67–68, and de Romilly 1971, 62 ff.

44. Even Reckford, who believes that she degenerates in the course of the play, admits (1985, 211, n. 7): "She uses persuasion from the first." Buxton 1982, 170–78, traces the development of *peithō* in the play prior to this passage.

45. She had even attempted a transfer of *charis* from herself to Polyxena, as here she attempts a transfer from Cassandra to herself.

46. This point is discussed by Luschnig 1976, 232–33. For the connection between status and free speech, see *Andromache* 153.

47. "Demeaning": Buxton 1982, 179. "Indecent": Reckford 1985, 121. Cf. also Michelini 1987, 151: "She is taking to herself the status of a pimp."

48. *Isōs kenon*, 824. Nauck's *isōs xenon*, adopted by Diggle, shows an editor inserting into the text his own judgment of the passage's relevance.

49. *Suppliants* 996–1009: Danaus warns his daughters not to be (unconsciously?) seductive. *Trachiniae* 1221 ff.: Heracles demands that his son marry Iole. *Antigone* 569: Creon says that his son must "plough other furrows." *Andromache* 370–71: Menelaus is prepared to act as an "ally" to his daughter, because he considers sexual deprivation a matter of great importance. *Trojan Women* 700: Hecuba advises her daughter-in-law Andromache to offer sexual enticement (*delear*) to her master, because such an attitude will ultimately benefit all the Trojans. Cf. also *Il.* 9.450–54 (Phoenix and his mother) and Herodotus 1.61 (Megacles and his daughter).

50. For a detailed comparison of the Homeric and Sophoclean passages see Easterling 1984.

51. Marriage entailed the forging of connections among all members of the *oikos*, not just between the two individuals concerned. This assumption is reflected in the *Andromache*, where the aged Peleus comes to the aid of his son's concubine, and the *Heracles*, where the aged Amphitryon lacks the strength but not the will to defend his daughter-in-law and grandchildren. In *Iphigenia in Aulis* (905–7), Clytemnestra successfully appeals to Achilles for help on the basis of an engagement to her daughter that both of them know to be fictitious.

52. At 859–60, reading, with Elmsley, *d'emoi* at 859. It would be pointless for Agamemnon to phrase *Hecuba's philos*-connection with Polydorus as a hypothesis, as the reading *soi* would suggest.

53. Cf. lines 685–87. As Reckford points out (1985, 211, n. 7), there is a play on two connotations of *nomos*, "law" and "tune."

54. Cf. Nussbaum 1986, 416, who, however, compares the two texts in terms of the Furies' progress from beasts to women as opposed to Hecuba's regress from woman to beast.

55. Buxton 1982, 64.

56. Cf. *Il.* 9.612–15. The same idea is expressed in oaths of *symmachia*: allies bound themselves "to have the same friends and enemies" (Thuc. 1.44.1).

57. Cf. 984–85 and 1226–27; also *Her.* 57–59, with the additional references in Bond's (1981) note.

58. At 957–58 Polymestor describes his own behavior as he laments the untrustworthiness of life, but he assumes that Hecuba will not make the connection. At 990, 1000, and 1021–22 Hecuba conveys her opinion and intentions to the audience, but Polymestor misunderstands because he believes her ignorant of his crime. At times the deception works on several levels, as when Polymestor tells Hecuba (993) that her son set out in secret to find her. This is presumably a lie on his part to explain to Hecuba why he cannot produce the boy. But the audience and Hecuba understand his words differently, since they know that Polydorus really did visit his mother in secret, in the form of a phantom haunting her dreams.

59. Cf. *onaimēn tou parontos*, 997 – a comment intended to suggest his modesty and integrity that has quite the opposite effect.

60. Cf. the use of *dikēn didonai/hypechein* at 853, 1024, 1052–53, 1253, and 1274. The line references are collected and discussed by Meridor 1978, 30, who comments: "The application of this expression to what is due (or given) to Hecuba from Polymestor . . . seems intended to represent 'Hecuba's Revenge' as an official act of justice. . . ."

61. Nussbaum 1986, 417, and Michelini 1987, 170, emphasize the reciprocity between the two.

62. E.g., by Matthaei 1918, 155; Daitz 1971, 222; Reckford 1985, 118; Nussbaum 1986, 416–17.

63. Meridor 1978, 33, argues that the metamorphosis has no symbolic meaning but rather is merely a piece of traditional information on a par with Polymestor's prophecy of the deaths of Agamemnon and Cassandra. That is to ignore, however, the imagery at 1173 and 1174 (where Polymestor describes the women as "bloodthirsty dogs" and himself both as a "beast" and as a "huntsman"), which implicitly links the vengeance with Hecuba's metamorphosis.

64. For a survey of dogs in Greek literature, see Lilja 1976. Obviously it is possible to pick and choose among the canine references: Nussbaum 1986, 414, and Kovacs 1987, 146, n. 68, offer their own selections, negative and positive respectively.

65. For discussion of these lines see Nagy 1985, 68, n. 1.

66. See 90, 142, 205, 337, and 526. These references are collected by Gellie 1980, 32. For the protectiveness of mothers cf. *Iph. Aul.* 918.

67. For animals' lack of *dikē*, cf. Hes. *W.&D.* 276–79.

68. Cf. the excellent discussion of "the betrayal of convention" in Nussbaum 1986, 408. She does not allow, however, that revenge is not a "new way of ordering the world" (409), but an old way, in fact one of the traditional *nomoi*.

69. At 836–840. Michelini 1987, 152, finds the image, like much else in the play, "astonishingly grotesque." While such judgments must ultimately be a matter of personal response, it is worth considering what Hecuba hopes to accomplish by this personification. She is trying, in the absence of any other supporters, to intensify her appeal to Agamemnon by multiplying herself – somewhat as Hippolytus (*Hipp.* 1078–79) wishes for "another self" to lament

his misfortunes. Kurtz 1985, 314, points out the effect of multiplication; he also calls attention to the "intensive rhetorical pathos" of the lines and the skill with which they are constructed. For me, the poignancy of Hecuba's situation and the artistry of her presentation endow the passage with a seriousness and passion far removed from the grotesque.

70. Cf. 581–82, 660, 667, 721, 786, and 811, and the discussion by Michelini 1987, 133.

71. For the change from allies to subjects cf. Meiggs 1972, 171, and Appendix 12, 425–27, where he discusses Mattingly's redating. For the tripling of the tribute see Meiggs-Lewis 1969, #69, pp. 188–201.

72. Thuc. 3.91.1. Melos was not perhaps entirely neutral, having contributed to the Spartan war fund. Cf. Meiggs-Lewis 1969, #67, 181–84, and Meiggs 1972, 314.

73. For parallels between the *Hecuba* and the more closely contemporary Plataean Debate, see Hogan 1972. For parallels to the Melian Dialogue elsewhere in Euripides, see Finley 1938, 56–58 — still unsurpassed for its study of the relationship between the two authors.

4

Heracles

Heracles was the most durable and beloved of the Greek heroes, as his many representations in art and literature attest. Though his origins were probably to be found in the Near East, the Spartan kings claimed him as their ancestor, and by the fifth century his legend had become the stuff of folktale, cult, literature, and art, and it had been dispersed throughout the entire Greek world. He had emerged, in fact, as "the one panhellenic hero."[1]

Heracles may have owed his popularity in part to the fact that he was no remote, inaccessible figure, but one who encountered more than his share of suffering and toil in the course of his journey toward apotheosis. His life was shaped by the hostility of divinity and the bitterness of service to a man inferior to himself. From infancy Heracles had to contend with the enmity of Hera—that enmity she harbored for Zeus' mortal children as well as their mothers.[2] Hera smuggled serpents into the cradle of the infant Heracles; when he grew to manhood she mounted a more sophisticated attack, visiting upon him an access of madness that provoked him to murder his children. But if Heracles' labors were undertaken in expiation of the murders inspired by Hera, and carried out at the behest of the cowardly Eurystheus, he accomplished them with such stunning success that their origins dwindled into insignificance.[3] For it was by dint of the labors that Heracles earned his place among the gods. He achieved immortality through the uniquely mortal means of sheer hard work, and the ultimate effect of Hera's malice was to launch him on the career that would win him glory and fulfill the promise of his name.[4]

Heracles was celebrated by Homer and Hesiod, Pindar and Bacchylides before he became a protagonist of tragedy, and sequences illustrating his labors figured on the temple of Zeus at Olympia, the Hephaestaeum at Athens, and the treasury of the Athenians at Delphi.[5] Although the outlines of Heracles' story were well known, his character resisted fixed definition; from the outset he was a protean figure who could serve a variety of artistic needs.[6] Each epoch and artist accorded him somewhat different treatment, emphasizing now his brute strength, now his human sympathy; now his propensities to excess, now his piety and reverence; now his struggles, and now his final reward.

Representations of Heracles in art suggest that he had come to be identified as the archetypal culture-bearer, the agent of civilization. The titles associated with his cult celebrated his extraordinary strength while also conveying the benevolent nature of his activities: he was the Defender against Evil, *Alexikakos*, and the Glorious Victor, *Kallinikos*.

Yet some of the early literary evocations of the hero suggest a different aspect—a Heracles whose apotheosis goes unmentioned, while the emphasis falls on his mortality; a hero whose experience summarized the poignancy of the human condition. When Achilles decides to reenter the fighting after Patroclus has been killed—an action that he knows will entail his own death—it is the example of Heracles that steadies him: he reflects (*Il.* 18.117-19) that "not even the strength of Heracles escaped destruction." When Bacchylides' Heracles meets Meleager in the underworld and hears his sad story he weeps for the first and only time in his life, "in pity for the fate of that unhappy man" (Bacchylides 5.157-58).

Euripides availed himself of this strain to construct his own version of the legend. Euripides not only omits any mention of immortality but reverses the traditional direction of Heracles' passage. Instead of a hero moving toward apotheosis he presents a Heracles who at first appears extraordinary, but who is subsequently reduced through an episode of bestial madness to mere mortality.

Euripides accomplishes this change of direction by his chronological arrangement of the mythical material, while underscoring it thematically by his treatment of the motif of Heracles' two fathers. In the *Heracles* the episode of madness is not the prelude to the labors but their climax. As the play begins Heracles is fetching Cerberus from the underworld—the final assignment imposed on him by King Eurystheus. After he has returned to Thebes and disposed of the tyrant who had seized power and threatened to kill Heracles' family, he has reason to believe that he has at last won respite from his toils. He seems well launched toward the immortality that was his traditional reward: he has passed every test devised by Eurystheus, nor has he neglected his familial obligations. The visitation of madness, coming with no warning, interrupts and reverses this triumphant progress. Heracles recovers his sanity to find that the episode has not only put his future in doubt but has given him a different perspective on his past. He no longer lays claim to the status of child of Zeus and solitary, invincible hero; instead he has recourse to the mortal heritage that is his legacy from Amphitryon.

Heracles' change of status incorporates a political message, for throughout the play immortality and heroic accomplishment are unobtrusively equated with aristocratic values, while mortality and ordinary human endeavor are linked to an egalitarian sensibility. Ultimately Heracles accomplishes a considerable shift of loyalties: he exchanges Zeus for Amphitryon, Thebes for Athens, solitude for fellowship, and elitist for egalitarian standards. In consequence of his suffering he develops a scheme of values consonant with the ideology of the democratic polis. Euripides has succeeded in appropriating the panhellenic hero for Athens.[7]

The Nature of Nobility

Because Heracles is absent from the stage, from Thebes, and indeed from the world of the living for the first five hundred lines of the play, it is left to secondary characters to introduce the issues that the hero's own experience will ultimately resolve. The action opens on a debate between Megara and Amphitryon that is taken up by Amphitryon and Lycus and eventually concluded by the original pair of disputants.[8] Each character has a different understanding of what constitutes the "superior man," *anēr aristos*, and a different definition of "nobility," *eugeneia*.[9] Elucidating these concepts is of immediate practical concern to Megara and Amphitryon, who try to guide their own conduct according to their understanding, but ultimately it is Heracles who provides an authoritative definition of nobility. At the moment when Heracles returns from the dead, rescues his family, and kills the tyrant Lycus, he seems to incorporate all the qualities of the traditional *eugenēs*. His identity is put into question, however, by the episode of madness, and in the end it is a revised understanding of *eugeneia* that prevails.

Eugeneia was one of the proudest badges of the aristocrat. The term evoked a whole nexus of qualities: inherited privilege, high standards of individual accomplishment, a sense of *noblesse oblige*, a transcendent concern for *eukleia* (honor and reputation), and, above all, the possession of innate excellence of character.[10] The *eugenēs* was by nature *agathos*, a term that conveyed both social and ethical superiority and conjoined the meanings of "noble" and "good."[11] In the course of the fifth century, however, and in the democratic context, these assumptions began to unravel, and the aristocratic equation of lineage with nobility of character came increasingly under attack.

Passages from tragedy suggest a concerted attempt at analysis and redefinition. Orestes in Euripides' *Electra* (367–85) draws attention to some of the difficulties inherent in the aristocratic claim to excellence when he notes that manliness (*euandria*) is not merely genetic. It is possible for the sons of a noble father to turn out badly; conversely, good judgment can reside in a humble man. He concludes that the noble (*eugeneis*) can only be recognized by their conduct—the criterion is not one of birth. Tecmessa in Sophocles' *Ajax* concurs, defining *eugeneia* in terms of gratitude and integrity (*Ajax* 522–24). Fragments of Euripides, while lacking a context, nonetheless unambiguously deny the special claims of lineage and affirm the inner, ethical character of *eugeneia*. "To me a good (*esthlos*) man is wellborn," says a character in the *Diktys*, "but the unjust man—even if descended from a better father than Zeus—seems lowborn." The chorus of the *Alexandros* takes note of the purely conventional nature of the aristocrat's claim to nobility: "Wellborn and lowborn are by nature one race. Time, joined with custom, makes birth a matter for boasting."[12]

By their different assessments of the situation created by Heracles' absence, Megara, Amphitryon, and Lycus contribute to the contemporary debate concerning the nature of *eugeneia*. At the opening of the play Amphitryon reports (22–25) that for his last labor Heracles descended to Hades in search of Cerberus. From this journey he has not returned, and his disappearance has had the gravest consequences for his family. The usurper Lycus has killed Megara's father, King Creon; has seized power in Thebes and now threatens the lives of Heracles' family. Amphitryon, Megara, and the children have been locked out of their house, deprived of food and other necessities, and forced to take refuge at the altar of Zeus (44–54). Their situation, critical enough to begin with, worsens when Lycus appears and threatens to burn them alive at the altar (240–45).

The crisis elicits a variety of responses. While Heracles' children trustfully await the momentary arrival of their father (73–75), the grown-ups' reactions are more complex. Amphitryon still hopes that

Heracles may reappear (95–97). Megara, Lycus, and the members of the chorus, however, assume that Heracles' failure to return – and from such a destination – can only mean that he is dead.[13] Even before Lycus arrives Megara has concluded that their own deaths are also a foregone conclusion (70–71), and she presses Amphitryon to admit that there can be no expectation of rescue.

Megara adduces a series of arguments to justify her pessimism. On the practical side she makes the point that the family has no means of escape, since the borders are guarded and there is no hope of help from friends (82–85). (Subsequently she will note that exile would in any case be difficult and painful, 302 ff.) Nor, as she points out, is there any chance of placating Lycus (298–99).

Megara's refusal to entertain any hope of rescue is fundamentally connected to the disappearance of Heracles. There can be, as she sees it, no expectation of his return (296): "What mortal has ever come back from Hades?" And with Heracles gone, all hope has died. Megara tells her children (460–61):

Truly, I am far removed from the optimistic
[*euelpidos*] fancies, which I once cherished [*ēlpisa*] as a
result of your father's talk!

Megara then recalls how the boys' "deceased father" (462) playfully promised one son that he would rule in Argos and the second that he would be king of Thebes, while to the third he allocated Oechalia. Each of these legacies, like the club that Heracles gave his second child to hold, now seems a "fictitious gift" (471). Because he was the touchstone of her hope, Heracles' presumed death is the source of her despair.

But Megara also has more theoretical reasons for urging on Amphitryon a prompt and voluntary death. Fatalism is for her an article of faith, almost an obligation. "One must not expect the unexpected," she tells Amphitryon (92). Only the obtuse, she believes, will resist necessity.[14] It is folly to "struggle one's way through fate" (*ekmochthein tychas*, 309), because "no one will ever convert what is necessary into what is not" (311).

Megara advocates swift and voluntary submission to Lycus not (as she points out, 280–82) because she does not love her children, and not because she does not think death terrible, but because she is convinced that a courageous death is what Heracles would wish for his family. Her "renowned husband" (*eukleēs posis*, 290) would not, she thinks, want his children to survive at the price of a bad reputation, for "the nobly born are afflicted by the shame of their children" (292–93). Megara considers it her duty to emulate her husband (294) by maintaining the family tradition of nobility. She reminds Amphitryon of the military renown he won in his youth and his obligation to uphold his reputation by the manner of his death (288–89, cf. 60–61). Finally she implores him (307–8): "Join me in braving death, which awaits you in any case! I appeal to your *eugeneia*, aged sir!"

Megara espouses the unyielding aristocratic attitude also adopted by Medea, Phaedra, Macaria, Polyxena, Iphigenia in the *Iphigenia in Aulis*, and Andromache in *Trojan Women*—all highborn women emulating a standard originally male.[15] It is in obedience to this code of conduct that Megara declares that she does not wish her enemies to have the last laugh; in fact that consideration, as she admits, is more important than death to her (285–86). Having concluded that Heracles is dead, Megara sees only one course of action that is consonant with nobility and with her emulation of her husband—not to struggle against fate but to die a hero's death, unhesitating and proud.[16] She loves Heracles and longs passionately for his return, even in the form of ghost or dream (490–95), but a combination of pride and fatalism blinds her to the truly exceptional capabilities of her husband. For Heracles is able, as no one else, to bring the unexpected to pass and "convert what is necessary into what is not" (cf. l. 311).

Amphitryon responds quite differently to the same set of constraints. His own nobility is beyond dispute—he introduces himself with a roll call of his heroic ancestors (2–3), and Megara, as remarked above, takes special note of his *eugeneia*—but he is far from espousing typical aristocratic values. In particular, he does not share the assumption that death is the only honorable course for those in trouble.[17] Like Pheres in the *Alcestis*, he clings tenaciously and unashamedly to life. "I rejoice in being alive," he tells Megara (91), "and I am fond of hope." He is inclined simply to delay, without having any specific plan in mind, in the expectation that some solution will present itself (87, 93). Instead of despair he prefers hopefulness—an attribute toward which the Greek tradition was equivocal, but which clearly had little place in the heroic scheme of values.[18] Far from apologizing for such an attitude, he challenges Megara with the revisionist claim that optimism is fundamental to the "superior man" (105–6): "He is superior who always trusts in hope. To be at a loss is the mark of a coward."

Amphitryon's hopefulness does not merely stem from an easygoing temperament: it is based on experience and philosophy. He trusts in the natural alternations of destiny (101–4):

> The troubles of mortals come to an end, and the blasts of
> the wind do not always keep the same force; the fortunate
> do not stay fortunate throughout, and everything parts
> company with everything else.

That change and alternation are part of the world of nature was a commonplace of Greek thought. Human beings, however, could imagine themselves as either embracing that natural pattern or resisting it. An eloquent statement of nonconformance is to be found in the monologue of the Sophoclean Ajax, another notable *eugenēs*:

> Winter's hard-packed snows
> Cede to the fruitful summer; stubborn night
> At last removes, for day's white steeds to shine.
> The dread blast of the gale slackens and gives
> Peace to the sounding sea; and Sleep, strong jailer,
> In time yields up his captive. Shall not I
> learn place and wisdom?[19]

Ajax does not answer his own rhetorical question, but his subsequent actions indicate that he declines to change his ways, preferring suicide to any accommodation with the Greek commanders who have dishonored him. In Ajax' world there is no room for compromise. "To live well or die well is the task of the *eugenēs*" (*Ajax* 479–80).

Megara would agree with Ajax. But Amphitryon holds that human beings and natural forces alike are subject to alternation; in consequence, to expect the unexpected seems to him no more than common sense. He is as concerned as Megara with honoring Heracles' wishes, but what comes to mind is Heracles' directive to keep his children safe (44–46, 317–18). He is far less intent on honor than is his daughter-in-law, and more concerned with survival.

Yet how is that to be accomplished? Painfully aware of his own age and helplessness (41–42, 228–31), Amphitryon can only look to others for help. He bemoans the indifference or inadequacy of the family's *philoi* (friends/relatives, 55–56), reproaches Thebes and all Hellas for failing to come to their aid (218, 222 ff.), and is particularly vociferous in his appeals to Zeus. For Zeus too is one of Heracles' *philoi*, one of the sources of his *eugeneia* and implicated in the complex question of his paternity.

The Dual Fatherhood

In the very first lines of the play Amphitryon alludes to a peculiarity of Heracles' heritage unique in Greek legend. He identifies himself as "the man who shared his bed with Zeus," and "the father of Heracles." Heracles is not the only mythological hero to boast two fathers— Phaethon, Theseus, Helen, and Ion can claim a similar distinction— but he is the only one whose two fathers seem in some sense to have merged. In order to seduce the virtuous Alcmena, Zeus was obliged to disguise himself as her husband. It was a simulated Amphitryon who deflowered her, although the real Amphitryon soon returned to claim his bride. Amphitryon thus played some crucial if biologically indefinable part in engendering the hero.

Far from concealing Zeus' role in his early married life, Amphitryon alludes to it repeatedly. The veracity of the story, an open question for the hostile Lycus and even the sympathetic members of the chorus, is for Amphitryon simply a fact of his own experience. He has not, however, forgiven the god for his conduct. Amphitryon seems to be engaged in a perpetual one-sided rivalry with Zeus; at every point he measures his own conduct against the god's and finds Zeus wanting. When he draws attention to the family's place of refuge at the altar of Zeus the Savior (Zeus *Sōtēr*, 48), and then remarks on their "want of safety" (*aporiai sōtērias*, 54), he seems to be hinting that Zeus has failed to live up to his name. He warns Lycus that he would not be able to proceed with impunity "if Zeus had a just disposition toward us" (212), and later, as death seems imminent, he addresses the god with unmistakable rancor (339–47):

Zeus, in vain I accepted you as sharer of my bed, in vain
I named you joint father of our son. You have proved
less a friend [*philos*] than you appeared. I, a mere

mortal, surpass you, a great god, in merit. For I have not
forsaken Heracles' children. You knew well how to come in
secret to my bed, and exploit another's marital rights
without consent, but you do not know how to preserve
[*sōizein*; cf. 48, 54] your kin [*philoi*]. You are a god
either uninformed or unjust.

Amphitryon keeps up the offensive when he directs his final prayer
to Zeus ("I labor in vain," he remarks bitterly, 501) while Megara is addressing hers to Heracles. Although the rivalry with Zeus has comic
potential—Amphitryon as cuckold would prove a fertile theme for
later playwrights—it is treated seriously in this play. The old man's accusations draw attention to a paradox basic to Heracles' existence,
which is scarcely questioned so long as he is successful, but which becomes critical the moment he encounters misfortune.

Heracles has two fathers, Zeus and Amphitryon—so, at least, runs
the story. He is "well born" (*eugenēs*, 50) but is his nobility attributable
to Zeus or to Amphitryon? This question points the way to a more
general query: does true nobility aspire to the divine, or is it a distilla-
tion of traits characteristically human? The same considerations are latent in the debate between Megara and Amphitryon. Is nobility
manifested in the aristocratic choice of a noble death, or in ordinary
optimism and persistence? Does the "superior man" make of the shift-
ing fortunes of human life the occasion for hope or for despair? Is it
life or death that is the coward's way out?

Megara and Amphitryon take opposite positions on these issues,
but their disagreement never flares into a quarrel, and is in any case
cut short by the appearance of Lycus. Their debate, thus broken off by
events, must await the end of the play for its resolution.

When Lycus arrives on the scene he is drawn into the discussion of
the nature of nobility. He castigates Amphitryon and Megara for their
"empty boasts: you, that you shared a bed with Zeus and had a part
in his child; you, that you were called the wife of a superior man"
(*aristou phōtos*, 150). Heracles' failure to return from the Underworld
gives his enemy license to deny Zeus' role in fathering Heracles; such
an outcome suggests that Heracles is no different from any other mortal.[20] As for Heracles' status as a "superior man," Lycus opens his attack by questioning the record. Killing animals, he remarks, scarcely

amounts to true courage. Heracles has never met bravery's true test, namely fighting in the hoplite line; instead, he has relied on his bow, the coward's weapon (*kakiston hoplon*, 161).

In thus belittling Heracles Lycus has the support of contemporary thinking. The bow was an implement of low status in comparison to the hoplite's spear; hoplite fighting was the choice of those who could afford the cost of the panoply.[21] But because the bow is fundamental to Heracles' heroic identity, Lycus is attacking far more than his choice of weapon. The exchange between Lycus and Amphitryon introduces a dialectic of solitude versus cooperative accomplishment that will figure importantly in the close of the play. Paradoxically, it will be the hateful Lycus who turns out to have had the clearer vision.[22]

Amphitryon does not deign to answer Lycus' slur on Heracles' parentage: that, he says pointedly, is Zeus' province (170–71). But he can and will defend Heracles against the "unspeakable" charge of cowardice (173–75). Amphitryon refutes Lycus by justifying Heracles' use of the bow in terms of the heroic tradition. He explains that the bow allows for an independence that the hoplite, who must rely on his companions for protection, cannot attain. With his bow Heracles is at once self-sufficient and invulnerable; not "moored to chance" (203), but free to shape for himself the course of battle.

Amphitryon's defense calls attention to Heracles' aristocratic independence from the rest of the human community. He has accomplished his labors in solitude, following the pattern of the individualistic heroes of epic. This self-sufficiency, however, has its drawbacks: although Heracles has benefited humanity in general by eradicating monsters and reclaiming land and sea, he has failed to forge a network of personal relationships that might benefit his family in their need.[23] His rescue of Theseus is an exception to the general pattern—no part of his heroic agenda but a personal, impulsive act of friendship. It delays Heracles in the Underworld until he is almost too late to rescue his family (619). But this deed will stand him in good stead when it becomes necessary for him to relinquish the independence signified by the bow and turn to the human community for support.

Amphitryon invokes prestigious witnesses to Heracles' valor—the gods, who had occasion to judge of Heracles' valor in the battle against the giants—and then asks Lycus angrily which individual the centaurs would judge the "superior man" (*andr' ariston*, 183)—would it not be his son, whom Lycus has just been disparaging? In fact it is Lycus, not

Heracles, who is open to the charge of cowardice (*deilia*; 210, 235). Lycus had earlier argued that it was not criminal shamelessness on his part, but merely good management, to eliminate Heracles' family: having killed Creon, he has no inclination to allow Heracles' children to grow up as their grandfather's avengers (165–69). Amphitryon now pours scorn on that argument. He explains that Lycus, "being personally base, fear[s] the offspring of the noble" (*tōn aristōn*, 208).

Amphitryon's words add up to a convincing refutation of the tyrant. Unfortunately the old man can win only verbal victories; both he and the chorus are too weak to take any effective measures (228–31, 268–69), and Lycus is the one who has the power to act (239). When the tyrant threatens the family with imminent death Megara's fatalistic interpretation seems to have won the day, and the old man and the young woman confront Lycus in a joint stand of dignity and courage. By voluntarily quitting the altar they hope to be able to die with honor, retaining control of at least some of the circumstances of their death (320–31).

The first stasimon expands on the theme of Heracles' nobility. Initially the members of the chorus waver in their ascription: should they call Heracles the child of Zeus or of Amphitryon (353–54)? Their hesitation reflects their pessimism over his fate; like Lycus, they cannot but see proof of Heracles' mortality in his continued residence in Hades. But even though they believe him dead, they still want to celebrate him, to create through song "a crown of praise for the labors."[24] For "the excellence of noble toils is a source of glory for mortals" (357–58).

The exalted language, with its linking of nobility, accomplishment, and the reward of song, sounds a distinctly epinician note. Heracles is portrayed in this stasimon as Pindar or Bacchylides might celebrate a victorious athlete.[25] His deeds are noble (*gennaioi*, 357) and the embodiment of excellence (*aretai*, 357). His "manliness" (*euanoria*, 407) has brought him into proximity with divinity—palpably so when, taking the place of Atlas, he "held up the starry dwelling of the gods" (405–6).

By placing the labors in an epinician context, the members of the chorus reinforce Amphitryon's portrayal of his son as traditional hero. They are trying to put Heracles' record in the best possible light, for every aspect of the labors, beginning with their origin, is subject to interpretation: up to this point it has been variously said that the labors were undertaken for Amphitryon's sake as part of a bargain with Eurystheus (17–19), on account of Hera (20), and out of necessity (21). We have already heard Lycus cite the labors as evidence of Heracles' cowardice, and it was also possible to view them as wearisome drudgery; Heracles himself, in fact, will so interpret them later in the play.[26] But this stasimon makes the claim that Heracles has transformed the labors into a blessing for the Greeks and a source of glory for himself. Only his expedition to Hades has not been rewarded with success, "the end of the labors" (427) having apparently also spelled the end of his life.

Heracles' disappearance has brought to light a disquieting fact. There is no one to help his family: "The house is empty of friends" (430). The members of the chorus cannot themselves come to the aid of the endangered suppliants. Echoing Amphitryon, they lament the age and physical weakness that render them helpless (436–41, cf. 268–69). Their complaints heighten the sense of the distance between ordinary people—too old, too weak, or too indifferent to offer any aid—and the youth, strength, and devotion of Heracles. The family looks to him—to his *hands*, as the chorus puts it (434–35)—but he is not there.

Heracles' Return

The most striking proof of Heracles' extraordinary stature—as hero, as "superior man," as son of Zeus—is furnished by his reappearance. He returns at the last possible moment to save his family, when Amphitryon, Megara, and the children have gathered in front of the palace already dressed in their grave clothes. By his miraculous arrival in the nick of time (532, 630) and from the place whence no mortal returns (cf. 297), he confirms Amphitryon's faith and refutes Megara's despair, the chorus' pessimism, and Lycus' sneers. Megara believed that it was futile to "struggle one's way through fate" (309), but that is precisely what Heracles has accomplished in returning from his last labor.

Because the episode of Heracles' return offers the audience its only direct view of the hero before he is struck down by madness, a full picture of his character must be compressed into its hundred-odd lines. He impresses as much by his intelligence as his decisiveness, and as much by his tenderness as his strength.

Heracles has no sooner arrived on stage than he notices that something is amiss. He is quick to demand an explanation; as in rapid dialogue (542–60) he gathers information on how Lycus seized power, why the family had abandoned hope for his own return, and whether any help was forthcoming from friends, he establishes himself as a man who informs himself of all aspects of the situation before taking action. A similar forethought (*pronoia*, 598) has governed the manner of his arrival in Thebes: noticing an ill-omened bird en route, he decided to make his entry in secret and unannounced (596–98). No mere musclebound bully, this Heracles possesses some distinctively modern traits. He manifests the capacity for "swift action based on intelligent reflection" admired by fifth-century Athens and characteristic of its best leaders.[27]

As might be expected, Heracles shows himself to be primarily a man of action. He wastes no time recounting his adventures in the Underworld, despite the rhetorical potential of the subject and the manifest curiosity of his auditors (cf. 610, 612). He is a hero cast in the same mold as the Sophoclean Ajax. Like Ajax, he is neither stupid nor incoherent, but words are of little value to him, deeds being his natural mode of expression. If such men are peculiarly vulnerable to madness, it is not because they are mentally deficient but rather because, by virtue of their physical strength, they are invulnerable to attack from any other direction. The gods must work with the material that comes to hand, and the strength of an Ajax or Heracles is such that it cannot be overcome, only misdirected.

As Heracles reacts angrily to the news of Lycus' usurpation, he offers ample evidence that Lycus was wrong to call his courage into question. Heracles proposes to accomplish his revenge as quickly and straightforwardly as possible. "I will take this in hand," is his remark once he has grasped the situation (565); his family, it appears, was well advised to look "to his hands" (434) for salvation. Heracles' language is distinctly violent: he threatens to raze the palace, cut off Lycus' head and throw it to the dogs, and make the stream of Dirce run red with the blood of disloyal citizens (565–73). There is no justification, however, for reading the savagery of incipient madness into his words.[28] Violence has been characteristic of Heracles throughout his career, but characteristically it has been perpetrated in a good cause: in this case, the defense of his family (574–75). His threats are proportionately more terrible than Amphitryon's (232 ff.) or the chorus' (254 ff.) as his strength is greater and his responsibility more direct. Heracles is acting in the tradition of the conscientious king who must, on his return home after a prolonged absence, purge his city of hostile elements. Aeschylus' Agamemnon announces but has no time to carry out a policy similar to Heracles', and Homer's Odysseus actually puts such a plan into effect upon his return to Ithaca from Troy.

Yet tenderness, not violence, is the dominant note of the scene. To Megara Heracles is her "most beloved" (514); for Amphitryon he is "the return of the light" (531). His children cling to him and will not let him go, nor does he try to shake them off. He assures them gently that he has no wings to fly away (628). Heracles fully reciprocates his family's affection. He affirms the importance of his personal ties (574–76):

> Whom should I better defend than my wife and children and
> [this] old man? Farewell to my labors! In vain I
> accomplished them rather than these.

Heracles' words are emphatic and rhetorical. He has, at this juncture, no intention of disavowing his labors; rather he is concerned to stress the equal importance of both aspects of his life, both his personal and his professional obligations.[29] In thus combining public responsibilities with familial commitment he conforms to the epic pattern of the complete hero. Hector in the *Iliad* (6.390–493) takes time out from fighting to hold a tender conversation with Andromache and dandle his infant son in his arms. Achilles in the *Odyssey* (11.494, 540), now resident in the Underworld, asks eagerly after his old father and is gladdened by news of his son. Sophocles even creates a domestic context (though the effect is somehow very grim) for his hero Ajax (*Ajax* 541–95).

In emphasizing Heracles' tenderness for his family Euripides does more than round out the traditional portrait of the hero. The motif functions as a structural element that bridges the discrete sections of the tragedy.[30] The familial affection Heracles displays throughout the episode will acquire additional significance in the light of the following scene: when the audience learns of Heracles' murder of his wife and children, it can look back on the episode of his return and understand that his crime is totally at odds with his own nature. There is no possible sense in which he could have wished to harm his family; the evidence is the protective love for them he expresses on his return. The madness that overwhelms Heracles uncovers no hidden truths of his nature; instead it entails an alienation (*xenōsis*, 965) from his former self.

The motif of domestic affection also lays the groundwork for the end of the play. Heracles himself makes the point that family feeling is something all men share (634–36): "Rich and poor alike love their children. Wealth is unequal; some have it, some not. But everyone loves his children." By emphasizing that universal quality here Euripides prepares for the transformed Heracles of the close, who will reject the proud isolation of the traditional hero in favor of communal life and the support of other human beings.[31]

At the moment of Heracles' reappearance, however, no one dreams of such a reversal. The hero's return from Hades establishes, in the chorus' eyes, his connection with divinity. "He is the son of Zeus," they proclaim (696). They take note of his outstanding *eugeneia* — a nobility that can now, it seems, confidently be traced to a divine father. After Heracles has killed Lycus they reiterate their admiration. If Heracles has proved his nobility, Lycus by his defeat has demonstrated his baseness or *dysgeneia* (810). Attempting violence toward his betters (741), he has paid the penalty. Heracles and Lycus have exchanged places (769–70), the one descending to the Underworld, the other returning to the light. Such an exchange confirms the chorus' belief in fortune's natural tides, in "the ebb flow of destiny" (739). The tyrant's death goes unmourned; the members of the chorus can only rejoice at the death of the impious man (760) and the happy alterations of fate (735, 765–66). Once more they reiterate their faith in the tale of the dual fatherhood (798–804). Time has worked in Heracles' favor; the truth of Zeus' role in his engendering has been confirmed against all expectation both by his reappearance from Hades and by his valor.[32] The pattern of events suggests an affirmative answer to the question of the gods' concern for justice (814–15).

Hera's Wrath

Yet even as the men of the chorus speak the word "justice," an event takes place that suggests either that justice concerns the gods not at all, or that their interpretation of the concept is very different from that of human beings — that Zeus, just as Amphitryon had suspected (347), is either uninformed or unjust. Two apparitions appear, throwing the members of the chorus into a state of terror. Of the two Iris speaks first, to reassure the old men that the polis is in no danger (824), and to identify the victim the goddesses are come to seek.

Iris announces that their business is with "one man, who they say is the son of Zeus and Alcmena." That brief reference to Heracles' parentage serves as her only explanation of Hera's wrath. Heracles is not, of course, the son of Zeus and Alcmena only; he is also the son of Amphitryon, and there is an allusion to these complexities in Iris' "they say" (*phasin*, 826). Like Lycus earlier, she belittles the hero by casting aspersions on his birth. But it seems clear that Hera herself considers Heracles the true son of Zeus. The origins of her anger are to be sought in his birth; such is the assumption of every major character in the play.[33]

No other justification is ever offered. Heracles cannot be charged with any wrongdoing that might have awakened the goddess' anger. Certainly he is not guilty of impiety; to the contrary, he erected an altar to Zeus Sōtēr (48) and dedicated the hind of Ceryneia to Artemis (375–79). Lyssa herself points out (852–53) that "single-handed he revived the worship of the gods." Madness will strike as he stands respectfully at the altar, poised to make sacrifice to his household deities.[34] Heracles will later describe himself as "the benefactor of Greece, a man utterly innocent" (1309–10), and his record confirms the claim.

In fact Heracles' own record, whether good or bad, is only in question insofar as his long engagement with the labors has shielded him from Hera's wrath (827 ff.). He poses a challenge because he has hitherto avoided her anger, and Iris explains that the gods will be "nowhere" (841) if Hera does not get her way. Hera's dispatching of Lyssa is simply one last maneuver in a hitherto unsuccessful campaign. The "gorgon-eyed serpents" (1266) sent to strangle the infant Heracles failed of their mission. This time Hera has dispatched "the Gorgon of the night with her hundredfold hissing of serpents" (883–84), and this final instrument of her wrath will prove effective.

The Greek gods were traditionally assumed to be vengeful, and it is not in fact Hera's role in Heracles' madness that raises questions, but rather that of Zeus. As Heracles' father Zeus might be expected to protect both his son and his son's family—a point made early on, and repeatedly, by Amphitryon. The old men of the chorus call Zeus' attention to the murders even as they are taking place (886–88); it is as if they cannot believe that Zeus might be apprised of the disaster, yet still decline to intervene. Amphitryon too is incredulous (1115, 1127). Only Iris offers a hint of the true situation.

Iris explains that so long as Heracles was busy with the labors,

Necessity preserved him, nor would Zeus allow either Iris or Hera to do him harm (827–29). At the beginning of the play Amphitryon had been uncertain whether Necessity or Hera was responsible for the labors (21–22). We may now conclude on Iris' authority that it was Necessity, acting in concert with Zeus—that is, that the labors formed a positive aspect of Heracles' destiny, constituting as much opportunity as travail. But has Zeus' power to help his son come to an end now that the labors are concluded? Iris does not say so directly, yet such appears the only explanation for the god's neglect of his son at this crisis.

The most limited inference to be drawn from the text is that the madness sent by Hera (or, as Heracles will put it [1393], "by the fortune of Hera") is tolerated by Zeus and Necessity according to the Olympian principle that gods must respect one another's spheres of influence.[35] Already in the *Iliad* Achilles acknowledges that Zeus' love for Heracles was no protection from Hera's anger (cf. *Il.* 18.118–19). Here responsibility is allocated along temporal lines: once Heracles' labors are at an end, Zeus yields the field to Hera. To put it another way, first Zeus-and-Necessity and then Fortune-and-Hera take charge of Heracles.[36] We may thus conclude that the hero's divine champions and adversaries are not at odds with one another, as the mortals imagine, but rather take turns in shaping his life. What to human beings looks like neglect or betrayal represents, from the divine perspective, the pattern of destiny—a hypothesis that casts a new light on the violent dislocations reflected in the structure of the play. At this point, however, any such conclusions still lie in the future. They will be suggested only obliquely toward the end of the play by Theseus, and they are never acknowledged by Heracles himself.

Iris cannot accomplish her task alone. She is accompanied by Lyssa, the goddess of madness, "of noble parents" (843) like Heracles himself, and like Heracles the product of two divergent elements. Lyssa is the daughter of Ouranos and Night: the one a celestial, the other a chthonic divinity. With this genealogy Euripides introduces a series of resemblances between the goddess of madness and her victim that gradually combine to blur the distinction between divine intervention and human impulse. By this device Euripides interiorizes Heracles' madness while retaining the traditional picture of madness as a force working from without.[37]

Lyssa's state of mind parallels that of her victim. Spirit of madness though she is, the goddess behaves initially in a strikingly reasonable fashion. As long as she remains sane, so too does Heracles. Lyssa's distaste for her task does not prevent her from carrying it out with the utmost thoroughness; and as she herself goes mad, Heracles keeps pace. As her meter changes from trimeter to tetrameter her tone also alters, becoming wild and charged with menace.[38] She promises to track Heracles like a hunting dog and likens the violence of her attack to the onset of tempest, earthquake, and thunderstorm (859–63). Because of the similarity already adumbrated between the goddess and her victim, Lyssa's transformation from calm to fury and her extended use of imagery from natural cataclysms facilitate the transformation of Heracles from hero to madman, from something more to something less than human.

As if to emphasize the shock and terror occasioned by Heracles' madness, Euripides gives the audience three descriptions of the attack. Lyssa's prophecy is succeeded by the chorus' impressionistic, almost hallucinatory evocation of the murders and by the messenger's sober after-the-fact report. The choral periods shape themselves into cycles of lament, description, and summation, each punctuated by Amphitryon's cries from within the palace. The stasimon begins with a lament for Heracles (875–79). There follows a description of Lyssa, the "Gorgon of the night" (883), whose attributes continue to coincide with Heracles'. For if Lyssa is a Gorgon, Heracles has eyes like a Gorgon's (868, 999). If Lyssa is a Bacchante (898), Heracles is a Bacchant of Hades (1119, 1122). Both Lyssa and Heracles figuratively ride chariots (760, 880). Both carry goads, Heracles' being self-imagined (949), Lyssa's the goad of madness (882). The language contrives to suggest that Heracles and his persecutor have in some sense fused.

Fundamental to Heracles' madness is a loss of humanity. The eyes are normally organs of expression and perception: Heracles' rolling, bloodshot eyes (868, 932–33) no longer perform either function. His hearing having gone awry, he is deaf to his family's pleas and warnings. His silence, followed by wild laughter (930, 935), signals a divorce from language. Even his breathing is no longer under control (869). His bearing has lost the expressiveness characteristic of a human being.

The messenger's account fills in gaps left by the other versions. It makes it clear, for example, that madness overtook Heracles in several stages.[39] When he first suspended the sacrifice he was already "no longer himself" (931), yet he still recognized Amphitryon as his father (cf. 936) and was still conscious of his surroundings. His announced plan was to kill Eurystheus—a project that is bloodthirsty but not yet insane. For Heracles seems always to have intended to seize Eurystheus' kingdom (he had promised it to his son, 463), and such a scheme could only entail the violent overthrow of the king.

Heracles calls for his weapons and then departs on an imaginary journey to Mycenae. The bystanders are still uncertain whether he is mad or merely playing a joke (952), but soon he leaves them no room for doubt. Heracles mounts an imaginary chariot and lashes on invisible horses, he breaks his putative journey to eat a nonexistent meal and win an imaginary victory, and he finally demolishes, as he believes, the walls of Mycenae (in reality the partitions of his own palace). He acts out the metaphor of wandering, which in Greek thought was closely associated with madness.[40] There is an especial pathos to his actions because they reiterate the activities that have filled his life: arrivals and departures, contests and banquets. But whereas his earlier journies were infused with purpose and gained him the title of *kallinikos*, this senseless labor leaves him *kallinikos oudenos* (961), "champion over nobody."

It is when he has arrived at his putative Mycenae that Heracles enters the final stage of his madness. He has now not only forgotten his surroundings and the identity of his victims, but has lost sight of the most compelling of human taboos. He ignores one suppliant, Amphitryon, and kills another, his own son. After shooting down the other two children and their mother, he advances on the old man. But now another goddess intervenes to bring the episode to an abrupt end. As Heracles takes aim against his father, Athena hurls a stone at the madman's breast that stuns him into unconsciousness (1002–6).

It is appropriate that Athena should put a halt to the carnage, for she is often represented in art (in four of the metopes of the temple of Zeus at Olympia, for example) as Heracles' guardian deity. Her intervention here, however, has additional connotations. The messenger describes her as decked out in full battle regalia, equipped with helmet and spear—an image that would presumably conjure up for Euripides' audience the great chryselephantine statue of Athena above them on the Acropolis, standing guard over the city of Athens.[41] Athena's intervention prefigures the role the city of Athens will perform for Hera-

cles at the end of the play. Mythic tradition constrains the goddess
from rescuing Heracles' wife and children, but by preventing him from
killing his father she saves him from the most extreme consequences
of his violence.[42] Amphitryon's survival is essential to that of Heracles,
for it is he, along with Theseus, who will sponsor the new sense of self
that Heracles discovers in the aftermath of madness.

Whether recounted from the perspective of Lyssa, the chorus, or
the messenger, the episode of madness seems to carry its own simple
and portentous lesson. It signifies a reversal that affects every aspect
of Heracles' existence. The heroic son of Zeus has been transformed
into a bestial creature, more like a bull than a man (cf. 869). His characteristic energy has mutated into destructive fury; the benefactor of all
mankind has become the murderer of his kin. The hero who held up
the world with his hand (403–7) now sprawls on the ground, propped
against a fallen pillar (1006–12).

Amphitryon's theory of natural succession can scarcely account for
this outcome. Amphitryon had envisioned a cosmic alternation in ac-
cord with justice: that was why he had trusted in the ultimate defeat
of the wicked Lycus (cf. 216). The chorus was of the same opinion,
since the function of time, in their theology, is to right any temporary
inequities, show up the excellence of the good man (805–6), and call
the wicked to account (739). Heracles' experience, however, suggests
a vertiginous absence of cause and effect in the workings of destiny.
Heracles has committed the very crime he killed Lycus to forestall;
there has proved, contrary to expectation, nothing to choose between
the good king and the tyrant, the savior and the destroyer, the noble
and the base-born.

If that is the case then human beings have every reason to
despair—and such, as we shall see, is Heracles' first response. But Euripides is not content to leave matters there. He moves beyond the
simple fact of reversal and beyond the temptations of despair to identify a margin for hope. The human community steps in to help Heracles, and the tenderness and generosity of Amphitryon and Theseus
are the more conspicuous when set against the cruelty and neglect of
Hera and Zeus. Heracles' misfortune gains him access to his other heritage, to resources undreamed of by Hera—that fund of human pity
and support that is proffered so lavishly in the last episode, and
summed up in the heartfelt repetitions of the word *philos*, friend.

Recovery and Reevaluation

The first thing that Heracles notices on awakening is "the sky and earth and arrows of the sun" (1090). This is true perception, "what [he] ought to see" (1089), and a signal that his madness is on the wane. As he awakens from his sinister and aberrant sleep (cf. 1061), he is prey to an amnesia that overleaps the episode of madness and casts him back to an earlier period. Heracles assumes that he has embarked on still another adventure for Eurystheus in Hades (1101–2), but he changes his mind when he cannot spot Sisyphus' rock or other landmarks of the Underworld. It is a further sign of recovery that he no longer orients himself by imaginary signposts. When Amphitryon steps forward Heracles recognizes him at once—final proof that his sanity has been restored.

Heracles' first word to the old man is "Father!" and Amphitryon replies, "My child! For you *are* mine even in your trouble" (1113). Far from disowning Heracles at this crisis, he emphatically lays claim to him. He is a model of tact and compassion as he instructs Heracles in his ignorance, guiding him first to the fact of his own responsibility for the disaster (1129), then to the identity of the corpses (1131), and finally to the full truth of the calamity (1135).

Heracles' grief and self-condemnation are manifested as straightforwardly as was his anger at the news of Lycus' usurpation. His impulse, now as earlier, is toward a violent consummation, this time directed against himself. In traditional aristocratic fashion he dreads the *dyskleia* or bad repute arising from his crime (1152). His solution is the same as Ajax' in far less drastic circumstances: self-destruction, whether by means of a suicide leap, fire, or the sword (1148–52).

Theseus arrives to thwart his project and to propose not only a solution to his practical difficulties but also a new way of interpreting his own history—a revision of the past made necessary, but also made possible, by the visitation of madness. Because Heracles' access of insanity is part of his history, it too becomes subject to reconsideration in the final episode. An event that had seemed entirely destructive turns out to contain the seeds of regeneration.

Theseus does not recognize the figure huddled on the ground, his head concealed in his cloak, as that of Heracles. Amphitryon identifies him with eager possessiveness as his son, and also—with an emphasis on his glorious past—as the giant-killer of Phlegra (1190 ff.). With this description he asserts that Heracles' heroic record remains a factor to be reckoned with. Theseus, however, answers in a different tone (1195): "Alas, was ever mortal so unfortunate?" The messenger, after recounting Heracles' murder of his family, had ended his tale on the same note: "I know of no mortal more wretched" (1015). If triumph brought Heracles' divine heritage to the fore, misfortune has sent him back to earth again.

Theseus is doubly a *philos*, both kinsman and friend (1154). He has journeyed to Thebes to offer Heracles his help against Lycus (1163–65), and he remains constant even though the terms of the battle have shifted. The first necessity, as Theseus sees it, is for Heracles to unveil himself, and he has recourse to four arguments in favor of this course. Each of his points, while intended to rally Heracles, simultaneously emphasizes the enormity of the disaster that has overtaken him.

Theseus' first argument is that self-concealment is useless: no cloud is dark enough to hide Heracles' misery (1216–17). In Heracles' conventionally humble posture Theseus reads a kind of arrogance, an assumption that he can devise a response commensurate to the disaster. Theseus undertakes to correct this misapprehension.

Theseus next assures Heracles that he himself does not fear pollution from intimate contact; on the contrary, he is eager to share in his friend's misfortunes as he had earlier shared in his triumphs (1220–25). Theseus thus incidentally refutes Megara's belief that "ill luck has no friends" (561). But Heracles has never had any misfortune worth sharing before, never required any return on his favors. Theseus' very decency underscores the enormity of the reversal that has taken place. As Theseus later remarks:

> Now you are in want of friends. When the gods give
> honor, there is no need for friends. The god is of
> sufficient help, when he so desires.[43]

Theseus' next remark revives the dispute over the characteristics of the *eugenēs* that had divided Megara and Amphitryon at the start of the play (1227–28):

> Stand up, uncover your poor head, and look at me. The
> nobly born of mortals endures what the gods deal out and
> does not resist.

Nobility as Theseus understands it is embodied in patience rather than pride, and it entails acknowledging divine power over mortal lives and submitting to destiny. His is a recasting of the traditional standard which, with its accent on endurance, lies closer to Amphitryon's point of view than Megara's. It is this sense of *eugeneia* that will prevail as the play draws to a close.

Theseus' final point is that Heracles' actions cannot in any case affect the divine order: "Mortal that you are, you cannot pollute what is the gods' " (1232). An argument that in another context could acquire a rationalistic, even sacrilegious tinge is here used in the service of a traditional lesson in humility.[44] Once more Theseus focuses on a strain of hidden arrogance he detects in Heracles' preoccupation with pollution, and chides his friend for placing himself on a level with divinity.

Theseus' strategy is to force Heracles to see himself for what he really is: a weak and pitiful mortal. As the two discuss Heracles' predicament Theseus repeatedly cuts his friend down to size. The only thing about Heracles that reaches heaven, he says, is his misfortune (1240). And when Heracles seems to hurl a challenge to divinity—"God is wilful toward me, and I toward the gods" (1243)—Theseus warns him to hold his tongue or risk punishment for his bravado.

Yet when Heracles takes these reproofs to heart and in discouragement reverts to the idea of suicide (1247), Theseus shifts his approach. Now he implies that suicide would be the way out for "just anybody" (1248). The choice of death over life, which Megara had seen as the hallmark of an aristocrat, is now branded as vulgar and cowardly. To deter Heracles from such a course Theseus reminds Heracles of his record of achievement and, by implication, of his obligation to live up to it (1250, 1252). But is Heracles a glorious hero or a wretched outcast? The two extremes of Theseus' characterization emphasize the contradiction between Heracles' triumphant past and his miserable present. The unity of his experience has been shattered by madness, and reassessment is in order.

That is precisely what Heracles undertakes in a long autobiographical excursus (1255 ff.). He proposes to demonstrate that his life has been a total loss: "Listen now, I will take issue with your reproaches and reveal to you that my life is not worth living now—nor was it before."

Like Megara, Heracles draws the most drastic conclusion from his plight. He reinforces his sweeping assertion by an appeal to his origins:

First of all, I am the son of Amphitryon here, who was guilty of
the murder of my mother's father and then married
Alcmena, who bore me. When the foundations of a family are
not solidly laid, there is bound to be sorrow for the
descendants. And then Zeus—whoever Zeus may be—fathered
me for Hera's hatred.

He inherited pollution from Amphitryon and the burden of Hera's
enmity from Zeus. Having explained this double handicap, he turns
to Amphitryon and adds, "Do not be pained, old man. I think of you
as my father, not Zeus" (1264–65).

With these words the question of Heracles' dual paternity finds its
resolution. Heracles has just articulated, with no sense of a biological
contradiction, the fact that he had two fathers. But he is aware of the
spiritual dilemma implicit in that circumstance, and at this moment of
anguish and defeat he makes his choice. Others may continue to see
Heracles as the son of Zeus (cf. 1020, 1289), but Heracles himself now
resigns his claims to semidivine status and acknowledges his share of
mortality, his human father.

Such an admission is what Theseus has had in mind for Heracles
all along. But Heracles is still far from finding sustenance in his identification with other mortals. Though he has relinquished his semidivine status, he adheres to the standards of the traditional *eugenēs*;
death still presents itself as the only solution to his troubles. Looking
back on his labors he sees them as no source of pride, only as a round
of dreary drudgery culminating in the murder of his children.[45] As he
considers the future he sees no mitigating factors in his situation. He
can neither stay in Thebes nor remove to Argos (1280 ff.). If he journies
to any other city he can imagine (1288–90) the suspicious glances and
contemptuous words that will greet him, signifying that loss of reputation so dreaded by the *eugenēs*. Hera may well rejoice, he concludes bitterly. She has had everything her way, since she has succeeded in
ruining "the first man in Greece" (1306), "the benefactor of Greece, a
man utterly innocent" (1310).

The chorus agrees that the disaster is Hera's work, but Theseus proceeds to imply a rather different line of reasoning.[46] Neither mortals
nor gods, he points out, live "untouched by destiny" (1314). The gods,
according to the myths, put up with ill treatment from one another,
and they continue to coexist under less than ideal circumstances. Why

should Heracles, "mortal that he is" (1320), be restive under fate, when the gods are not?[47]

What has happened to Heracles, Theseus obliquely suggests, cannot simply be attributed to Hera. Rather than looking for someone to blame, Heracles should realize that his whole life comprises the pattern of his destiny. Zeus and Hera work in combination—a partnership that infuriates Amphitryon (1127) but is nonetheless binding on Heracles as on all mortals. The will of Hera (1305) that arouses Heracles' ire is ultimately scarcely separable from the more familiar will of Zeus. That being the case, Heracles will do best to accept his destiny—an attitude that is, in Theseus' view, in any case the mark of the *eugenēs* (1227–28).

Theseus does not openly rebuke Heracles for blaming Hera, and he soon turns to Heracles' immediate difficulties and offers some practical solutions. He invites him to travel to Athens, undergo purification there, and live out the rest of his life in enjoyment of Theseus' patronage and his gifts of land. There is not a word about immortality, but Theseus makes it clear that Heracles can look forward to a hero's special status.[48] After he is "dead [and] gone to Hades" (1331), he will be honored with a cult in Athens. Theseus concludes:

> It is a pleasing crown [*stephanos*] for the citizens,
> through helping a fine man, to attain glory [*eukleia*]
> from the Greeks.

Theseus' initial counsel to Heracles, like Amphitryon's dialogue with Megara, had contained elements of revisionist social definition: the *eugenēs*, he had suggested, is not the traditional aristocrat who prefers death to defeat, but the man who understands the nature of endurance. The same revisionist element is in evidence here, as Theseus makes two claims in highly compressed form. The first is that, contrary to Heracles' own interpretation, something has been preserved from his past accomplishments. His reputation has not been shattered by the deeds committed in madness; the absolute standards of the aristocratic code no longer apply, for Heracles remains an *anēr esthlos* even in disaster.[49] Nobility, in Theseus' understanding, depends on character rather than circumstances.

Theseus' second inference is that the crown and glory that had been Heracles' possession (cf. *stephanōma*, 355; *eukleēs*, 290; *eukleia*, 1370) will

now become the prerogative of all the citizens of Athens. Such a
change accords with the ideology of a political system that champi-
oned the interests of the collective over those of the individual. A
study of Athenian funeral orations has demonstrated how in the fifth
and fourth centuries themes and attributes previously associated with
aristocratic individuals were newly applied to the polis.[50] The same
transference is discernible here, as the crown that adorned epinician
athletes is now promised to the city of Athens, the reward not for victory but for compassion.

But we are not yet done with Heracles himself. Heracles answers
Theseus with a speech that shows how carefully he has attended to his
friend. He begins by denying Theseus' tales of Olympian misconduct;
these, he says, can only be the invention of the poets. "God, if he is
truly god, needs nothing" (1345–46). Though Heracles harbors a deep
resentment against Hera, his fundamental faith in the gods remain un-
shaken, and he chooses to condemn the false stories that have been
told about the gods rather than the gods themselves.[51]

Although Heracles speaks in direct reference to the examples
offered by Theseus, his conclusion also applies to his own situation.
Heracles here summarizes, even as he lays aside, the standard that
had regulated his earlier career. As the son of Zeus and in pursuit of
immortality, he had lived a life of self-sufficient heroism in emulation
of the gods. Heracles had long flourished in solitude; he had striven
to bring benefits to his family, Thebes, and all Greece while asking—
and requiring—nothing in return. "God, if he is truly god, needs nothing." Human beings, on the other hand, are weak and vulnerable;
they need to join together to compensate for their individual helplessness.[52] Heracles' acknowledgment of his neediness and his acceptance
of Theseus' companionship are a crucial part of recognizing himself as
mortal, truly the son of Amphitryon.

Heracles had always been willing to perform acts of friendship; now
he is willing to accept them.[53] He has adopted Theseus' argument that
suicide would be cowardly, as well as his definition of *eugeneia* as endurance (1347–57):

Even in the midst of troubles I have considered whether it
would not be labelled cowardice to quit the light. For the
man who does not stand up under misfortune would not be able
to withstand the weapons of an adversary. I will endure

life.[54] I am going to go to your city, and I am infinitely grateful
for your gifts. Yet I have also tasted of
infinite labors, which I never refused, nor did I weep, nor
ever thought that I would come to weeping. But now I must,
it seems, be a slave to destiny.

Heracles' words reveal the pain of transition as they mingle old assumptions with new. He still phrases his decision to live in heroic terms,
still evinces concern for his reputation as a warrior. At the same time his
tears and his acceptance of Theseus' favors constitute a recognition of
his altered status and his characteristically mortal need for succor.[55]

Heracles' resolution of the problem posed by his weapons recalls
the earlier dispute between Lycus and Amphitryon and gives an indication of where Heracles now stands: precariously balanced between
pride and despair, resentment and tolerance, nobility in the old sense
and the new. Heracles wonders whether to leave his weapons behind
when he travels to Athens, but he eventually decides to take them,
even though they will serve as a perpetual reminder and reproach
(1376–85). Heracles' bow has throughout been identified closely with its
owner, becoming at times a sort of totem. Now Heracles decides to
keep it, but on new and reduced terms: "wretchedly" (*athliōs*, 1385),
like his father's life (1365) and his own (1375). His bow has not permitted
him to live unencumbered by destiny, as Amphitryon had claimed
(203); to the contrary, he now understands that he must be a slave to
destiny.[56] Yet he will abandon neither his bow nor his life; that would
be cowardice, and to link cowardice with Heracles is, as Amphitryon
had recognized, to speak the unspeakable (174–75).

Heracles' acceptance both of Theseus' arguments and Theseus' aid
is more wholehearted than his friend had bargained for. He asks for
Theseus' companionship as he disposes of the dog Cerberus; in view
of his grief and his bereavement, he is uneasy about his own state of
mind (1385–87). He, who never wept before, now yields to grief beyond
the point Theseus thinks proper, and Theseus feels himself once again
obliged to remind him of his heroic past (1410 ff.). In his final exchange
with Amphitryon Heracles promises to attend to his burial—the final
duty a son could perform for his father. At last Heracles departs, lean-
ing on Theseus. Even his posture is consistent with his acceptance of
mortality. In accepting Theseus' physical support he reiterates his distance from the gods and his dependence on mortal help.

If there is a lingering sense of incompleteness, it is because Heracles himself seems to misinterpret his experience. To the end he continues to view his life as one continuous disaster and to blame everything on Hera and *tychē*: "We have all been wretchedly destroyed by a single blow of fortune—Hera's" (1392–93). Yet the audience needs to consider not so much what Heracles says as what he does: it is typical of this hero that his actions speak louder than his words. In the end he decides to go on living, and to have arrived at this decision is to have discovered some reason for hope. The fatalism of the traditional *eugenēs* is rejected and the values of hopeful endurance and generous reciprocity exalted by way of Heracles' final choice.

The audience can understand, even if the protagonist does not, that the two aspects of Heracles' destiny—Zeus and Hera, necessity and fortune—are really one. It is no new discovery but a return to archaic wisdom to recognize that what the gods deal out to mortals is sometimes mixed and sometimes overwhelmingly evil, but never wholly good.[57] What is new is the demonstration that the human community can serve to counterbalance the inconsistent patronage of the powers above.

In its critique of divinity the *Heracles* is reminiscent of the *Alcestis* and the *Hippolytus*. All three plays demonstrate that the gods inhabit an entirely different plane from mortals and that the help forthcoming from other human beings is more consistent, more generous, and more consonant with mortal needs than is the uncertain favor of the gods. Yet while Euripides exposes the disparity between divine promise and performance, he is not primarily concerned to castigate the gods' behavior, much less to question their existence.[58] The shortcomings of divinity are not the focus of Euripides' attack, but they become the occasion for purely human remedies.

These remedies may involve a reshaping of traditional understandings. Heracles at the end of the play is still a *eugenēs*, still an *esthlos*—so much Theseus makes clear—but the terms have acquired a different resonance as a result of his madness and suffering. Heracles has turned away from the aristocratic value system with its emphasis on individual glory and solitary accomplishment. His projected residence in Athens is emblematic of a change of attitude, as is his decision to accept Theseus' help and patronage.

The *Heracles* must have conveyed a heartening message to Euripides' war-weary compatriots.[59] At the close of the play the references to Theseus, and through Theseus to Athens, become increasingly lavish. "Happy in its offspring," says the chorus (1405),"is the fatherland that produced this man!" When Heracles chooses Athens as his domicile and Theseus' friendship as his resource, he seems to affirm that one cannot do better than to live as an Athenian.

NOTES

1. Galinsky 1972, 4. For Heracles' origins see Burkert 1985, 207–11. On Spartan claims to Heracles see also Goossens 1962, 347.

2. Mattes 1970, 37–38, lists Hera's victims, pointing out that Hera's anger extended even to Athamas and Ino, the nurses of the infant Dionysus.

3. Bond 1981 (henceforth "Bond"), xxviii–xxx, reviews the evidence—suggestive but not conclusive—for a pre-Euripidean tradition that placed the murders anterior to the labors. Prior to Bond's edition scholars followed the lead of Wilamowitz 1895[2], (vol. 2, 109) in assuming such a traditional chronology. The persistence of that tradition in post-Euripidean accounts suggests that Euripides had at least a choice of chronologies, so that his placement of the murders after the labors looks like a purposeful thematic emphasis.

4. Pötscher 1971 argues that Heracles' name preserves an early stage of the legend that made Hera Heracles' patron—a tradition subsequently lost sight of. Euripides' treatment gives an unexpected turn to this version: by driving Heracles back on his mortal heritage, Hera proves his unintended benefactor.

5. For artistic representations of the labors see Brommer 1953. Galinsky 1972 surveys the literary tradition on Heracles.

6. Galinsky 1972, 1–2; he points out that not every mythological figure is so adaptable.

7. So Goossens 1962, 6–7 and 347–48; followed by Foley 1985, 189 and 195.

8. On the structure of the debate see Hamilton 1985.

9. While Chalk 1962 makes many excellent and perceptive observations on the play, in my view he misstates its major theme when, following Wilamowitz, he concentrates on *aretē* rather than *eugeneia*, which is in fact the reference point for many of the passages he discusses. The word *aretē* does not recur in the play after 659 (whereas *eugenēs* appears as late as 1227) and for good reason: as Adkins 1966, 209 ff., points out, there is no evidence for a revisionist definition of *aretē* (as there is of *eugeneia*) that would make it applicable to Heracles in defeat. Chalk also claims, 9–10, that Heracles in the course of the play moves from Amphitryon's activism to Megara's philosophy of endurance, a formulation that seems to me to reverse the attitudes exemplified by the two. It is Amphitryon who wants to wait and hope, Megara who argues in favor of a precipitous death.

10. Cf. Donlan 1973, who notes (65): "[*Eugeneia*] was the emblem of aristocratic exclusiveness par excellence, the one characteristic that could not

be imitated or adopted by nonaristocrats." This play, however, shows how the term could be redefined so as to make it available to nonaristocrats.

11. For discussion of *agathos* and other evaluative terms, see Adkins 1960, 30 ff.

12. Fr. 336 N^2 and 52 N^2; cf. also 495 N^2, 40–43. For the themes of *eugeneia* and *dysgeneia* in Euripides' Trojan trilogy, see Scodel 1980, 84–89 and 108–9.

13. Amphitryon refrains from drawing any conclusions about Heracles' prolonged absence (25), in contrast to Lycus (145–46), Megara (295–96), and the chorus (420 ff.). At 553 Megara tells Heracles that Eurystheus' heralds announced his death.

14. Her term is *skaios* (283), which, as Bond explains, conveys aristocratic as well as aesthetic, intellectual, and moral disdain.

15. Adkins 1966, 211, argues that as a female Megara cannot aspire to masculine *aretē*. While it is true that *aretē* can be defined differently for men, women and children, slave and free, etc. (cf. Plat. *Meno* 71e), so many tragic heroines aspire to the "masculine" version that we should perhaps conclude not that these women are aberrations, but that heroic *aretē* is an "unmarked" category available to women as well as men. On Medea's heroism, see Knox 1977, 196–98. On perceived equivalences between male and female experience, see Loraux 1981A.

16. On the *Heldentod* as Homeric ideal, if not Homeric reality, see Renehan 1987.

17. Amphitryon shows that he is aware of the *Heldentod* ideal when he justifies his continued survival at 316 and 1073–75.

18. See Bond *ad* 105. for some of the diverse judgments on hope attested in Greek literature.

19. *Ajax* 670–77, translation by Moore 1957. For a comparison of Heracles and Ajax see de Romilly 1983.

20. Chalk 1962, 10.

21. Goossens 1962, 348–54. Cf. also Snodgrass 1965.

22. For the relationship between this scene and the themes of the play, see Hamilton 1985.

23. Heracles' failure to involve others in his exploits may also have worked to dull the beneficiaries' sense of danger, and hence their gratitude. Even his victory over the Minyans, which gained the Thebans their freedom, is here presented as a solitary combat: see 220, and cf. 50, 560.

24. At 355–56. Bond *ad* 348 ff. points out the ode's double function; it is "a *thrēnos* for the dead Heracles," but its "predominant tone is not lamentation."

25. Parallels are collected by Bond *ad* 355–58.

26. At 1269–78. For a survey of the range and connotations of *ponos*, see Boegehold 1982. The specific political reference of the word as part of a slogan, however, even if operative during the 420s as Boegehold maintains, is not relevant to the *Heracles*, which most probably belongs to the late teens.

27. Knox 1957, 23. For *pronoia* cf. Thuc. 1.138.3, 2.65.5, and 2.65.13.

28. As proposed by Wilamowitz 1895^2, vol. 2, 129. He later recanted, but the interpretation was revived by, e.g., Pohlenz 1954, 299, and Burnett 1971, 168. For discussion see Bond, xix.

29. I do not agree with Bond *ad* 575 that these words show Heracles breaking conclusively with his past. Kamerbeek 1966, 14, has it right: "The uselessness of his *ponoi* strikes him, in the event of his failing to rescue his children."

30. For discussion of the unity of the *Heracles*, see Gregory 1979, 259–60, with bibliographical references in notes 2 and 3. For Bond's interpretation of the play's structure see xvii–xxii.

31. Cf. Bond's discussion of *isotēs ad* 634–36; see also Foley 1985, 189.

32. Reading Murray's *son ep' ouk elpidi* at 804: the members of the chorus are presumably referring to their earlier belief that Heracles was dead, hence an ordinary mortal with a questionable connection to Zeus. Having once accepted his immortal parentage, however, they remain faithful to their conviction: cf. 1019 and 1086–87.

33. Cf. 1127, 1189, 1263–64, 1309–10. Burnett 1971, 176 ff., does not give these lines their proper weight when she argues that it is Heracles' hybris, not his parentage, that excited Hera's wrath. She puts faith in Iris' (and Hera's) claim to be acting on behalf of "the gods" (841) in punishing Heracles, but in the context *theoi* seems to be a convenient and self-serving plural that turns Hera's particular grudge into a general crusade and also balances the equally vague plural of *ta thnēta* in 842. For refutation of the hybris theory, see Bond xxiv–xxvi and *ad* 841.

34. For discussion of the ritual see Foley 1985, 152–55, who does not however convince me that the motif of perverted sacrifice is central to the play. Euripides seems to have brought together the act of sacrifice with the onslaught of madness for maximum dramatic contrast, rather than to suggest any relationship of cause and effect.

35. This principle is explained by Artemis at *Hipp.* 1328–30.

36. The temporal explanation is Bond's, who suggests *ad* 827 ff., citing Apollo's patronage of the house of Admetus in the *Alcestis*, that there is a time limit for divine protection. He might have added that divine hostility can also have a time limit: in the *Ajax* (756–57) Athena's persecution of Ajax lasts for one day only. To conclude, however, that Zeus and Hera combine—one to preserve, the other to persecute Heracles—is not the same as saying, with Burnett 1972, 175, that Zeus "sanctioned everything" because Heracles by his greatness posed a threat to all the gods.

37. For Greek conventions of madness, see Mattes 1970.

38. Iris shifts to tetrameter at 855 and is immediately followed by Lyssa. For the emotional effect of tetrameter see Drew-Bear 1968.

39. Mattes 1970, 85.

40. Becker 1937, 156–77.

41. At 1002–3. For Phidias' statue, see Paus. 1.24.5–7. Bond *ad* 1002 reports an attractive emendation by D. S. Robertson (*PCPhS* 1937, 1), which by the addition of a *de* makes explicit the comparison of the apparition of Athena to the statue. Herington 1955, 55, discusses "the close personal connection of Athena with Athens."

42. The story of the stone that saved Amphitryon was not invented by Euripides; Bond *ad* 1004 cites Pausanias (9.11.2), who had seen the very stone on display at the Herakleion in Thebes. However, it was not a standard element

of the Heracles legend: according to Pausanias, neither Stesichorus nor Panyassis treats this event. Euripides seems to be emphasizing a rather arcane detail—the narrow escape of Amphitryon from death—both to emphasize the all-encompassing violence of Heracles' madness and to bring the old man into the foreground, thus preparing for Heracles' affirmation of Amphitryon as his father at the close of the play.

43. At 1337–39. Bond follows Nauck and Wilamowitz in bracketing 1338–39, which are admittedly similar to *Or.* 667–68, as "irrelevant." I would argue for their retention: the contrast between divine patronage and human friendship, between invulnerability and need is distinctly relevant to Heracles' experience. For the motif of friendship in the play, see Sheppard 1916. For the tendency of editors to bracket "general reflections," see de Romilly 1983; she gives a representative list of such bracketed passages, 415–16.

44. Cf. *Ant.* 1043–44, where Creon's argument that no man can pollute the gods serves as a justification for leaving Polyneices unburied. Michelini 1987, 258–60, has an excellent discussion of Theseus' words as a criticism of traditional attitudes toward pollution. Associated with this criticism, however, is a note of old-fashioned piety—a combination that is characteristic of Theseus.

45. Hangard 1975, 127, notes: "Il les voit comme une conglomération de travaux sans nombre, intolérables, dont la séquence et le caractère n'ont plus d'importance."

46. It makes sense for lines 1311–12 to be spoken by the chorus (so Camper, adopted by Bond) rather than Theseus, although it is necessary to assume that an introductory line or two is missing from the beginning of Theseus' speech. Theseus has already acknowledged Hera's role (1189). He here moves on to make the point in the body of his speech that mortals and gods alike are subject to fate and should learn endurance: that is, he is attributing Heracles' suffering to fate rather than simply blaming it on Hera.

47. At 1315–21. Bond *ad* 1314–22 points out the resemblance between Theseus' reasoning here and the nurse's sophistic argument from divine analogy in the *Hippolytus* (456 ff.). Theseus and the nurse have very different outcomes in mind, however, when they speak of endurance and putting up with fate: Theseus intends that Heracles should forego suicide, the nurse that Phaedra should make a sexual proposition to Hippolytus. As Michelini notes (1987, 273), the nurse uses a sophistic technique to argue for the rejection of traditional moral standards; Theseus uses the same updated technique to argue for a traditional posture of humility vis-à-vis the gods.

48. Meridor 1984, 207–8, revives Burnett's suggestion (1971, 182, n. 39) that there are references to Heracles' apotheosis in the chorus' discussion of second youth at 655 ff. (an allusion to Hebe) and in Heracles' wish to die by fire at 1151 (an allusion to his traditional funeral pyre on Mt. Oeta). But these references, if such they are, are so brief and obscure that they are unlikely to be picked up by an audience. Stinton 1986, 67, makes the sensible point that "insofar as an allusion was dramatically important the poet made it readily understandable, obscure or oblique allusions being of little or no importance for the understanding of the play as a play."

49. So Bond *ad* 1335, against Adkins 1966.

50. Loraux 1985, 56.

51. Much speculative discussion has resulted from treating this passage either as an attack on the gods or as a self-referential allusion to the poetic process (for a review of the literature see Halleran 1986, and also Michelini 1987, 275 with n. 194). But as Bond emphasizes (*ad* 1341–46), it is essential to take it in context as a reply to Theseus. (Grube 1961², 58, already pointed out that "Heracles, like Theseus, is thinking of life on *Olympus*.") Heracles' essential point is that the gods cannot serve as models for men (so Burnett 1971, 174). Heracles means to base his decision to live not on an analogy with the gods, as Theseus suggested, but on a new understanding of what it means to be human, as noted by Halleran 1986, 177. I am not convinced, however, by Halleran's additional contention that the passage invites the audience to frame their own indictment of the gods.

52. On *chreia* as the force behind the formation of communities and the development of civilization, see Plat. *Prot.* 322b and Diodorus 1.8.

53. The motif of *philia* is broadly political, in that it directs attention to the value of the human community, but *philia* in the play should not, in my view, be explained with reference to the "political friendship" discussed by Connor 1971 and Hutter 1978. In the *Heracles* Euripides does not use the term *hetairos* (as he does at, for example, *Or.* 804), which does convey a specifically political sense (for the *hetaireiai* or aristocratic "clubs," see Connor 1971, 25 ff. and 75 ff.). *Philia* is a far less specific term than *hetaireia*, though it could on occasion be used in the same factional sense.

54. Reading Wecklein's *bioton* at 1351, adopted by both Wilamowitz and Bond and central to the play's redefinition of courage and nobility as endurance.

55. A detail of this passage shows Euripides simultaneously acknowledging and transforming his literary sources. It will be recalled that the Heracles of Bacchylides (5.155–58) wept for the first and only time in his life when he encountered Meleager in the underworld. As Richard Garner has pointed out to me, "Heracles' first tears" becomes a *topos* taken up by both Sophocles and Euripides. Euripides adapts elements from both other versions, but on the whole his greater debt is to Bacchylides. Bacchylides' Heracles weeps unselfconsciously, in spontaneous pity for the human condition as exemplified by Meleager. He has yet to encounter personal misfortune (although the context, with its mention of Deianira, strongly hints at disaster to come). Sophocles' Heracles succumbs to tears in the last trial of his life; he weeps from physical pain, even as he condemns himself for his womanish weakness (*Trach.* 1070–75). Euripides' Heracles is chronologically intermediate: he is neither untouched by misfortune nor on the point of death. Heracles borrows some of his language from the Sophoclean Heracles (cf. Bond *ad* 1353–57), and like him comments on his own weeping. But he does so without condemnation; as he describes his own tears he sounds a Bacchylidean note of quiet but intense poignancy. Bacchylides' Heracles proceeds to tell Meleager, in a traditional gnomic vein, that "it would be best for mortals never to be born," but then

sturdily sets such thoughts aside; this combination of theoretical despair with individual resolve would seem to prefigure Euripides' portrait of the hero.

56. At 1357. Hamilton (1985, 23) points out: "The arguments put forth by Lycus . . . turn out to be unexpectedly relevant to Heracles: fighting in the hoplite line is true bravery—friendship outweighs independence—and Heracles lives by that code."

57. Cf. Achilles' story of the two jars of Zeus, *Il.* 24.527–33.

58. Burnett 1971, 176, n. 24, notes that Euripides "has never for a moment shown that he found the existence of evil on earth incompatible with the idea of the existence of god in heaven." Cf. also Lefkowitz 1989.

59. Bond (xxxi) dates the play to 416 or 414.

5

Trojan Women

The Trojan Women has often been described as a study in despair.[1] Like the *Hecuba* it adopts a somber perspective on the Trojan War, concentrating on the defeated Trojans rather than the victorious Greeks.[2] Yet in this tragedy (produced in 415 as last in a trilogy devoted to the matter of Troy) the condition of the captive women is even more desperate. Because their defeat is still so recent they have not had a chance to accommodate themselves to misfortune; indeed, the opening of the play finds them in a condition of psychic shock. As Andromache explains (639–40): "Someone who has been fortunate and falls into misfortune wanders in spirit from [the memory of] former happiness."

In practical terms the situation could scarcely be more terrible. The war has just ended and the royal captives have not yet been divided up among the Greeks: they are not entitled to even the minimal protection that slaves could expect from their masters. Their sphere of action, as befits prisoners of war, is severely restricted. They can give vent to grief by beating their breasts and tearing their hair: such gestures, as Hecuba notes (793–95), they still command. They can render one another limited service, as when Andromache offers the last rites of the dead to Polyxena (626–27), and Hecuba does the same for Astyanax. But as the herald Talthybius is quick to point out, they are essentially without power (729). Even death is forbidden them, for Talthybius is on the lookout against attempted suicide (299–305, 1284–86). Only in the realm of speech do they retain any independence, and even that is precarious: Talthybius does his best to rob Cassandra's prophecies of their force (417–19) and to reduce Andromache to silence (734–36).

The action of *Trojan Women* unfolds a series of disasters, each more gratuitous than the last. The play opens when the city of Troy has fallen; the men have been killed, the women reduced to slavery. The Greeks then proceed to additional outrages in the sacrifice of Polyxena, the murder of Astyanax, and the firing of Troy. There is no relief, no variation from the relentless litany of horrors. Although the audience learns from the prologue that the Greeks will soon be punished for their sacrilegious crimes, that knowledge is not shared by the Trojans, who despair of any justice emanating from the gods. In terms of the action the play is one of the darkest Euripides ever wrote.

Yet such a description fails to take other dramatic elements into account. The physical and temporal frame seems designed to mute the violence of the action and establish a sense of pause and suspension. The setting is an encampment by the sea, lying between the ruined city of Troy where the women once made their homes and the ships that will soon transport them to new destinies in Greece. Troy presents a scene of desolation—*erēmia*, as Poseidon calls it in the prologue (26, cf. 15)—but the remnants of a Trojan community have been reconstituted on the seashore.

The play encompasses a time of transition for both conquered and conquerors. As the action begins, the Greeks are loading the ships with spoil while awaiting the favorable wind that they expect will bear them home (18–22). As for the Trojan captives, they have already suffered terrible losses (of fatherland, children, and husbands, as Hecuba notes, 107), and they anticipate further separations (484–88, 1089–99), which indeed inexorably take place in the course of the play. But for the moment they are still together. The presence of a leader, the sharing of lamentation and the exchange of mutual support, and the very persistence of old tensions and differences contribute to a sense of community and postpone the final break with the past.

This period of waiting offers the Trojan women a rare chance for reflection. They have not been idle in the past: to remember Troy is to remember work at the looms (199–200). Nor do they expect to be idle in the future: they anticipate service as concierges or nursemaids, as concubines, water bearers or bakers for their Greek masters (194–95, 202–6, 491–94). Their present leisure is that of slaves whose time is at their masters' disposition: that point is underscored when Cassandra is ordered both on and offstage by Talthybius and when Andromache is forced to embark, leaving her child unburied, because an emergency has summoned Neoptolemus back to Greece. Nevertheless, even this precarious leisure affords the women a chance to pause and take stock. The reflections that originate in psychic disorientation, in Andromache's "wandering of the spirit," prove far-reaching in their consequences, offering not just a defense against psychic dissolution but a positive means of self-assertion and of maintaining communal ties.

Reflection constitutes the major business of this curiously introspective play, which by its tone and structure invites interpretation as an extended discussion carried on among the Trojan women and interrupted, but never broken off, by the atrocities of the Greeks.[3] The common denominator of each episode is the attempt to interpret the present in the light of the past. In the series of exchanges among Hecuba and her daughter and daughters-in-law, each of the younger women (Cassandra the prophetic virgin, Andromache the faithful wife, and promiscuous Helen) embodies a different experience and ethos, which reflects itself in her interpretation of events.

Hecuba has her differences with each of her interlocutors, and as she answers each in turn her own fundamental attitudes emerge. Her point of variance with Cassandra lies in the choice of an attitude appropriate to misfortune: Hecuba has settled on lament, Cassandra on celebration. Hecuba at least initially finds Cassandra's attitude inexplicable; yet she modifies that position in the course of her dialogue with Andromache. If she is unwilling to join Cassandra in thanksgiving, she equally rejects Andromache's intransigent despair. Hecuba urges Andromache, instead, to adjust to her situation and make the best of her altered circumstances. That Hecuba sets limits to flexibility is established, finally, in the debate with Helen, where she draws a firm distinction between submission to necessity and mere opportunism.

The very diversity of the women's responses confirms the audience's sense of an enduring connection between past and present. The veering destiny (*metaballomenos daimōn*, 101) that has wrecked the women's fortunes has not destroyed their individual standards or perspective—a circumstance that suggests that the play has to do not with "total disaster" but with the oscillations of despair and fortitude characteristic of human beings in extreme situations.[4] The Trojan women assume that they have lost everything—that their very identity has disappeared along with their city, their families, their fortune, and their freedom. "Nobility is come to slavery," says Andromache, "through such great changes" (614–15). The episodes demonstrate, however, that nobility remains intact, for the women have brought

with them from the past the individual resources to survive and to
endure.[5]

These resources are embodied in each woman's use of *logos*—a term
encompassing reason and reflection, speech and language, poetry and
incantation, argument and explanation.[6] Around the time that Euripides wrote his trilogy on the Trojan War, Gorgias the sophist composed
his *Encomium of Helen*, an artful and elaborate rhetorical exercise in
praise of Helen of Troy. Euripides may well have been influenced by
this work, for *Trojan Women* touches repeatedly on Gorgianic themes.[7]
In fact, the play might be described as an "Encomium of *Logos*" that
reflects on the uses, though also on the limitations, of tragic poetry for
the city of Athens.

The Power of *Logos*

In extolling the power of *logos* Euripides was scarcely introducing an
unfamiliar topic. As early as the *Iliad* language and action are recognized as equal and complementary spheres of human accomplishment: Phoenix reminds Achilles that his father wished him to grow up
"a speaker of words and a doer of deeds" (*Il.* 9.443). Subsequently this
pairing becomes firmly established as one of the binary oppositions so
characteristic of Greek thought.[8] The antithesis *logōi men . . . ergōi de*
("on the one hand, in word . . . but on the other hand, in deed")
turns up with monotonous regularity (and sometimes without any
logical justification) in any number of contexts. Not uncommonly
these collocations reflect a certain suspicion of *logos*, for they imply
that language requires validation in the realm of action. It is all very
well to propose a course of action "in word," but the true test comes
when it is put into practice.[9]

Logos assumed a particular importance in democratic Athens,
where the ability to speak lucidly and persuasively in the assembly or
the law court was vital to citizens ambitious of public advancement.
Political decisions were arrived at only after extended debate, although the value of this practice was a matter of some controversy.
Thucydides' Cleon is of the opinion that the Athenians' refined appreciation of words has an adverse affect on their assessment of deeds:
an over-valuation of fine speaking, Cleon claims, is an obstacle to political judgment (3.38.4–7). On the other hand Thucydides' Pericles

describes the Athenian method of formulating policy as a felicitous combination of "words" and "deeds":

> It is our wont to make accurate judgments or assessments of issues, not considering words as an impediment to deeds, but considering it far more damaging not to receive instruction in advance through argument [*logoi*] before proceeding to appropriate action.[10]

Such passages exploit the traditional antithesis of word and deed. But the fifth century also saw a new interest in *logos* for its own sake. The sophists taught techniques of persuasive speech applicable in the political or the judicial spheres, but they also took the phenomenon of language as an object of scholarly study.[11] Gorgias in particular concerned himself with the psychological effects of *logos*, which he portrayed as operating on the soul with all the power generally ascribed to *ergon*.[12] "Speech," he wrote (*Encomium of Helen*, 9), "is a great monarch, which accomplishes divine results with its minute, even invisible body. For it is able to put a stop to fear, and banish grief, and produce joy and increase pity."

That *logos* could be assigned an essential civilizing function is apparent from a passage in Euripides' *Suppliants*, in which Theseus offers a list of the factors that enabled human beings to transcend their original primitive state. Speculation about the process of human development seems to have been a characteristic feature of the fifth-century "enlightenment," and similar lists are to be found in the *Antigone* and the *Prometheus*.[13] But only Euripides gives reason and language pride of place in his catalog (*Suppl.* 201–4):

> I praise whichever of the gods it was who marked our lives
> off from chaos and brutishness, first implanting reason
> [*synesis*], and then giving us language [*logos*], the
> messenger of communication. . . .

For Theseus reason and language are the primary gifts of the gods; they distinguish human beings from the brute animals and lay the basis for future progress. This notion would later be taken up by Isocrates (*Nicocles* 5 = *Antidosis* 256), who makes the additional point that *logos* is useful not only in communicating with others but in private deliberation:

> With this faculty we both debate on controversial questions and on our own account investigate matters unknown; for we use the same modes of argument with which we persuade others in public discourse when we take counsel for ourselves. . . .

Logos as alternative to action, as defense against chaos, as a means of guiding the self and influencing others—all these aspects figure in *Trojan Women*. The captive women's meditations originate in *logos*, reflection, and issue forth in *logos*, speech and language. *Logos* in turn helps to stem the tide of loss, reminding the audience that certain human qualities can survive a change of fortune and resist enslavement. Euripides' interest in nobility as an attribute independent of external circumstances is familiar from the *Hecuba* and the *Heracles*.[14] Here the theme is subordinated to the demonstration of how character manifests itself through language.

Hecuba and Lamentation

It is Hecuba's laments, often taken as evidence for her psychic collapse, that provide the first illustration of the sustaining power of *logos*. As Poseidon speaks the prologue, he draws attention to the stricken figure of the former queen (36–39):

> If anyone can have the desire to look upon the pitiful
> woman, here is Hecuba, prostrate before the [tent] doors,
> weeping many tears for many losses.

Hecuba raises herself half off the ground to deliver her first lament (98) but sinks back again after Cassandra's exit (462). In the course of the play she will often be found collapsed or kneeling on the ground, the image of helpless desolation.[15]

It is made clear from the outset, however, that Hecuba's is an attitude deliberately, even willfully adopted. Her body's language reinforces her verbal laments: she does not lie prostrate from lack of help or because she is too shattered to stand upright, but because she deems such a posture appropriate to her situation. When the women of the chorus attempt to raise her Hecuba refuses their help, explaining that she finds it unwelcome, though well-intended (466). "Let me lie where I am fallen," she tells them. "What I am suffering and have suffered and am yet to suffer deserves to beat me down."

Hecuba's words as well as her posture are meticulously chosen to convey an accurate sense of her plight. What can she not mourn, she demands—she who has lost country, children, and husband (105–7)? What should she keep to herself, what should she bewail (110–11)? These questions are far from reflecting uncertainty; they signal the start of a traditional lament or *thrēnos*, which frequently opens on a note of interrogation.[16] Hecuba's habitual contrasting of past prosperity with present wretchedness is also appropriate to the *thrēnos*.[17] Hecuba has found a way to impose some form on her bereavement.

Euripides is not merely drawing on the conventions of lament to offer an artistic representation of a wretched old woman's inchoate sorrow. The rhetorical element is presented as the accomplishment of Hecuba herself, who self-consciously manipulates language both to comfort herself and to affect others. Hecuba comments that she longs to rock her body back and forth while pouring out "ceaseless elegies of tears" (119), and adds that "this is poetry for the unfortunate, to sing of woes not fit for the dance" (120–21). After Cassandra's departure Hecuba initiates a lament that once more evokes her vanished happiness—in order, as she ingenuously explains, to inspire more pity for her present misery (472–73). The banishing of grief and the enhancement of pity, we may recall, were among the uses of *logos* identified by Gorgias. Like Gorgias, Hecuba is aware of language's psychic power; she grieves aloud not only because she has every reason to grieve, but because her lamentation serves as an antidote to the losses that inspired it. She is not alone in her awareness of the healing power of *logos*. "How sweet," exclaim the women of the chorus, "are tears to the unfortunate, and wails of lamentation, and the poetry of sorrow."[18]

Lamentation traditionally had two well-recognized functions: to appease the dead and to relieve the living.[19] In this play the emphasis falls on the second. Not surprisingly, the Trojan women fluctuate in their concept of the situation of the dead. In moods of high emotion they invoke them as if they were still alive underground. Cassandra calls out to her father and brothers, while Andromache appeals to the shade of Hector. Hecuba addresses the corpse of Astyanax, assuring him that his father will take thought for him in the Underworld, and later invokes her children who, the chorus quickly reminds her, are all among the dead.[20]

At calmer moments the women recognize that the dead are without consciousness. That is the crux of Andromache's demonstration that Polyxena is better off than Andromache herself (636–42). When Hecuba reminds Andromache that her tears cannot save Hector (697–98), she is suggesting that the living cannot be of much use to the dead. Nor can the dead help the living: Andromache tells her son that Hector is not going to return from the Underworld to rescue him (752–54). Rich grave-ornaments scarcely matter to those who have perished, Hecuba observes; such displays are "an empty vaunt for the survivors" (1248–50). But the psychic relief afforded the living by attending to the last rites of the dead, and by giving voice to their grief, is very real. As we have seen, the characters themselves are conscious of its efficacy.

Lamentation does not merely comfort the women; it also serves to maintain their links with the past. Even though all the men of Troy have perished, Hecuba still views the Trojans as a community with herself as leader. It is in keeping with this role that, when Talthybius arrives with the news of the distribution of the captives, she inquires about the fate of each of the younger women before asking about her own (235 ff). Later she urges Andromache to propitiate her new master and thus save her child's life: in this way she will bring joy to "the community of her *philoi*" (701). Lamentation allows Hecuba to sustain social bonds and uphold her former authority. When she initiates or "leads out" the lament (147, cf. 152), she is resuming a role that, as the audience would remember from the *Iliad*, had also occupied her at Troy.[21] Lamentation was a social function normally reserved for women. The absence of the men, therefore, will be felt less sharply so long as the women occupy themselves with the rituals of mourning, despite the fact that it is their own menfolk's loss they are lamenting. That is an additional reason why throughout the play lamentation continues to reverberate, the most enduring of the women's diverse responses to misfortune.

Cassandra and Celebration

If Cassandra adopts a different mode, it is one that is intelligible in terms of her history and ethos, even if the other Trojan women find it difficult to comprehend. When Talthybius announces the disposition of the Trojan captives, Hecuba is appalled by the contradiction between the consecrated existence granted Cassandra by Apollo and Agamemnon's decision to take her as his concubine (251–58). But she is even more appalled by Cassandra's gleeful reception of her fate. Cassandra comes on stage dancing, singing a marriage hymn, and brandishing a pine torch. She contrasts her joy to Hecuba's tears and invites her mother to join her in the dance (315–40). In her choice of tone and topics she is as selective as her mother, but with a different aim. Her muse is reluctant to be a "singer of evils."[22] Cassandra is inspired to use *logos*, in the form of a *hymenaios* or marriage song, for yet another of the purposes identified by Gorgias: to produce joy.

Hecuba had initially sought to prevent Cassandra's entrance altogether (169–73). Now she tries to quell her daughter's exultation and reestablish the mood of lament. "Take in the torches," she orders, "and exchange tears for these wedding songs" (351–52). She sees Cassandra's rejoicing as entirely inappropriate, and can think of only one explanation: misfortune has not restored Cassandra's wits, and she is just as mad as she always was (349–50). It is actually the case, of course, that Cassandra is just as sound as she always was, just as unerring in her visions of the future. By linking her predictions with the plan of action agreed to by Poseidon and Athena in the prologue, the audience will be able to envisage the full extent of the ruin awaiting the Greeks.

Yet Cassandra remains, as ever, incapable of inspiring belief. Her words would be ominous — and provocative — if anyone took them seriously. If Cassandra were not mad, notes Talthybius, she would not be allowed to send the Greek generals forth under such auspices (407–10). As it is, he "cast[s her words] to the wind" (419) — a turn of phrase that suggests at once careless dismissal and an uneasy apotropaic impulse. Even though Cassandra will in the course of the scene divest herself of the physical trappings of a priestess of Apollo (451–54), she retains both the privileges and the limitations of her former condition. Her marriage song is thus a sign — as were Hecuba's lamentations — of her continuing links to her own past.

Cassandra rejoices because her prophetic gift affords her the certainty of future suffering for the Greeks and vengeance for the Trojans, all emanating from her union with Agamemnon. On her first entrance she sardonically evokes the conventional emblems of Greek marriage: the god Hymen, the torch, the dance, and the wreath. She even imagines herself as the modest bride traditional to marriage songs, who is reluctant to leave her mother (355–56). At the end of the episode and with a radical change of imagery, she envisions herself as an Erinys who will arrive victorious in the Underworld, having vindicated her father and brothers by becoming the instrument of Agamemnon's destruction (456–61). She alludes cryptically to future events — to Hecuba's death, the wanderings of Odysseus, to her own murder and Agamemnon's. But for much of the episode she puts aside the lyric mode, puts aside her "possession," her "Bacchic ravings" (366, 367), to pursue a line of reasoning (first in sober trimeters, then in impressive tetrameters) that is designed to be fully intelligible to her mother and the other Trojan women. She sketches an ironic encomium of the Greeks (*epainos*, 383; Talthybius recognizes it as more truly abuse, *oneidē*, 418), and a serious benediction of the Trojans.[23]

Cassandra bases her assessment on a distinction, well established in contemporary thought, between actions performed voluntarily and under compulsion. Contrasting the invading Greeks with the Trojans who died for their fatherland (387), she explains that the Trojans are more blessed than the Greeks because they fought a defensive, not an offensive war. She observes that Agamemnon gave up his child for no compelling reason, for the sake, in fact, of a woman who had herself left her husband "of her own free will, and not constrained by force" (370–73). She describes war as something to be shunned by men of good sense but which, "if it should come to that" (401 — that is, if it proves unavoidable), still holds out opportunities for glory. Cassandra implies that the Greeks bear the full responsibility for everything that occurred: that war, the sacrifice of children, and the exchange of husbands are all outrages forced upon the Trojans but voluntarily undertaken by the Greeks.

To reason in this way is to absolve the Trojans of any blame for the conflict, for by the time Euripides composed his play the argument from compulsion commanded judicial as well as psychological force. Archaic Greek thought, to be sure, had paid scant attention to such matters, disregarding motives and intentions in favor of action and results.[24] In the course of the fifth century, however, the agent's intentions came increasingly under scrutiny, and it became possible to establish mitigating circumstances for even the most heinous crimes by pleading the existence of some constraint: force or the threat of force, external necessity, or even compelling social norms.[25] Gorgias, for example, argues in the *Encomium of Helen* (6) that Helen was innocent of wrongdoing no matter what her motive, for in each and every case she was acting under compulsion:

> She acted as she acted either through the wishes of Chance and the designs of the gods and the decrees of Necessity, or seized through violence, or persuaded by words, or ensnared by love.

Like Gorgias, Cassandra examines the relationship between compulsion and moral responsibility, although in the case of Helen she arrives at very different conclusions. Her distinction between voluntary and enforced action will figure importantly later in the play, again with specific reference to Helen. In its immediate context the argument serves to free Cassandra from the charges of aberration and callousness levelled at her by Hecuba and the chorus (348–50, 406–7). The audience understands both that she is justified in her mood of defiant rejoicing and that her intention is to console, not aggravate, her mother. The past, Cassandra argues, is not to be mourned, for it was a source of glory. Nor is the present to be regretted, for it holds the potential for future vengeance. Two unexpected forms of *logos*—marriage hymn and benediction—have served Cassandra to articulate her sense of an enduring connection between past, present, and future.

Andromache and the "Very Beautiful Argument"

Andromache is not so heterodox as Cassandra: on her entrance she merges smoothly with Hecuba into antiphonal lament. However, she presently abandons that mode for a *rhēsis* or extended speech addressed to Hecuba, a "very beautiful argument" (*kallistos logos*) designed to "cast pleasure into [Hecuba's] mind."[26] Here, as elsewhere in the play (386, 1282), the word *kallistos* signals an appeal to the aristocratic tradition. As was the case with Cassandra, a speech intended to comfort its hearer has the ancillary effect of illuminating the *ēthos* of the speaker. Like Hecuba and Cassandra, Andromache brings to her new situation the same attitudes that had characterized her during her time of prosperity.

As she informs Hecuba of Polyxena's death, Andromache speaks of *logos* in terms reminiscent of Theseus in the *Suppliants*. She tries to soften her news by assuring the bereaved mother that Polyxena is in fact better off than Andromache herself: death has brought Polyxena oblivion, while the living remain painfully conscious of their misfortunes (636–40). Turning to her own situation, Andromache uses a vivid analogy to explain her resistance to the notion of coming to love a second husband. She explains that it is difficult even for a horse to be parted from its yokefellow; how much more so should it be for human beings! She has in mind the yoke of marriage, the yoke of slavery, the yoke of necessity, so her imagery seems entirely apposite (667–72):

> I loathe the woman who, casting out her previous
> husband in favor of a new union, loves another man. Not
> even a horse which has been unharnessed from its partner
> bears the yoke patiently. And yet animals are without
> speech [*aphthongos*], and lacking in reason [*synesis*], and
> deficient in their nature.

In speaking of Polyxena Andromache had just declared that to be alive is to possess consciousness, a powerful source of misery. But she simultaneously recognizes that human beings, as opposed to beasts, are to be defined in terms of language and reason. That which hurts can also heal: the gift of *logos* can temper the pain arising from consciousness of evils. The play illustrates this very process of suffering and consolation.[27]

Andromache cherishes the convictions we have seen displayed by other Euripidean heroines such as Megara and Polyxena. She is, first and foremost, an aristocrat—well-matched to her husband, whom she considered "outstanding in intellect, rank, wealth, and manliness" (674). Her assertion that Polyxena is better off than she is herself, since death is preferable to the consciousness of misfortunes, is a by now familiar manifestation of an aristocratic viewpoint that admits no compromises with regard to the quality of life. Taking their cue from the heroic tradition, women like Andromache adapt themselves only minimally to the exigencies of the female lot. The humiliations they fear may be specific to a woman's life, but the solution they propose—a noble death, in preference to a diminished life—recognizes no distinctions of gender.

Yet Andromache has also shaped her conduct in accordance with feminine codes. She has labored hard, as she explains, at "whatever is approved as *sōphrōn* for women" (645). *Sōphrosynē* was a term of broad semantic range; in its sense of modesty, chastity, and rectitude it was the prime virtue of the Greek female.[28] Andromache explains how she cultivated modesty in her former existence even as she makes it clear that she continues to be faithful to Hector in the present: she dreads the prospect of union with her Greek master (659–68). Entering wedded life as a virgin (675–76), she lived a secluded life after marriage to avoid the ill repute that attaches to a woman who goes about in public.[29] She admitted no "superficial talk" into the house (651–52), thus avoiding the kind of corrupting gossip so dreaded by Hippolytus (*Hipp.* 645–50). Her *sōphrosynē* was not all self-denial, for she had a clear sense of the divisions of responsibility within a marriage and knew when to assert herself and when to give way (655–56). All this added up to a good reputation, the aristocrat's most prized possession—to *eudoxia*, her goal from the outset (643).

Andromache's description of her former life makes clear how much thought, effort, and calculation went into the achieving of *sōphrosynē*. She knew how to keep her own counsel: "I was satisfied with having in my own mind a good teacher" (652–53). Andromache has, it is clear, a pronounced intellectual bent. She also values intelligence in a husband. Summarizing Hector's qualities (674), she mentions not only his birth, rank, and manliness but also his *synesis* or intellect—an unusual attribute to head the list of aristocratic virtues.

Incorporating all the qualities to which Phaedra could only aspire, Andromache also matches Gorgias' ideal of womanly excellence (Diels-Kranz B22): "Not the appearance, but the reputation of a woman should be known to many." Therein, as she explains, lies her misfortune. Andromache's reputation, coming to the attention of the Greeks, prompted Neoptolemus to claim her as his own (657–60).

Andromache brings her intellect to bear on her present situation. In discussing the plight of women who, like herself, are forced to accept new mates, Andromache glances at Cassandra's categories of volition and compulsion. She refuses (665–66) to put faith in the common belief that a single night with a new partner is sufficient to change a woman's hatred to love. She feels nothing but scorn for the woman who is emotionally unfaithful to her former spouse, who "opens her heart" to another man and "loves" her new master (662, 668). Andromache's own loyalty to the past, to Hector's memory, is as characteristic and unwavering as Cassandra's reliance on the future. She believes that her emotions if not her physical circumstances are subject to her own control, and she is resolved not to be guilty of emotional betrayal even though she knows that she will be compelled to perform sexual services for her Greek master.

Everything has turned out contrary to expectation, but in this very circumstance Andromache sees a kind of reversed causation at work. Not only does she consider her good reputation the cause of her present plight (657–60), she also will later reflect that Hector's noble rank, which saved so many others, has contributed to the ruin of Astyanax (742–43), and that the child born to rule Troy will instead become a sacrifice to the Greeks (747–48). These are grim paradoxes, but their very articulation enables Andromache to preserve in her own fashion a sense of connection between past, present, and future, just as Hecuba and Cassandra had done in theirs.

To Hecuba, however, Andromache's position seems based on an overvaluation of the past. Attempting to put matters in perspective for her daughter-in-law, Hecuba marks a shift in her own attitude. Whereas earlier she had refused to abandon her prostrate position because she had, as she explained, nothing to hope for (505), she now maintains that merely to be alive is to possess hope (633). And if Andromache attempts to "cast pleasure" into Hecuba's mind, Hecuba herself abandons her mute (*aphthongos*, 695) sorrow for Polyxena in order to offer some advice.

Hecuba raises the prospect of leaving the past behind and conforming to new realities. She urges her daughter-in-law not to cling to Hector's memory but to ingratiate herself with her new master. In this way she might succeed in raising Astyanax to adulthood so that he could found a new Trojan dynasty (702–5). Her syntax suggests that she has little confidence in these possibilities, yet she advances them nonetheless.[30] Hope, fragile but tenacious, is another of the resources of *logos* available to victims of misfortune. Hecuba defends hopeful expectation not because it is likely to be realized in fact, but as an attitude intrinsic to life itself.

Hecuba's hopes are no sooner enunciated than they are shattered by Talthybius. With his announcement of the sentence passed on

Astyanax, the women are once more cast back on lamentation. Although Talthybius forbids any form of active protest, Andromache's keen intelligence suggests to her a way to vent her emotions through a fresh and powerful form of language—malediction.

When Talthybius announces that the Greeks have decided to kill Astyanax, he recommends that Andromache limit herself to restrained, aristocratic manifestations of grief.[31] He warns against any form of resistance, physical or verbal (731–36):

> We are [fully] capable of standing up to a
> single woman. So I don't want you to be eager for
> confrontation or try anything shocking or invidious or
> cast curses at the Greeks. For if you say anything that
> angers the army, your child might not get his burial . . .

With these threats he tries to curb her tongue, but Andromache finds a way of circumventing him. She lays a curse not on the army as a whole, but on the one Greek whom the Greeks themselves can be counted on to hate and distrust. Helen becomes the focus for Andromache's displaced hatred of all the conquerors (766–73):

> Offspring of Tyndareus, you were never child of
> Zeus, but are the issue, I am convinced, of many fathers:
> of Ruin foremost, then of Envy and Murder and Death and as
> many ills as the earth rears up. I shall never admit that
> Zeus bore you, you spirit of destruction for many
> barbarians and Greeks as well. May you perish! For with
> those exquisite eyes of yours, you brought—to your
> shame—destruction on the famous plains of Troy.

Because Andromache holds Helen responsible for the destruction of Troy, her vehement denial of any connection between Helen and Zeus also signifies a rejection of any divine involvement in the Trojan War.[32] Yet the audience knows from the prologue that Andromache is mistaken. It is too simple to make Helen the scapegoat for the war; what the repeated allusions to external forces and internal inclination, necessity and volition rather suggest is a complex pattern of responsibility not easily discernible by the mortal actors in the drama. The debate between Hecuba and Helen will return to this problem of causation.

Although Andromache's words do not provide an accurate description of the origins of the war, they supply her with an outlet for her otherwise helpless rage. They also act as a cue to Hecuba, who in the following scene develops Andromache's curse into a formal indictment. Hecuba takes up not only the question of Helen's guilt, but also the issue of Zeus' involvement in mortal affairs. Andromache's curse thus forms one of the transitions to the next episode. Another is the natural contrast suggested between the chaste Andromache, notable for her reputation, and the wanton Helen, notable for her beauty. When Talthybius reminds Andromache that she is only "one woman" with whom the Greeks can easily contend (731–32), we are reminded of Helen, the "one woman" (372, 498–99, 781) who succeeded in destroying all the Trojans. The audience is put in mind both of the diverse choices made by the two women and of their unpredictable consequences. Virtuous though she is, Andromache is powerless to influence events. Helen, in contrast, has exercised an influence disproportionate to her worth.

Helen has posed something of a puzzle throughout: is she to be treated as Greek or Trojan, victor or captive? Poseidon noted at the outset that Helen had been grouped "with justice" among the Trojan prisoners (34–35). The Trojan women, however, disown her: Hecuba insists on her Greek heritage when she calls her "the detestable spouse of Menelaus, Castor's shame and the disgrace of the Eurotas" (131–33), and as we have seen, Andromache assigns her a lineage neither human nor divine, but monstrous.[33] As for Menelaus, he finds it unpleasant even to pronounce the name of "the woman who at one time was my wife."[34] Departure now approaches, and the issue of Helen's allegiance comes to a head in the confrontation of Hecuba and Helen. Hecuba here uses *logos* for persuasive purposes against an opponent; in so doing, she tries to propel language as far as it will go in the direction of action.

Helen, Hecuba, and Persuasion

When Menelaus enters, Hecuba seizes his attention with a remarkable prayer (884–88):

O support of the earth with your seat upon the earth,
whoever you are, difficult to comprehend, Zeus, whether

you are necessity of nature or mind of mortals, I address
you in prayer. For traveling with silent tread you
guide all mortal outcomes according to justice.

Hecuba addresses Zeus as the principle of causation. Her assertion
that the god guides mortal outcomes according to justice is hopeful
and persuasive, reflecting her aspirations for the project at hand—that
Menelaus will have his wife put to death—rather than her customary
despairing skepticism about divine assistance.[35] Hecuba is clearly not
speaking at random; rather, she is sharply concentrated on the requirements of the situation. Thus when she proposes *ananke physeos*,
"necessity of nature," and *nous broton*, "mind of mortals," as alternative descriptions of Zeus, there is no reason to assume that Euripides
is making a "patently undramatic" display of his recondite philosophical knowledge.[36] The alternatives suggested by Hecuba are applicable
in the first instance to her debate with Helen, but also to the play as
a whole.

Although Hecuba speaks in highly compressed fashion and the
sense of each term is debatable, when thus juxtaposed "necessity of
nature" and "mind of man" seem to refer to the by now familiar antinomy of volition and compulsion. If Zeus, or causation, is identical
to "the mind of man," then Hecuba seems to be suggesting that certain
events, conveniently explained (and thereby excused) as divine in origin, are in fact the result of human intention. Although they are the
product of individual impulse, the perpetrator tries to exculpate himself by invoking divine agency.

An illustration of what Hecuba has in mind will be provided by the
upcoming episode. Helen's strategy will be to seek forgiveness on the
grounds that she was the victim of divine compulsion: she will attribute her erotic attraction for Paris to the irresistible influence of Aphrodite (940–50). Hecuba, however, will refute that explanation with her
crisp paraphrase: "Your mind turned into Aphrodite" (*nous epoiēthē
Kypris*, 988). By suggesting at the outset of the scene that what human
beings call "Zeus" (or, for that matter, Aphrodite) may in fact be only
their own volition, Hecuba anticipates Helen's argument and deprives
it of much of its force.

Hecuba is not, however, denying the power of the gods to affect human destinies—she shows at other points in the play that she fully understands that principle—or rejecting the notion of compulsion as an

extenuating circumstance.[37] Hecuba does not assert that Zeus is only or invariably "the mind of man." By alternatively identifying him with "necessity of nature" she seems to acknowledge that there are compulsions to which human beings have no choice but to submit, since they originate outside individual agency. (She had earlier [616] used the term *ananke*, necessity, in just this sense with reference to slavery.) If the compulsion is indeed genuine, Hecuba can make allowances. Thus she urges Andromache to make conscious use of her erotic charm (700), while later denouncing Helen for the same behavior (892–93). The situation of the two women is entirely different, for Andromache is an authentic, Helen a simulated victim of force.

To be sure, at the outset Helen appears as helpless as any of the other captives. Like Cassandra, Andromache, and Astyanax, she is handled roughly by the Greek soldiers (895–97; cf. 617, 774–78). But differences immediately make themselves felt. Helen seizes the initiative, addressing Menelaus intimately and directly, complaining of her violent treatment and asking to "debate in argument" (*ameipsasthai logōi*, 903) on her own behalf.

Menelaus initially denies Helen's request on the grounds that he is concerned with deeds, not words: "I came not for arguments [*logous*], but to kill you" (905). Hecuba, however, urges Menelaus to let Helen have her say and then allow Hecuba herself the opportunity for rebuttal. Hecuba is certain that her words will find issue in action, that "the argument as a whole" (*ho pas logos*, 909) "will put [Helen] to death." She has reason for her confidence, for Menelaus has already announced his intention to kill Helen once he and she arrive back in Argos (878).

Helen speaks first, adopting a number of self-serving and mutually incompatible strategies. Her first is to attribute crimes to other people that detract and distract from her own. Thus Helen claims that Hecuba "gave birth to the source of the evils" when she bore Paris; next that Priam is at fault, because he failed to destroy Paris at birth. Finally she labels Menelaus "very wicked" because he set off to Crete during Paris' visit, leaving Helen on her own to contend with Paris and that even more troubling houseguest, Aphrodite.[38]

Helen also glances at her own responsibility for the war. In this connection she argues that she is not only innocent of crime but has actually behaved exceptionally well throughout. Harking back to the Judgment of Paris, she contends that Greece would have been conquered by the barbarian Trojans if either Hera or Athena had won the contest. She essentially sacrificed herself for her country (932–34), and so deserves reward rather than punishment (936–37). In the same vein she claims that after Paris' death she behaved precisely as a virtuous woman should, making repeated efforts to rejoin her husband (955–58).

Helen's final line of argument is that although she did betray her home and country (947), she was throughout the victim of force. Her definition of force is vague and generous. She claims that she was impelled to follow Paris by the superior power of Aphrodite; after all no one, not even Zeus himself, can resist Aphrodite.[39] Hers was, in fact, a marriage of violence (*bia*, 962). Later on, after the death of Paris, she was forcibly prevented from escaping by the guards.[40] Like her advocate Gorgias, Helen is well aware that the plea of compulsion — especially if the compulsion can be shown to emanate from the gods — is her strongest suit, the argument most likely to win her pardon (*syngnōmē*, 950, cf. 1043).

Hecuba in rebuttal directs most of her energy to the role of the gods in Helen's abduction. She not only challenges Helen's version of the Judgment of Paris, but she also applies to the gods what has previously been demonstrated about the stability of character in human beings. Helen's version makes no sense, Hecuba claims, because the Olympians are consistent in their desires. There was no reason for Hera, securely wedded to Zeus, to aspire to superior beauty, or for the virginal Athena to develop a sudden desire for a husband. Furthermore, if Aphrodite had wished to bring Helen to Troy, she could have done so without ever leaving Olympus. Hecuba concludes that it is not the gods who were responsible for the abduction, but Helen herself (987–88): "My son was extraordinary for his beauty, and your mind, on seeing him, was changed into Cypris."

It is no accident, Hecuba continues, that the name for the goddess of love and the word for folly begin with the same syllables: *Aphroditē*, *aphrosynē*. In etymology she finds the true link between concepts that Helen had tried to connect via cause and effect. *Aphroditē* and *aphrosynē*, she is suggesting, are essentially identical — different names for the same phenomenon.[41]

Hecuba maintains that Helen was not forcibly removed from Sparta (*biai*, 998). At Troy she exploited every turn of fortune to her own advantage with little regard for integrity (1004–9). She had the options of escape or suicide but availed herself of neither; far from remaining at Troy against her will (*akousiōs*, 1011), she chose to stay. Far from being a slave, Helen enjoyed playing the Oriental queen (1020–21); moreover, she has not altered in misfortune, for she is still elegantly decked out, still bold and unashamed (1022–27). The example of Helen suggests that evil as well as virtue is consistent in human beings.

Hecuba seems to have won the argument, as Menelaus, addressing the crucial issue of Helen's motivation, concludes that his wife left him *hekousiōs*, of her own free will, and has simply introduced Aphrodite into the case as a distraction (1037–39). But Hecuba suspects that his decision is not final. She ends the scene as she began it, warning the king against any proximity to his wife (1049, cf. 891). Desire, as Hecuba well knows (cf. 988), is transmitted through the eyes, and Menelaus has only to look on Helen for *erōs* to prevail: "There is no lover who does not always love."[42] Menelaus replies that such an outcome depends on the mind (*nous*, 1052) of the beloved. He seems to have accepted Hecuba's arguments about the role of volition in activating desire. He also reiterates his intention of having Helen put to death upon his homecoming (1055–57, cf. 876–79).

Yet as the audience will remember from Homer, Menelaus never acted to punish Helen. The Odyssean references introduced by Cassandra earlier in the play will have primed the spectators to recall at this juncture the Helen who welcomes Telemachus to Sparta in Book 4 of the *Odyssey*—a gracious hostess presiding in Menelaus' palace, surrounded by luxury, speaking boldly of the past while plying the company with amnesia-inducing drink. The audience will recognize that although Hecuba has won the debate, the ultimate triumph will be Helen's.[43]

But if Hecuba prevails in words only, that is less a comment on the hollowness of *logos* than on the insufficiency of a causal framework that would make an individual responsible for the entire war. Hecuba, like Helen and Andromache, has fallen into the habit of looking for a scapegoat. For the individuals caught in the catastrophe of war such a quest seems reasonable enough. The more remote perspective of the gods or of Cassandra, however, suggests a different version of events. Divine intervention may appear to hinge on the crimes of individuals: so, for instance, Athena turned against the Greeks after Ajax the son of Oileus violated her temple. But in fact it is the Greeks as a whole whom Athena holds responsible for the sacrilege; as she emphasizes to Poseidon (71), it was the communal failure to chastise Ajax that prompted her change of heart. So too Helen was only the catalyst for the expedition to Troy; it is the Greeks who embarked on a bloody, costly, and protracted war "for the sake of one woman" (368, 781) who must ultimately bear the responsibility.

The members of the audience have been given a glimpse of the cosmic point of view in the prologue, as well as an assurance of the gods' continued involvement with the matter of Troy. Poseidon rises from the sea depths, "where the troop of Nereids trace the graceful circles of their dance" (2–3), to describe his sorrow at Troy's ruin. When Athena asks him to join her in persecuting the Greeks, he rebukes her for her wanton change of mind (67–68):

> Why do you thus leap about now to one mood, now to
> another, and hate too much and love too much, just as
> chance would have it?

Athena justifies her change of heart by reminding Poseidon of Ajax' sacriligious act, and by the end of their interview Poseidon seems won over to her view that the Greeks have provoked their punishment (95–97). The audience is thus assured that justice will ultimately be served. The prologue provides a kind of warranty of cosmic order; Euripides declines to indict the gods of anything more than a somewhat narrow concern for their own affairs and a certain inevitable remoteness from the suffering of human beings.[44]

Yet the assurances offered by the prologue are superseded by the action of the play, for it is Poseidon's question rather than Athena's answer that occupies the Trojan women. In words that echo Poseidon's, Hecuba describes destiny as a skittish madman (1203–5). After Helen's departure the women of the chorus describe Zeus' forsaking of Troy (cf. *proudokas*, 1062) and their own sense of abandonment (1071–80):

> Vanished are your sacrifices and the auspicious strains of
> choral song and the night-long festivals under the dark
> sky. . . . It troubles me, it does trouble me, lord, [to
> wonder] if you think of all this as you sit enthroned in heaven
> —of the burning of the ruined city, undone by fire's
> flaming onrush.

Zeus might have been expected to harbor a special fondness for Troy, since his beloved Ganymede was a Trojan.[45] Instead he has merely looked on as the city was sacked and burned. Divine justice, the audience is assured, will come in time, but the prospect is too remote to help the Trojan women in their suffering. They can only despair of the gods and look to their own emotional and intellectual resources.

Hecuba, Astyanax, and Lamentation

In the last episode Hecuba, presented with the corpse of the child Astyanax, turns once more to lamentation. It is at this point that her fragile equilibrium is most severely threatened. She is confronted by the terrible actuality of her grandson's shattered corpse; moreover, as she prepares to bury Astyanax in his father's shield she must also relive the loss of Hector.

Hecuba's last *logos* is a bitter epitaph for the dead boy: "This child the Greeks killed out of fear" (1190–91). Though Hecuba scoffs at the Greeks for being afraid of Astyanax, she herself had seen in him the possible harbinger of a new Troy (703–5). His death thus signifies the death of hope, which she had earlier defended as intrinsic to human existence (633). Throughout her speech Hecuba trembles on the verge of breakdown, and she closes on a vision of chaos—the very prospect that *logos* has tried to keep at bay (1203–6): "Destinies have the ways of a crazy man, and leap now in this direction, now in that, and no one is ever fortunate in himself."

Hecuba is barely steadied by the ritual of tending the corpse and by the recollection of *logoi* addressed to her earlier. Andromache and Cassandra had both shaped their discourse with the aim of consoling Hecuba, and Hecuba now recapitulates some of their arguments, though in broken and fragmentary form. In the manner of Andromache, Hecuba takes note of the oblivion that comes with death (1172) and of the reversal of expectations. She recalls that Astyanax had promised to bring offerings to her grave; instead she, an old woman, is laying the child to rest (1182–86).

In the manner of Cassandra, Hecuba offers a benediction of those who died for Troy in the full flower of youth. Such a death would have rendered Astyanax blessed (*makarios*, 1170), "if," she adds doubtfully, "any of these things is blessed." She also falls back on Cassandra's traditional consolation of the compensations of fame.[46] Cassandra had noted (395–99) that both Hector and Paris owed their reputations to Helen. Now Hecuba asserts:

> If the god had not turned everything topsy-turvy, we should be lost to view, and not the subject of song, giving inspiration to generations yet to come.[47]

As Hecuba envisages the poetic immortality that awaits the Trojans she momentarily achieves something of Cassandra's prophetic objectivity. As she speaks the boundaries between her present and her future, between the world of the play and the world of the audience, waver and then dissolve. The audience cannot but be aware that Hecuba's prophecy is being brought to fulfillment even as she utters it: the words Hecuba speaks in her own time make her the subject of song for the audience in theirs. By distilling her sorrows into art, *Trojan Women* grants Hecuba the poetic immortality she predicts. Although Hecuba herself, having once articulated this insight, slips back into her own piteous present, her prophecy reinstates for the spectators the remote perspective established in the prologue, and it offers them some consolation as the action draws to its close.

The Greeks' final atrocity is the firing of Troy. Already a smoking ruin at the start of the play (cf. 8–9), the city that was once great (*megalopolis*, 1291) will now be reduced to nothing (*apolis*). Such is the despairing conclusion of the chorus; to the audience, of course, it will be apparent that Troy's name did not vanish but proved sturdier than its physical entity.[48] Hecuba now contemplates, as the most "beautiful" end to her life, mingling her own fate with that of the city by casting herself into the flames. The impulse is a measure of her desperation but also of her undiminished nobility of spirit: Talthybius had earlier (302) recognized suicide as a manifestation of freedom.

Talthybius seizes Hecuba before she can carry out her impulse (1284–86). Checked in her desire, she is somehow still able to persevere; having flung herself to the ground (1305) she struggles to her feet of her own volition, and unordered by Talthybius. Her final words consist of an exhortation to endure. The women of the chorus imitate her gesture of abandonment (1307), but in the last words of the tragedy they also echo her resigned tone: "O unhappy city. But walk forward, nevertheless, to the Greek ships." Their "nevertheless" (*homōs*, 1331) signals a decision to carry on. The victory of endurance, hardly won, is still a victory.

The end of the play leaves no doubt about the sternness of Euripides' tragic vision. He never suggests that the pleasures of lamentation, the assurance of punishment for the Greeks, or the prospect of poetic immortality constitutes any equal compensation for the sufferings of the Trojan women. But although *logos* does not weigh in the balance against *ergon*, neither is it a mockery or a deception.[49] *Trojan Women* testifies to the power of *logos* to help human beings endure the unendurable. It is thus in their own present, not just in the remote future envisaged by Hecuba, that language mitigates the women's suffering.

Logos assumes many forms for the Trojan women, each enabling them to view their situation in a different light—threnody, marriage song, benediction, encomium, abuse, curse, prayer, debate, epitaph. It enables them to articulate, and thus maintain, points of view arrived at in the past. It permits them to impose order on a universe whose intelligibility is otherwise hidden from them. There are as many versions of this order as there are characters in the play, but the process of representation through language is extolled as a characteristic and redeeming human activity.

Euripides and *Logos*

Of course it was not the women of Troy but their creator who had the skill to shape *logos* into such artful forms. The language of sorrow was what Euripides understood best, for the transmuting of anguish into pleasurable poignancy is part of tragedy's own alchemy. He also knew at first hand the limitations of *logos*. Euripides could offer his fellow Athenians a poet's perspective on events—in this play, a view of the consequences of war more cautionary than any they might hear in the assembly—but he could neither expect nor desire to have a direct influence on the events themselves. For the poet, as opposed to the rhetorician, words did not have consequences in action.

Still there were exceptions. *Trojan Women* was produced on the eve of the expedition to Sicily, an imperialist adventure that ended in disaster for Athens. Of the forty thousand Athenians who survived the final battle in the harbor of Syracuse, the majority were butchered during an attempted retreat by land. The survivors, some seven thousand, were taken prisoner and sent to the stone quarries of Syracuse.[50]

In recounting how some managed to survive, Plutarch tells a story so moving that we yearn to believe it true:

> Several were saved for the sake of Euripides, whose poetry, it appears, was in request among the Sicilians. . . . Many of the captives who got safe back to Athens are said, after they reached home, to have gone and made their acknowledgments to Euripides, relating how some of them had been released from their slavery by teaching what they could remember of his poems, and others, when straggling after the fight, had been relieved with meat and drink for repeating some of his lyrics.[51]

It must have gladdened the heart of Euripides to know that his *logoi* had saved his fellow Athenians in their hour of need.

NOTES

1. Cf. Wilamowitz 1906, vol. 3, 263; Havelock 1968, 127; Poole 1976.

2. The choice of perspective is noted by Sĭcǎlin (1983, 105), who reads into it Euripides' protest against the Peloponnesian War. But in view of the fact that Aeschylus in the *Persians* also eschews a purely patriotic or celebratory approach to military victory, Euripides' concentration on the victims rather than the victors of war seems likely to reflect the ethical complexity characteristic of the genre rather than a specific political reference. Murray 1946 connects the Trojan trilogy with the destruction of Melos in 416, while Maxwell-Stuart 1973 sees in it a protest against the Sicilian expedition. A trilogy about war produced in wartime would obviously have a general topical interest, and the proposed expedition to Sicily may well have been "uppermost in the minds of [Euripides'] audience" (Maxwell-Stuart, 397) as they watched the play. However, as van Erp Taalman Kip (1987) has shown, chronology makes specific allusion to the fate of Melos all but impossible. Specific reference to the Sicilian expedition must also be ruled out on chronological grounds (see Parmentier 1925, 14).

3. For this dual aspect see Scodel 1980, 11 and 121; also Lloyd 1984, 303.

4. The phrase "total disaster" is from the title of Poole's article (1976).

5. For the contrary view — that the play shows how war drives human beings to acts of expediency — see Waterfield 1982. He sees this theme as summed up by Hecuba's self-exhortation (102-4) to "sail with the current." But the counsel of flexibility need not suggest expediency: cf. Soph. *Ant.* 710-18 and Eur. *Hipp.* 1115-18.

6. For succinct discussions of the range of the term, see Kerferd 1981, 83-84, and MacDowell 1982, 12-13; for attitudes toward *logos* in the fifth and fourth

centuries, see de Romilly 1975. Goldhill 1986, 3–31 and passim, discusses *logos* as a concern of tragedy, but with an emphasis on its deceptive and treacherous aspects.

7. For views on the relationship of the two texts see Segal 1962, 137, n. 11. Scodel 1980, 90, n. 26, suggests Gorgias' *Palamedes* and *Encomium of Helen* as sources for the Trojan trilogy—an unprovable but plausible and attractive suggestion.

8. For a study of Greek polarities see Lloyd 1966. For a brief history of the *logos-ergon* antithesis, see Heinimann 1945, 43–58; see also Parry 1981, 15–57.

9. This suspicion of *logos* is connected by Parry (1971, 15–16 and passim) with the "popular" strand of thinking, as opposed to the "literary" strand that takes *logos* and *ergon* as complementary and the "philosophical" strand that ultimately sees the realm of *logos* as more true and more real than the realm of *ergon*. Parry's labels do not convince (since any particular writer—as Parry demonstrates in the case of Thucydides—was capable of adopting any of these three views at different times), but the distinctions themselves are interesting and useful.

10. Thuc. 2.40.2, reading *autoi* (not *hoi autoi*).

11. For a discussion of these specialized and technical studies, see Classen 1976; see also Kerferd 1981, 68–77.

12. Parry 1981, 79–80. For an account of the psychological processes involved see Segal 1962.

13. See *Prom.* 447–68, 478–502; *Ant.* 332–75. Other passages illustrative of "antiprimitivism" are collected and discussed by Lovejoy and Boas 1935, 192–221.

14. For *eugeneia* as a theme of the *Alexander*, the first play of the trilogy, see Scodel 1980, 83–89, who is I think overly cautious in evaluating the belief in natural equality expressed here and elsewhere by Euripidean characters. That Euripides' noble slaves still behave like slaves, not like free men, testifies to Euripides' psychological acuity and his understanding of the effects of upbringing; it does not mean that he is accepting or defending the institution of slavery.

15. Hecuba's changes of posture are catalogued by Steidle 1968, 51.

16. Alexiou 1974, 161.

17. Alexiou 1974, 165.

18. At 608–9. For the pleasure of lamentation cf. Eur. *Andr.* 93–95, *Elec.* 125–26, *Suppl.* 79, fr. 573 N^2. As Denniston 1939 points out (*ad Elec.* 125–26), the idea is already present in Homer (*tetarpomestha gooio*, *Il.* 23.98).

19. Alexiou 1974, 165.

20. Cassandra: 459–60. Andromache: 587 (Hecuba in response reminds her that Hector is dead; the chorus will remind her of the same fact at 1304). Hecuba: 1188 ff. (Her address to the corpse of Astyanax parallels Andromache's farewell to the living child, 740 ff.) Hecuba mentions Hector at 1234, and addresses her children at 1303.

21. Cf. *Il.* 24.748–59. Cassandra's compressed summary of the wanderings of Odysseus (431–43) indicates that Euripides could take for granted the au-

dience's intimate knowledge of Homer. This knowledge will come in useful at the conclusion of the Helen *agōn*.

22. At 384–85. In keeping with the theme of *logos*, the word *mousa* appears frequently in the play, at 120, 384, 512, 609, and 1245. I agree with Parmentier 1925, Biehl 1970, and Lee 1976 (henceforth "Lee"), against Diggle 1986 (henceforth "Diggle"), that 384–85 should be retained; they are appropriate because Cassandra is making a transition from the Greeks' evil to the Trojans' glorious destiny.

23. Benediction (*makarismos*) is implied by *makariōteran*, 365. Cassandra's benediction is of course paradoxical, since the Greeks have won the war and the Trojans have lost it; however, Cassandra looks beyond temporary failure and success to the ultimate value of the undertaking. She also knows that the Greeks' present felicity will not last; a point further emphasized by what Scodel (1980, 115) calls the "reverse *makarismos*" of Poseidon's judgment on the Greeks at 95–97.

24. Cf. Adkins 1970, 29–42; this, the received view of archaic thinking on moral responsibility, is qualified and criticized by Rickert 1985.

25. For these categories see Rickert 1985, 6–33; also Saïd 1978, especially 178–98.

26. At 634–35. Diggle, following Dindorf, brackets these lines on the grounds that they are foreign to the context and because Andromache should not address Hecuba as her mother. I hope to have established in what way the notion of a *kallistos logos* that brings *terpsis* is relevant to the themes of the play. With respect to the second objection, there is no need to assume that Andromache is addressing Hecuba as her own mother rather than as the mother of many others (so Lee *ad loc.*).

27. For an exhaustive analysis of this process see Pucci 1980, 21–45.

28. Cf. North 1966, 252–53, for *sōphrosynē* as a virtue celebrated in women's epitaphs. For *sōphrosynē* in the political sense see chapter 2 above, pp. 54–55.

29. At 647–50. For the norm that women should stay indoors, cf. Eur. fr. 521 N^2; see also *Medea* 214–15 and *Phoen. W.* 88–100.

30. At 703–4 I would read, with Diggle, *hin' hoi . . . ex sou* which is at any rate a little more confident than *einai . . . ex hou*, adopted by Lee (Lee explains the optatives of 705 as cupitives). The clearest indication of Hecuba's attitude comes in the cautious *ekthrepsaias an* of 702: she is by no means confident that Andromache can raise Astyanax to adulthood, much less of the remoter consequences. Meridor 1989, 33, seems to disregard Hecuba's uncertainty when she argues that Euripides is at great pains to heighten the contrast between Hecuba's "real and urgent" hopes and Talthybius' brutal announcement.

31. Cf. 727: *eugenōs . . . algei kakois*. Polyxena in *Hecuba* (404–8) similarly tries to dissuade her mother from clinging to her; evidently there was felt to be something vulgar about physical resistance.

32. Scodel 1980, 135.

33. At 766–73. The exception to the Trojan women's denigration of Helen is

398, where Cassandra calls her "the daughter of Zeus" in order to enhance the glory of Paris' marriage.

34. At 869–70. Lines 862–63, which contain mention of Helen's name, should be deleted (so Diggle, following Herwerden), because they conflict with 869–70 and are also weak and unnecessary.

35. She is elsewhere quite explicit about her lack of faith in the gods: see 469–71, 1240–42, and 1280–81.

36. The accusation is Lee's (ad 884–88). For further discussion of the prayer, with attention to its philosophical background, see Ebener 1954, Scodel 1980, 93–97, and Lloyd 1984.

37. Cf. 612–13 and 1240–42.

38. The same strategy of far-fetched accusation is used by Orestes (Or. 585–88), blaming Tyndareus for fathering Clytemnestra. For other examples of the strategy and a more sympathetic account of Helen's position, see Lloyd 1984, 305.

39. At 948–50. Helen is the most self-serving of all the tragic protagonists who use "l'excuse de l'invincible amour," for which see de Romilly 1976.

40. Lines 959–60 should be deleted (so Diggle, following Wilamowitz). As Lloyd 1984, 309, points out, the masculine pronoun at 962 must refer to Paris, since Hecuba picks up on it with her mention of Paris at 998–1001, and it cannot so refer if preceded by lines that apply to Deiphobus.

41. Gorgias (Encomium of Helen 19) also considers the possibility that love is either "a god, with divine power," or "a human disease"; but he exculpates Helen in either case.

42. At 1051. For the connection between vision and desire, cf. Gorgias, Encomium of Helen 18–19, and the discussion of Dover 1973, 59.

43. Meridor 1984, 211, makes the attractive suggestion that the chorus' evocation of Helen as holding a golden mirror (1107–9)—an incongruous implement for a captive—constitutes an additional allusion to her escape from punishment.

44. Meridor 1984, 210, protests that the prologue "puts into strong relief the fact that the gods do not exact any penalty for offences against human beings." But Greek gods never do exact such penalties, unless the offenses against human beings (e.g., the denial of burial) simultaneously infringe on divine prerogatives.

45. Cf. 820–38. For a study of this ode see Burnett 1977.

46. The motif is Homeric: cf. Il. 6.357–58 (where it is expressed by Helen!) and Od. 8.579–80. References noted by Lee ad 1242–45.

47. At 1242–45. At 1242 Stephanus' ei de mē theos (adopted by Biehl 1970 and Diggle) seems preferable to the manuscripts' ei d'hēmas theos (accepted by Parmentier 1925 and Lee). There seems no reason to introduce at this juncture a distinction between swift and slow destruction; on the other hand a reference to the overturn of destiny is thematically appropriate. Ebener 1954 identifies twenty-three examples of the "Einst und Jetzt" motif in the play.

48. On the name of Troy cf. 1278, 1319, and 1322. Scodel 1980, 141, notes that

"the name is not really lost," and draws attention to the theme of "famous Il-ium" running through the trilogy.

49. For reasons against attributing to Gorgias the view that *logos = apatē*, see MacDowell 1982, 13–14.

50. Thuc. 7.75–87.

51. Plut. *Nic. 29*, in Dryden's translation revised by A. L. Clough, Boston 1906, vol. 3, 329. A doublet in the *Life of Lysander* (ch. 15) unfortunately casts doubt on the story: Plutarch recounts that when the Spartans were tempted to destroy the city of Athens after the Peloponnesian War, they were dis-suaded by a Phocian quoting from the parodos of Euripides' *Electra*.

Conclusion

It has been the premise of this study that Aristophanes' account of the goals of tragedy is a trustworthy guide for analysis; that the plays of Euripides, like those of his fellow tragedians, were intended for civic instruction, and that the tragedians' most urgent task was to reconcile traditional aristocratic values with the democratic order. Because its raw material is drawn from tradition but its idiom is that of the fifth century, tragedy allows us to glimpse the subtle process of adjustment—of assumptions, values, terms, and paradigms—that accompanied the establishment of a new social structure in Athens. Through the medium of the drama we can see both "the emergence of a new society from the old," and "the persistence of the old society in the new."[1]

I have tried to show also that Aristophanes is correct in identifying the "democratization" of tragedy (*Frogs* 952) as the distinctive contribution of Euripides. It is not merely that Euripides gives faces and voices to a whole spectrum of humanity, to "women and slaves, masters, young girls and crones" (*Frogs* 948–49). More fundamental is his demonstration that certain political categories reverberate at a level far deeper than the political. A society's vision of freedom and compulsion, equality and privilege, individual and community will affect how its members regard death, influence their erotic responses, and determine how they comport themselves in victory and defeat. Four of the plays studied here impart this lesson. The fifth, *Trojan Women*, turns the mirror on tragedy itself and considers the role of language as an instrument for interpreting and memorializing experience.

There is a distinct correlation between a society's attitude toward death and the standards it upholds for its living, and the *Alcestis* encourages the audience to reflect on one realm through the medium of the other. Apollo the aristocrat devises special privileges for his favorite mortal, securing for Admetus exemption from the common condition of unforeseen, unavoidable, and irrevocable death. Thanatos objects strenuously to this arrangement, which was brought about through trickery and against his will. Its consequences prove disastrous for Admetus, and by the end of the play the *status quo ante* has been restored. Admetus' experience invites the conclusion that Apollo's favor is in reality no favor at all, that an ordinary death is preferable to any exceptional arrangements. This lesson in democracy is readily transferable to the domain of life, although the parallel is never explicitly drawn in the play.

Historians have noted that in Athens "the accepted scale of values remained aristocratic throughout" and that the democracy "never acquired a language of its own."[2] This state of affairs has been interpreted in two ways: either it is claimed that Athens was a democracy in name only, while the aristocratic element continued to prevail, or else it is explained that the aristocratic vocabulary was "subverted," "captured," or "harnessed" for the uses of the new democratic order.[3] The evidence of the *Hippolytus* points toward linguistic appropriation carried out in a different spirit: respectfully and discreetly, through the medium of mythical paradigms.

Sōphrosynē, one of the cardinal Greek virtues, had by the fifth century acquired an oligarchic and even Spartan coloration. In the *Hippolytus* Euripides undertakes a critical exploration of this and other values clustering around the concept of moderation. The *sōphrōn* Hippolytus is portrayed as a young oligarch; his adversary Phaedra guides her conduct according to the equally aristocratic standards of *aidōs* and *eukleia*. At the opposite end of the spectrum stands the nurse, whose debased moral sense permits infinite accommodations and adjustments. In the spirit of the proverb *mēden agan*, which becomes emblematic for the play, Euripides mediates between these two extremes. Ultimately he proposes a revised standard of moderation applicable to both individuals and the polis—"neither inflexible," as the chorus puts it, "nor yet false-stamped" (*Hipp.* 1115).

Athens was internally a democracy but externally—as its leaders were prone to remind the citizens—a kind of tyranny whose rule depended on force.[4] Even without such reminders, the problematical nature of Athenian dominance would have been brought home by the repeated revolts of the subject allies over the seventy-odd years of Athenian hegemony. In the *Hecuba* Euripides turns his attention to the moral implications of power, warning the Athenians against excessive reliance on their strength. The possession of might, he reminds his audience, does not justify its abuse. The weak also possess certain rights and recourses, and those who press their advantage too far will receive their ultimate check not from the gods, but from their oppressed victims.

The concept of nobility or *eugeneia* was inherited from the past and imbued with aristocratic glamor, yet in need of revision to suit the conditions of a democratic social structure. Euripides' Heracles incorporates both traditional and innovative aspects. When he returns from the dead and rescues his family he seems a hero cast in the traditional mold, but by the end of the play he has renounced his divine heritage and heroic aspirations in favor of a way of life characterized by patience, endurance, and reliance on the human community. When Heracles decides that self-destruction would be cowardly and resigns himself to serving *tychē*, rather than Eurystheus, for the rest of his life, he signals a departure from the heroic standards exemplified by a traditional aristocrat such as Sophocles' Ajax. Heracles embodies a definition of nobility accessible to the ordinary Athenians watching the play.

The Athenians had a special appreciation for *logos*, for speech and argument played a significant role in the life of their polis. Operating within this context, *Trojan Women* illuminates the sustaining role of *logos* for both individuals and community. Euripides himself was a playwright and thus quintessentially a man of words; he may well be commenting on the services a poet could perform for his city. Just as the Trojan women impose order on their universe through language, so the poet depicts a world in which issues are posed with a clarity foreign to real life and consequences normally unknowable are presented in the form of mythical paradigms. How the audience chose to act on these insights was their own affair; Euripides could only set forth his instruction for all to see and hear.

Euripides the Athenian

This study points toward some conclusions about Euripides himself—necessarily partial because based only on five plays, but not, I believe, contradicted by the rest of his extant work. Euripides emerges as a playwright more in tune with his profession and his society than has been generally acknowledged. Although his plays differ in tone from those of Aeschylus and Sophocles, they do not differ in intent. His affection for the mythical tradition is as real as theirs, his allegiance to the tragic genre as strong, his ethical concerns as profound.[5]

Since antiquity it has been customary to appeal to Euripides' religious attitudes as testimony to his deviance.[6] The evidence of the five plays studied here suggests, not that Euripides was an atheist, but that the morality of the gods is something of a side issue in his plays. When Euripidean characters blame heaven for their misfortunes they are either the victims of a misunderstanding or attempting to evade their own responsibility. The gods are an aspect of Necessity or *Anankē*, and *Anankē*, as noted at the outset, is only the point of departure for Euripidean drama. It is human beings' responses to Necessity that are of primary concern to the playwright, and his dramatic portrayal of those responses cumulatively suggests his own liberal and idealistic temper. Euripides' attentiveness to personal responsibility, his insistence that character—not birth or station—defines the noble or slave, his protest against abuses of power, his championing of the rights of the weak—these motifs figure in play after play, not as isolated lines or passages but incorporated into the dramatic texture of the whole. They testify to an abiding passion for social justice that took as its point of departure the democratic principles of equality and freedom.

The Euripides whose lineaments we have sketched here has little in common with the Euripides of the biographical tradition—a man who, in contrast to Sophocles, is not known to have held public office; who avoided the company of his fellow Athenians, preferring to spend his time in a cave near Salamis; and who finally abandoned Athens for Macedonia. But even if we could accept these anecdotes as fact, we still would not be entitled to conclude that Euripides was unhappy in Athens or indifferent to its political affairs. A man who chose to spend his life in Athens is not likely to have felt himself alienated from his city.[7] A poet who twenty-two times was chosen to compete at the City Dionysia can scarcely have been held in contempt by his fellow citizens.[8] Euripides was not one of the *achreioi*, the nonparticipants castigated by Thucydides' Pericles (2.40.2); his plays serve notice of an engagement with the democratic polis no less strong for being so often critical.[9] Euripides' political contribution can be summed up in the words of his own Amphion, defending his patriotism before his reproachful brother Zethus: "If I am able to think well, that is better than a strong right arm."[10]

NOTES

1. Finley 1966, 2.

2. Arnheim 1977, 131; Loraux 1986, 334. Both are cited by Ober 1989, 290, n. 74, to whose discussion I am indebted.

3. For the first explanation see Arnheim 1977 and Loraux 1986. For the second see Ober 1989, 289–91 and 339.

4. Thuc. 2.63.2 and 3.37.1. For the connotations and development of the metaphor, see Raaflaub 1979.

5. Cf. Kovacs 1987, 117–21, and Kamerbeek 1960, 7: "En ce qui concerne le role du mythe chez Euripide, le moins qu'on puisse dire, c'est bien qu'il a été touché par son charme, sans doute dès son enfance, et qu'il est resté sous son charme jusqu'à sa mort."

6. See Lefkowitz 1989 for a detailed account and refutation of the charge of atheism.

7. Cf. Plato's *Crito* (521e), where the Laws argue that Socrates' long sojourn in Athens implies contentment with its way of life and its laws.

8. Cf. Stevens 1956, 91–94.

9. Such is also the conclusion of Carter 1986, 150.

10. *Antiope*, fr. 18 Kambitsis = 199 N^2.

Abbreviations

A&A	*Antike und Abendland*
AJP	*American Journal of Philology*
AJAH	*American Journal of Ancient History*
ASNP	*Annali della Scuola Normale Superiore di Pisa*
BICS	*Bulletin of the Institute of Classical Studies*
CA	*Classical Antiquity*
CJ	*Classical Journal*
CP	*Classical Philology*
CQ	*Classical Quarterly*
CR	*Classical Review*
CRAI	*Comptes rendus de l'Académie des Inscriptions et Belles-Lettres*
Diels-Kranz	H. Diels and W. Kranz, eds., *Die Fragmente der Vorsokratiker*
FGH	F. Jacoby, ed. *Die Fragmente der griechischen Historiker*
G&R	*Greece and Rome*
GRBS	*Greek, Roman and Byzantine Studies*
JHS	*Journal of Hellenic Studies*
HSCP	*Harvard Studies in Classical Philology*
Page	D. L. Page, ed., *Poetae Melici Graeci*
PCPhS	*Proceedings of the Cambridge Philological Society*
REG	*Revue des Études Grecques*
RFIC	*Rivista di Filologia e di Istruzione Classica*
SO	*Symbolae Osloenses*
TAPA	*Transactions of the American Philological Association*
West	M. L. West, ed. *Iambi et Elegi Graeci*
YCS	*Yale Classical Studies*

Bibliography

Adkins, A. W. H. 1960. *Merit and Responsibility*. Oxford.

———. 1963. " 'Friendship' and 'Self-Sufficiency' in Homer and Aristotle." *CQ* 13:30–45.

———. 1966. "Basic Greek Values in Euripides' *Hecuba* and *Hercules*." *CQ* 16:193–219.

———. 1970. *From the Many to the One*. Ithaca.

———. 1972. *Moral Values and Political Behaviour in Ancient Greece: From Homer to the End of the Fifth Century*. New York.

———. 1976. "*Polypragmosyne* and 'Minding One's Own Business': A Study in Greek Social and Political Values." *CP* 71:301–27.

Aélion, R. 1983. *Euripide héritier d'Eschyle*. Paris.

Alexiou, M. 1974. *The Ritual Lament in Greek Tradition*. Cambridge.

Allison, J. W. 1979. "Thucydides and *Polypragmosyne*." *AJAH* 4:10–22, 157–58.

Arnheim, M. T. W. 1977. *Aristocracy in Greek Society*. London.

Arrowsmith, W. 1959. "The Criticism of Greek Tragedy." *Tulane Drama Review* 3, 3:30–57.

———. 1968. "Euripides' Theater of Ideas." In *Euripides: A Collection of Critical Essays*, edited by E. Segal, 13–33. Englewood Cliffs, N.J.

Barlow, S., trans. and comm. 1986. *Euripides: Trojan Women*. Warminster, Wiltshire.

Barrett, W. S., ed. 1964. *Euripides: Hippolytos*. Oxford.

Becker, O. 1937. *Das Bild des Weges und verwandte Vorstellungen im frühgriechischen Denken*. *Hermes* Einzelschriften 4. Berlin.

Behler, E. 1986. "A. W. Schlegel and the Nineteenth-Century *Damnatio* of Euripides." *GRBS* 27, 4:335–67.

Benedetto, V. di. 1971. *Euripide: teatro e società*. Turin.

Bers, V. 1985. "Dikastic Thorubos." In *Crux: Essays Presented to G.E.M. de Ste Croix on his 75th Birthday*, edited by P. A. Cartledge and F. D. Harvey, 1–15. London.

Biehl, W., ed. 1970. *Euripidis Troades*. Leipzig.

Blumenthal, H. J. 1974. "Euripides' *Alcestis* 282 ff. and the Authenticity of *Antigone* 905 ff." *CR* 24:174–75.

Blundell, M. W. 1989. *Helping Friends and Harming Enemies: A Study in Sophocles and Greek Ethics*. Cambridge.

Boegehold, A. L. 1982. "A Dissent at Athens ca. 424–421 B.C." *GRBS* 23, 2:147–56.

Bond, G., ed. 1981. *Euripides: Heracles*. Oxford.

Bowersock, G. W., ed. and trans. 1968. *Constitution of the Athenians*. In: *Xeno-phon VII: Scripta Minora*, translated by E. C. Marchant. The Loeb Classical Library. Cambridge, Mass.

Bradeen, D. W. 1969. "The Athenian Casualty Lists." *CQ* 19:145–59.

Bremer, J. M. 1975. "The Meadow of Love and Two Passages in Euripides' *Hip-polytus*." *Mnemosyne* 28:268–80.

Brommer, F. 1953. *Herakles: Die zwölf Taten des Helden in antiker Kunst und Liter-atur*. Münster.

Burian, P. 1977. "Euripides' *Heraclidae*: An Interpretation." *CP* 72:1–21.

——. 1985. "Logos and Pathos: The Politics of the *Suppliant Women*." In *Direc-tions in Euripidean Criticism: A Collection of Essays*, edited by P. Burian, 129–55. Durham.

Burkert, W. 1955. *Zum altgriechischen Mitleidsbegriff*. Diss. Erlangen, 1955.

——. 1966. "Greek Tragedy and Sacrificial Ritual." *GRBS* 7:87–121.

——. 1985. *Greek Religion*. Translated by J. Raffan. Cambridge, Mass.

Burnett, A. P. 1965. "The Virtues of Admetus." *CP* 60:240–55.

——. 1971. *Catastrophe Survived: Euripides' Plays of Mixed Reversal*. Oxford.

——. 1977. "*Trojan Women* and the Ganymede Ode." *YCS* 25:291–316.

Butts, H. R. 1947. *The Glorification of Athens in Greek Drama*. Iowa Studies in Classical Philology XI.

Buxton, R. G. A. 1982. *Persuasion in Greek Tragedy: A Study of Peitho*. Cam-bridge.

Carter, L. B. 1986. *The Quiet Athenian*. Oxford.

Cartledge, P. 1985. "The Greek Religious Festivals." In *Greek Religion and Soci-ety*, edited by P. E. Easterling and J. V. Muir, 98–127. Cambridge.

Chalk, H. H. O. 1962. "*Aretē* and *Bia* in Euripides' *Herakles*." *JHS* 82:7–18.

Classen, J. 1976. "The Study of Language amongst Socrates' Contemporaries." In *Sophistik*, edited by J. Classen, 215–47. Darmstadt.

Claus, D. 1972. "Phaedra and the Socratic Paradox." *YCS* 22:223–38.

——. 1975. "*Aidōs* in the Language of Achilles." *TAPA* 105:13–28.

Collard, C., ed. 1975A. *Euripides: Supplices*. 2 vols. Groningen.

——. 1975B. "Formal Debates in Euripides' Drama." *G&R* 22:58–71.

Conacher, D. J. 1967. *Euripidean Drama*. Toronto.

——. 1980. *Aeschylus' "Prometheus Bound": A Literary Commentary*. Toronto.

Connor, W. R. 1971. *The New Politicians of Fifth-Century Athens*. Princeton.

Cropp, M. and G. Fick. 1985. *Resolutions and Chronology in Euripides: The Frag-mentary Tragedies*. BICS Supplement 43. London.

Daitz, S. 1971. "Concepts of Freedom and Slavery in Euripides' *Hecuba*." *Hermes* 99:217–26.

——, ed. 1973. *Euripides: Hecuba*. Leipzig.

Dale, A. M., ed. 1954. *Euripides: Alcestis*. Oxford.

Davies, J. K. 1981. *Wealth and the Power of Wealth in Classical Athens*. Salem, N.H.

Delebecque, E. 1951. *Euripide et la guerre du Péloponnèse*. Paris.

Denniston, J. D. 1929. "Epexegetic *ge*." *CR* 43:59–60.

——, ed. 1939. *Euripides: Electra*. Oxford.

Détienne, M. 1974. "Orphée au miel." In *Faire de l'histoire*, edited by J. Le Goff and P. Nora, vol. 3, 56–75. Paris.

Devereux, G. 1985. *The Character of the Euripidean Hippolytus: An Ethno-Psychoanalytical Study*. Chico, Calif.

Diels, H. and W. Kranz, eds. 1951–52[6]. *Die Fragmente der Vorsokratiker*. 3 vols. Berlin.

Diggle, J., ed. 1986[2]. *Euripidis Fabulae*, vol. 2. Oxford.

———. 1987[2]. *Euripidis Fabulae*, vol. 1. Oxford.

Dimock, G. E. 1977. "Euripides' *Hippolytus*, or Virtue Rewarded." *YCS* 25:239–58.

Dodds, E. R. 1925. "The *Aidōs* of Phaedra and the Meaning of the *Hippolytus*." *CR* 39:102–4.

———. 1929. "Euripides the Irrationalist." *CR* 43:97–104.

———. 1960[2]. *Euripides: Bacchae*. Oxford.

———. 1973. "The Ancient Theory of Progress." In *The Ancient Theory of Progress and Other Essays in Greek Literature and Belief*, 1–25. Oxford.

Donlan, W. 1973. "The Role of *Eugenia* in the Aristocratic Self-Image During the Fifth Century B.C." In *Classics and the Classical Tradition: Essays Presented to Robert C. Dengler on the Occasion of his Eightieth Birthday*, edited by E. N. Borza and R. W. Carubba, 63–78. University Park, Pa.

———. 1980. *The Aristocratic Ideal in Ancient Greece: Attitudes of Superiority from Homer to the End of the Fifth Century B.C.* Lawrence, Kans.

Dover, K. J. 1973. "Classical Greek Attitudes Toward Sexual Behavior." *Arethusa* 6:59–73.

———. 1974. *Greek Popular Morality in the Time of Plato and Aristotle*. Berkeley and Los Angeles.

———. 1983. "The Portrayal of Moral Evaluation in Greek Poetry." *JHS* 103:35–48.

Drew-Bear, T. 1968. "The Trochaic Tetrameter in Greek Tragedy." *AJP* 89:385–405.

Easterling, P. E. 1973. "Presentation of Character in Aeschylus." *G&R* 20:3–19.

———. 1977. "Character in Sophocles." *G&R* 24:121–29.

———. 1984. "The Tragic Homer." *BICS* 31:1–8.

———. 1985. "Anachronism in Greek Tragedy." *JHS* 105:1–10.

Ebener, D. 1954. "Die Helenaszene der Troerinnen." *Wissenschaftliche Zeitschrift der Martin-Luther-Universität Halle-Wittenberg* 3, Heft 4:691–722.

Edmunds, L. 1975. *Chance and Intelligence in Thucydides*. Cambridge.

Ehrenberg, V. 1947. "Polypragmosynē." *JHS* 67:44–67.

Else, G. F. 1957. *Aristotle's Poetics: The Argument*. Cambridge, Mass.

Erffa, C. E. von. 1937. *Aidōs und verwandte Begriffe in der Entwicklung von Homer bis Demokrit*. *Philologus* Supplementband 30, 2. Leipzig.

Erp, M. A. Taalman Kip. 1987. "Euripides and Melos." *Mnemosyne* 15:3–4.

Euben, P. 1986. "Political Corruption in Euripides' *Orestes*." In *Greek Tragedy and Political Theory*, edited by P. Euben, 222–51. Berkeley and Los Angeles.

Farrar, C. 1988. *The Origins of Democratic Thinking*. Cambridge.

Figueira, T. J. 1985. "The Theognidea and Megarian Society." In *Poetry and the Polis*, edited by T. J. Figueira and G. Nagy, 112–58. Baltimore.

Finley, J. H. 1938. "Euripides and Thucydides." *HSCP* 49:23–66.

——. 1942. *Thucydides.* Cambridge, Mass.

——. 1966. "Politics and Early Attic Tragedy." *HSCP* 71:1–13.

Finley, M. I. 1981. "Politics." In *The Legacy of Greece*, edited by M. I. Finley, 22–36. New York.

Fisher, N. R. E. 1976. *Social Values in Classical Athens.* London and Toronto.

Foley, H. 1985. *Ritual Irony: Poetry and Sacrifice in Euripides.* Ithaca.

Forrest, W. G. 1975. "An Athenian Generation Gap." *YCS* 24:37–52.

——. 1986. "The Stage and Politics." In *Greek Tragedy and its Legacy: Essays Presented to D. J. Conacher*, edited by M. Cropp, E. Fantham, and S. Scully, 229–39. Calgary.

Fraenkel, H. 1946. "Man's 'Ephemeros' Nature According to Pindar and Others." *TAPA* 77:131–45.

——. 1975. *Early Greek Poetry and Philosophy.* Translated by M. Hadas and J. Willis. New York.

Frischer, B. 1970. "*Concordia Discors* and Euripides' *Hippolytus.*" *GRBS* 11, 2:85–100.

Fritz, K. von. 1962. "Euripides' Alkestis und ihre modernen Nachahmen und Kritiker." In *Antike und moderne Tragödie*, 256–321. (= *A&A* 5:27–70.) Berlin.

Galinsky, K. 1972. *The Herakles Theme: The Adaptations of the Hero from Homer to the Twentieth Century.* Oxford.

Garland, R. 1985. *The Greek Way of Death.* Ithaca.

Garner, R. 1987. *Law and Society in Classical Athens.* New York.

——. 1990. *From Homer to Tragedy: The Art of Allusion in Greek Poetry.* London and New York.

Garton, C. 1957. "Characterisation in Greek Tragedy." *JHS* 77:247–54.

Gellie, G. H. 1980. "Hecuba and Tragedy." *Antichthon* 14:30–44.

Gill, C. 1990. "The Character-Personality Distinction." In *Characterization and Individuality in Greek Literature*, edited by C. Pelling, 32–59. Oxford.

Girard, R. 1977. *Violence and the Sacred.* Translated by P. Gregory. Baltimore.

Goldhill, S. 1986. *Reading Greek Tragedy.* Cambridge.

——. 1987. "The Great Dionysia and Civic Ideology." *JHS* 107:58–76.

Goossens, R. 1962. *Euripides et Athènes.* Brussels.

Gould, J. 1978. "Dramatic Character and 'Human Intelligibility' in Greek Tragedy." *PCPhS* 24:43–67.

——. 1985. "On Making Sense of Greek Religion." In *Greek Religion and Society*, edited by P. E. Easterling and J. V. Muir, 1–33. Cambridge.

Graham, A. J. and G. Forsythe. 1984. "A New Slogan for Oligarchy in Thucydides III.82.8." *HSCP* 88:25–45.

Greenhalgh, P. A. C. 1972. "Aristocracy and its Advocates in Archaic Greece." *G&R* 19:190–207.

Gregory, J. 1977. "Euripides' *Heracles.*" *YCS* 25:259–75. Rewritten here as Chapter 4.

——. 1979. "Euripides' *Alcestis.*" *Hermes* 107:259–70. Rewritten here as Chapter 1.

———. 1985. "The Power of Language in Euripides' *Troades*." *Eranos* 84:1–9. Re-written here as Chapter 5.

Griffin, J. 1990. "Characterization in Euripides: *Hippolytus* and *Iphigeneia in Aulis*." In *Characterization and Individuality in Greek Literature*, edited by C. Pelling, 128–49. Oxford.

Griffith, M. 1977. *The Authenticity of the Prometheus Bound*. Cambridge.

Grossmann, G. 1950. *Politische Schlagwörter aus der Zeit des Peloponnesischen Krieges*. Zürich.

Grube, G. M. A. 1961². *The Drama of Euripides*. New York.

Guthrie, W. K. C. 1971. *The Sophists*. Cambridge. (= Volume 3, Part 1 of *A History of Greek Philosophy*. Cambridge, 1969.)

Halleran, M. R. 1985. *Stagecraft in Euripides*. Totowa, N.J.

———. 1986. "Rhetoric, Irony and the Ending of Euripides' *Heracles*." *CA* 5, 2:171–81.

Halliwell, S. 1986. *Aristotle's Poetics*. Chapel Hill.

———. 1987. *The Poetics of Aristotle*. Chapel Hill.

Hamilton, R. 1978. "Prologue Prophecy and Plot in Four Plays of Euripides." *AJP* 99:277–302.

———. 1985. "Slings and Arrows: The Debate with Lycus in the *Heracles*." *TAPA* 115:1–25.

Hangard, J. 1976. "Remarques sur quelques motifs répétés dans l'Héraclès d'Euripide." In *Miscellanea tragica in honorem J. C. Kamerbeek*, edited by J. M. Bremer, S. L. Radt, and C. J. Ruijh, 125–46. Amsterdam.

Havelock, E. A. 1968. "Watching the *Trojan Women*." In *Euripides*, edited by E. Segal, 115–27. Englewood Cliffs, N.J.

Heath, M. 1987. *The Poetics of Greek Tragedy*. Stanford.

Heinimann, F. 1945. *Nomos und Physis*. Reprinted 1960. Basel.

Henderson, J. 1990. "The *Dēmos* and the Comic Competition." In *Nothing to Do with Dionysos? Athenian Drama in its Social Context*, edited by J. J. Winkler and F. I. Zeitlin, 271–313. Princeton.

Henrichs, A. 1986. "The Last of the Detractors: Friedrich Nietzsche's Condemnation of Euripides." *GRBS* 27, 4:369–97.

Herington, C. J. 1955. *Athena Parthenos and Athena Polias*. Manchester.

———. 1986. *Aeschylus*. New Haven.

Hermassi, K. 1977. *Polity and Theater in Historical Perspective*. Berkeley and Los Angeles.

Hogan, J. C. 1972. "Thucydides 3.52–68 and Euripides' *Hecuba*." *Phoenix* 26:241–57.

Humphrey, S. 1983. *The Family, Women and Death: Comparative Studies*. Boston and London.

Hutter, H. 1978. *Politics and Friendship*. Waterloo, Ontario.

Jacoby, F. 1923–. *Die Fragmente der griechischen Historiker*. Berlin and Leiden.

Jones, A. H. M. 1957. *Athenian Democracy*. London.

Jones, J. 1962. *On Aristotle and Greek Tragedy*. Oxford.

Kambitsis, J., ed. 1972. *L'Antiope d'Euripide*. Athens.

Kamerbeek, J. C. 1960. "Mythe et réalité dans l'oeuvre d'Euripide." In *Euripide: Entretiens sur l'antiquité classique* VI, 1–25. Vandoeuvres-Genève.

——. 1966. "The Unity and Meaning of Euripides' *Heracles*." *Mnemosyne* 19:1–16.

Kerferd, G. B. 1981. *The Sophistic Movement*. Cambridge.

King, K. C. 1985. "The Politics of Imitation: Euripides' *Hekabe*." *Arethusa* 18:47–64.

Kirkwood, G. 1947. "Hecuba and Nomos." *TAPA* 78:61–68.

Kleve, K. 1964. "*Apragmosyne* and *Polypragmosyne*: Two Slogans in Athenian Politics." *SO* 39:83–88.

Knox, B. 1952. "The *Hippolytus* of Euripides." *YCS* 13:1–31 (= *Word and Action*, 205–30. Baltimore, 1971).

——. 1957. *Oedipus at Thebes*. New Haven.

——. 1977. "The *Medea* of Euripides." *YCS* 25:193–225.

——. 1983. "Sophocles and the Polis." In *Sophocle: Entretiens sur l'antiquité classique* XXIX, 1–27. Vandoeuvres-Genève.

Konstan, D. 1985. "*Philia* in Euripides' *Electra*." *Philologus* 129:176–85.

Kovacs, D. 1980A. "Shame, Pleasure and Honor in Phaedra's Great Speech (Euripides, *Hippolytus* 375–387)." *AJP* 101:287–303.

——. 1980B. "Euripides' *Hippolytus* 100 and the Meaning of the Prologue." *CP* 75:130–37.

——. 1987. *The Heroic Muse*. Baltimore and London.

Kuch, H. 1983. "Individuum und Gesellschaft in der tragischen Dichtung der Griechen." In *Die griechische Tragödie in ihrer gesellschaftlichen Funktion*, edited by H. Kuch, 61–84. Berlin.

Kullmann, W. 1967. "Zum Sinngehalt der euripideischen Alkestis." *A&A* 13:127–49.

Kurtz, D. and J. Boardman. 1971. *Greek Burial Customs*. London.

Kurtz, E. 1985. *Die bildliche Ausdrucksweisen in den Tragödien des Euripides*. Amsterdam.

Lanza, D. 1963. "*Nomos* et *Ison* in Euripide." *RFIC* 41:416–39.

Lattimore, R. 1939. "The Wise Adviser in Herodotus." *CP* 34:24–35.

——, trans. 1951. *The Iliad of Homer*. Chicago.

——, trans. 1955. *Greek Lyrics*. Chicago.

Lee, K. H., ed. 1976. *Euripides: Troades*. Basingstoke.

Lefkowitz, M. 1979. "The Euripides *Vita*." *GRBS* 20, 2:187–210.

——. 1989. " 'Impiety' and 'Atheism' in Euripides' Dramas." *CQ* 39:70–82.

Lennep, D. F. W. van, ed. 1949. *Alcestis*. Leiden.

Lesky, A. 1925. "Alkestis, der Mythus und das Drama." *Sitzungsber. Akad. Wien*. 203, 2:1–86.

——. 1966. "Der angeklagte Admet." In *Gesammelte Schriften*, 281–94. Bern and Munich. (= *Maske u. Kothurn* 10 [1964]:203–16.)

Lilja, S. 1976. *Dogs in Ancient Greek Poetry*. Helsinki.

Lloyd, G. E. R., 1966. *Polarity and Analogy*. Cambridge.

Lloyd, M. 1984. "The Helen Scene in Euripides' *Trojan Women*." *CQ* 34:303–13.

——. 1985. "Euripides' *Alcestis*." *G&R* 32, 2:119–31.

Long, A. A. 1970. "Morals and Values in Homer." *JHS* 90:121–39.

Longo, O. 1990. "The Theater of the *Polis*." In *Nothing to Do with Dionysos? Athenian Drama in its Social Context*, edited by J. J. Winkler and F. I. Zeitlin, 12–19. Princeton.

Loraux, N. 1978. "Sur la race des femmes et quelques-uns de ses tribus." *Arethusa* 11:43–87.

——. 1981A. "Le lit, la guerre." *L'Homme* 21:37–67.

——. 1981B. *Les enfants d'Athéna*. Paris.

——. 1985. *Façons tragiques de tuer une femme*. Paris.

——. 1986. *The Invention of Athens: The Funeral Oration and the Classical City*. Translated by A. Sheridan. Cambridge, Mass.

Lovejoy, A. O. and G. Boas. 1935. *Primitivism and Related Ideas in Antiquity*. Baltimore.

Lucas, D. W., ed. 1968. *Aristotle: Poetics*. Oxford.

Luschnig, C. A. E. 1976. "Euripides' *Hecabe*: The Time is Out of Joint." *CJ* 71:227–34.

MacDowell, D. M., ed. and trans. 1982. *Gorgias: Encomium of Helen*. Bristol.

Macleod, C. W. 1982. "Politics and the *Oresteia*." *JHS* 102:124–44.

Martin, R. P. 1990. *The Language of Heroes: Speech and Performance in the Iliad*. Ithaca.

Mason, P. G. 1959. "Kassandra." *JHS* 79:80–93.

Mattes, J. 1970. *Der Wahnsinn im griechischen Mythos und in der Dichtung bis zum Drama des fünften Jahrhunderts*. Heidelberg.

Matthaei, L. 1918. *Studies in Greek Tragedy*. Cambridge.

Maxwell-Stuart, P. G. 1973. "The Dramatic Poets and the Expedition to Sicily." *Historia* 22:397–404.

Meier, C. 1983². *Die Entstehung des Politischen bei den Griechen*. Frankfurt.

——. 1988. *Die politische Kunst der griechischen Tragödie*. Munich.

Meiggs, R. 1972. *The Athenian Empire*. Oxford.

Meiggs, R. and D. Lewis, eds. 1969. *A Selection of Greek Historical Inscriptions to the End of the Fifth Century*. Oxford.

Meridier, L., ed. and trans. 1926. *Euripide*, vol. 1. (Collection Budé.) Paris.

——. 1927. *Euripide*, vol. 2. (Collection Budé.) Paris.

Meridor, R. 1978. "Hecuba's Revenge." *AJP* 99:28–35.

——. 1983. "The Function of Polymestor's Crime in the *Hecuba* of Euripides." *Eranos* 81:13–20.

——. 1984. "Plot and Myth in Euripides' *Hecuba* and *Troades*." *Phoenix* 38:205–15.

——. 1989. "Euripides' *Troades* and the Andromache Scene." *AJP* 110:17–35.

Mette, H. J. 1933. *MĒDEN AGAN: Ein Vortrag*. Munich.

Michelini, A. 1987. *Euripides and the Tragic Tradition*. Madison.

Moore, J., trans. 1957. *Ajax*. In *Sophocles II*, edited by D. Grene and R. Lattimore, 7–62. Chicago.

Morris, J. 1989. "Attitudes toward Death in Archaic Greece." *CA* 8, 2:296–320.

Motte, A. 1973. *Prairies et jardins de la Grèce antique. De la religion à la philosophie.* Brussels.

Murray, G. 1946. "Euripides' Tragedies of 415 B.C.: The Deceitfulness of Life." In *Greek Studies*, 127–46. Oxford.

Murray, O. 1980. *Early Greece.* Stanford.

Nagy, G. 1979. *The Best of the Achaeans.* Baltimore and London.

——. 1985. "Theognis of Megara: A Poet's Vision of His City." In *Theognis of Megara: Poetry and The Polis*, edited by J. Figueira and G. Nagy, 22–81. Baltimore and London.

Nauck, A., ed. 1889². *Tragicorum Graecorum Fragmenta.* Leipzig.

Nielson, R. 1976. "Alcestis: A Paradox in Dying." *Ramus* 5:92–102.

North, H. 1966. *Sōphrosynē: Self-Knowledge and Self-Restraint in Greek Literature.* Ithaca.

Norwood, G. 1930. "The *Babylonians* of Aristophanes." *CP* 25:1–10.

Nussbaum, M. 1986. *The Fragility of Goodness: Luck and Ethics in Greek Tragedy and Philosophy.* Cambridge.

Ober, J. 1989. *Mass and Elite in Democratic Athens: Rhetoric, Ideology and the Power of the People.* Princeton.

Ober, J. and B. Strauss. 1990. "Drama, Political Rhetoric and the Discourse of Athenian Democracy." In *Nothing to Do with Dionysos? Athenian Drama in its Social Context*, edited by J. J. Winkler and F. I. Zeitlin, 237–70. Princeton.

O'Conner-Visser, E. A. M. E. 1987. *Aspects of Human Sacrifice in the Tragedies of Euripides.* Amsterdam.

Ostwald, M. 1969. *Nomos and the Beginnings of the Athenian Democracy.* Oxford.

——. 1986. *From Popular Sovereignty to the Sovereignty of Law.* Berkeley and Los Angeles.

——. 1988. *Anankē in Thucydides.* Atlanta. (American Classical Studies.)

Page, D. L., ed. 1962. *Poetae Melici Graeci.* Oxford.

——. 1964⁵. *Euripides: Medea.* Oxford.

Parke, H. W. 1977. *Festivals of the Athenians.* London.

Parke, H. W. and D. E. W. Wormell. 1956. *The Delphic Oracle.* 2 vols. Oxford.

Parmentier, L. and H. Grégoire, ed. and trans. 1923. *Euripide*, vol. 3. (Collection Budé.) Paris.

——. 1925. *Euripide*, vol. 4. (Collection Budé.) Paris.

Parry, A. 1956. "The Language of Achilles." *TAPA* 87:1–7.

——. 1971. *Logos and Ergon in Thucydides.* New York. Diss. Harvard, 1957.

Pickard-Cambridge, A. W. 1968². *The Dramatic Festivals of Athens.* Revised by J. Gould and D. M. Lewis. Oxford.

Podlecki, A. J. 1986. "Polis and Monarch in Early Greek Tragedy." In *Greek Tragedy and Political Theory*, edited by P. Euben, 76–100. Berkeley and Los Angeles.

Pohlenz, M. 1954. *Die Griechische Tragödie.* 2 vols. Göttingen.

Poole, A. 1976. "Total Disaster: Euripides' *The Trojan Women*." *Arion* n.s. 3, 3:257–87.

Pötscher, W. 1971. "Der Name des Herakles." *Emerita* 39:169–84.

Pucci, P. 1980. *The Violence of Pity in Euripides' Medea.* Ithaca and London.

Raaflaub, K. 1979. "Polis Tyrannos: Zur Entstehung einer politischen Metapher." In *Arktouros: Hellenic Studies Presented to Bernard M. W. Knox*, edited by G. W. Bowersock, W. Burkert, and M. C. J. Putnam, 237–52. Berlin and New York.

Race, W. H. 1981. "The Word *Kairos* in Greek Drama." *TAPA* 111:197–213.

Radt, S. 1983. "Sophokles in seinem Fragmenten." In *Sophocle: Entretiens sur l'antiquité classique* XXIX, 185–231. Vandoeuvres-Genève.

Reckford, K. 1985. "Concepts of Demoralization in the *Hecuba*." In *Directions in Euripidean Criticism: A Collection of Essays*, edited by P. Burian, 112–28. Durham.

Redfield, J. 1975. *Nature and Culture in the Iliad*. Chicago.

Reinhardt, K. 1957. "Die Sinneskrise bei Euripides." *Die Neue Rundschau* 68:615–46.

——. 1960. *Tradition und Geist*. Göttingen.

Renehan, R. 1987. "The 'Heldentod' in Homer." *CP* 82:99–116.

Rhodes, P. J. 1972. *The Athenian Boule*. Oxford.

Rickert, G. A. 1985. *Hekōn and Akōn in Early Greek Thought*. Ann Arbor. Diss. Harvard, 1985.

Rivier, A. 1968A. "Remarques sur le 'nécessaire' et la 'nécessité' chez Eschyle." *REG* 81:5–39.

——. 1968B. "Sur un motif de l'Alceste d'Euripide." *Actas del III Congreso Español de Estudios Clásicos*, 286–95.

——. 1972. "En marge d'Alceste et de quelques interprétations recentes." *Museum Helveticum* 29:124–43.

Romilly, J. de. 1961. *L'évolution du pathétique d'Eschyle à Euripide*. Paris.

——. 1966. "Thucydide et l'idée de progrès." *ASNP* 35:143–91.

——. 1971. *La loi dans la pensée grecque*. Paris.

——. 1975. *Magic and Rhetoric in Ancient Greece*. Cambridge, Mass.

——. 1976. "L'excuse de l'invincible amour dans la tragédie grecque." In *Miscellanea Tragica in honorem J. C. Kamerbeek*, edited by J. M. Bremer, S. L. Radt, and C. J. Ruijh, 309–21. Amsterdam.

——. 1979. *La douceur dans la pensée grecque*. Paris.

——. 1980. "Le refus du suicide dans l'Héraclès d'Euripide." *Archaiognosia* I, 1:1–9.

——. 1983. "Les réflexions générales d'Euripide: analyse litteraire et critique textuelle." *CRAI* 405–18.

——. 1986. *La Modernité d'Euripide*. Paris.

Rosenmeyer, T. 1963. *The Masks of Tragedy: Essays on Six Great Dramas*. Austin, Tex.

Rösler, W. 1980. *Polis und Tragödie: Funktionsgeschichtliche Betrachtungen zu einer antiken Literaturgattung*. Konstanz.

Saïd, S. 1978. *La faute tragique*. Paris.

——. 1985. *Sophiste et tyran: le problème du Prométhée enchaîné*. Paris.

Ste Croix, G. E. M. de. 1972. *The Origins of the Peloponnesian War*. Ithaca.

——. 1981. *The Class Struggle in the Ancient Greek World from the Archaic Age to the Arabic Conquests*. Ithaca.

Scodel, R. 1979. "ADMĒTOU LOGOS." *HSCP* 83:51–62.

——. 1980. *The Trojan Trilogy of Euripides.* Göttingen.

Schreckenberg, H. 1964. *Anankē: Untersuchungen zur Geschichte des Wortgebrauchs.* Zetemata Heft 36. Munich.

Schwinge, E. R. 1962. *Die Stellung der Trachinierinnen im Werk des Sophocles.* Göttingen.

——. 1968. *Die Verwendung der Stichomythie in den Dramen des Euripides.* Heidelberg.

——. 1970. "Zwei sprachliche Bermerkungen zu Euripides' *Alkestis.*" *Glotta* 48:36–39.

Seeck, G. A. 1985. *Unaristotelische Untersuchungen zu Euripides: ein motivanalytischer Kommentar zur 'Alkestis'.* Heidelberg.

Segal, C. 1962. "Gorgias and the Psychology of the *Logos.*" *HSCP* 66:99–155.

——. 1965. "The Tragedy of the *Hippolytus.* The Waters of Ocean and the Untouched Meadow." *HSCP* 70:117–69.

——. 1970. "Shame and Purity in Euripides' *Hippolytus.*" *Hermes* 98:278–99.

Sheppard, J. T. 1916. "The Formal Beauty of the *Hercules Furens.*" *CQ* 10:72–79.

Šičalin, J. 1983. "Die Krise der traditionellen Weltanschaung in den trojanischen Tragödien des Euripides." In *Die griechische Tragödie in ihrer gesellschaftlichen Funktion,* edited by H. Kuch, 103–14. Berlin.

Sinclair, R. K. 1988. *Democracy and Participation in Athens.* Cambridge.

Smith, W. 1960A. "The Ironic Structure of the *Alcestis.*" *Phoenix* 14:127–45

——. 1960B. "Staging in the Central Scene of the Hippolytus." *TAPA* 91:162–77.

Snodgrass, A. M. 1965. "The Hoplite Reform and History." *JHS* 85:110–22.

Solmsen, F. 1975. *Intellectual Experiments of the Greek Enlightenment.* Princeton.

Sourvinou-Inwood, C. 1981. "To Die and Enter the House of Hades." In *Mirrors of Mortality,* edited by J. Whaley, 15–39. New York.

Stanford, W. B., ed. 1958. *Aristophanes: Frogs.* London.

——. 1963. *Sophocles: Ajax.* New York.

Starr, C. G. 1986. *Individual and Community: The Rise of the Polis, 800–500 B.C.* New York and Oxford.

Steidle, W. 1968. *Studien zum antiken Drama.* Munich.

Stevens, P. T. 1956. "Euripides and the Athenians." *JHS* 76:87–94.

Stinton, T. C. W. 1986. "The Scope and Limits of Allusion in Greek Tragedy." In *Greek Tragedy and its Legacy: Essays Presented to D. J. Conacher,* edited by M. Cropp, E. Fantham, and S. E. Scully, 67–102. Calgary.

Straten, F. T. Van. 1981. "Gifts for the Gods." In *Faith, Hope and Worship: Aspects of Religious Mentality in the Ancient World,* edited by H. S. Versnel, 65–151. Leiden.

Sutton, D. 1980. *The Greek Satyr Play.* Meisenheim am Glan. (Beiträge zur klassischen Philologie, 90.)

Synodinou, K. 1978. "Some Cases of 'Oxymoron' in Euripides." *Dodone* 7:351–58.

Taplin, O. 1977. *The Stagecraft of Aeschylus.* Oxford.

——. 1978. *Greek Tragedy in Action.* Berkeley.

———. 1983. "Tragedy and Trugedy." *CQ* 33:331–33.

———. 1986. "Fifth-Century Tragedy and Comedy: A *Synkrisis*." *JHS* 106:163–74.

Tarkow, T. 1977. "The Glorification of Athens in Euripides' *Heracles*." *Helios* 5:27–35.

Verdenius, W. J. 1970. "Homer, the Educator of the Greeks." *Mededelingen der Koninklijke Nederlandse Akademie van Wetenschappen* 33.5:207–31.

Vermeule, E. 1979. *Aspects of Death in Early Greek Art and Poetry*. Berkeley and Los Angeles.

Vernant, J.-P. 1970. "Greek Tragedy: Problems of Interpretation." In *The Languages of Criticism and the Sciences of Man: The Structuralist Controversy*, edited by R. Macksey and E. Donato, 273–95. Baltimore.

———. 1980. *Myth and Society in Ancient Greece*. Translated by J. Lloyd. Atlantic Highlands, N.J.

Vernant, J.-P. and P. Vidal-Naquet. 1981. *Tragedy and Myth in Ancient Greece*. Translated by J. Lloyd. Atlantic Highlands, N.J.

Vickers, B. 1973. *Towards Greek Tragedy*. London.

Vlastos, G. 1953. "Isonomia." *AJP* 74:337–66.

Walsh, G. 1978. "The Rhetoric of Birthright and Race in Euripides' *Ion*." *Hermes* 106:301–15.

Warner, R., trans. 1954. *Thucydides: History of the Peloponnesian War*. Harmondsworth and Baltimore.

Waterfield, R. A. H. 1982. "Double Standards in Euripides' *Troades*." *Maia* 34:139–42.

Webster, T. B. L. 1967. *The Tragedies of Euripides*. London.

West, M. L., ed. 1971. *Iambi et Elegi Graeci*. 2 vols. Oxford.

Whitman, C. 1974. *Euripides and the Full Circle of Myth*. Cambridge, Mass.

Wilamowitz-Moellendorf, U. von, ed., trans., and comm. 1895². *Euripides: Herakles*. 3 vols. Reprinted 1969. Darmstadt.

———. 1904–6. *Griechische Tragödien*. 3 vols. Berlin.

Wilkins, E. G. 1917. '*Know Thyself* in Greek and Latin Literature'. Chicago.

———. 1926. "*Mēden Agan* in Greek and Latin Literature." *CP* 21:132–48.

Will, E. 1978. "Un nouvel essai d'interprétation de l'*Athenaiōn politeia* pseudo-xénophontique." *REG* 91:77–92.

Willink, C. W. 1968. "Some Problems of Text and Interpretation in the *Hippolytus*." *CQ* 18:11–43.

Wilson, J. R. 1980. "*Kairos* as 'Due Measure.' " *Glotta* 58:177–204.

Wilson, N. 1982. "Observations on Aristophanes' *Lysistrata*." *GRBS* 23, 2:157–63.

Winkler, J. J. 1985. "The Ephebe's Song: *Tragoidia* and *Polis*." *Representations* 11:26–62.

Winnington-Ingram, R. P. 1960. "Hippolytus: A Study in Causation." In *Euripide: Entretiens sur l'antiquité classique* VI, 170–91. Vandoeuvres-Genève.

Winton, R. I. and P. Garnsey. 1981. "Politics and Political Theory." In *The Legacy of Greece*, edited by M. I. Finley, 37–64. New York.

Woodbury, L. 1986. "The Judgment of Dionysus: Books, Taste and Teaching in the *Frogs*." In *Greek Tragedy and its Legacy: Essays Presented to D. J.*

Conacher, edited by M. Cropp, E. Fantham, and S. E. Scully, 241–57. Calgary.

Wolff, C. 1982. "Euripides." In *Ancient Writers: Greece and Rome*, edited by T. J. Luce, vol. 1, 236–66. New York.

Wyckoff, E., trans. 1954. *Antigone*. In *Sophocles I*, edited by D. Grene and R. Lattimore, 161–209. Chicago.

Zeitlin, F. 1985. "The Power of Aphrodite: Eros and the Boundaries of the Self in the *Hippolytus*." In *Directions in Euripidean Criticism: A Collection of Essays*, edited by P. Burian, 52–111. Durham.

Zuntz, G. 1955. *The Political Plays of Euripides*. Manchester.

——. 1965. *An Inquiry into the Transmission of the Plays of Euripides*. Cambridge.

Index

Achilles: in *Iliad*, 21–22, 24, 76, 103, 122, 137, 158; in *Odyssey*, 134
Aeschines, 55
Aeschylus: in Aristophanes, 1–4; relationship of, to Euripides, 9. Works: *Oresteia*, 107–8, 110, 134; *Prometheus*, 22–23, 46, 47n.11, 159
aidōs (respect), 51, 53, 54, 71, 72–74, 186
Alcestis, 12, 19–50, 148, 185–86
anankē. *See* Necessity
Archelaus, 99
Aretē (excellence), 131, 149n.9, 150n.15
Aristocratic values, 52–54, 62–64, 68, 70, 76, 123, 126–27; and Athenian democracy, 7–8, 186; vocabulary of, 165, 186; and women, 96, 126, 166–67. *See also* Heredity; Nobility; Reconfiguration of values; Reputation
Aristophanes, 1–4, 11, 19, 62–63, 90, 185
Aristotle, 1, 33, 52
Asclepius, 19, 26, 42
Avarice, 92–93, 109

Bacchylides, 19, 22, 41, 121, 122, 131, 153–54n.55
Barbarians, 85, 100
Bee, 59, 60, 66
Benediction, 164, 165, 176, 178
Binary oppositions, 158
Bow, 130, 147

Callinus, 22
Causation, 89, 169, 171, 174. *See also* Responsibility

Characterization, conventions of, 30, 32–34, 87, 133
Characters: as exemplars, 3, 55, 60, 67, 70, 75, 78, 112; psychological interpretation of, 20, 30, 33–34, 54–55
Charis (favor, gratitude), 42, 43, 113; and betrayal, 27, 39; erotic, 104, 106–7, 113
Cleisthenes, 4, 7–8, 45, 49
Comedy, 3–4, 6
Community, 7–8, 97, 146, 162, 175; as dramatic element, 86–87; support of, 130, 148, 156, 187
Compulsion, argument from, 91–92, 164–65, 171–72, 173
Cowardice, 27, 37, 127, 129, 131, 146–47
Curse, 77, 169, 170, 178

Dale, A. M., 32
Dead: situation of, 161–62; treatment of, 45, 93, 99–100, 108, 109
Death, 26–27, 43–44, 166, 176; in literary tradition, 20–24; politics of, 44–45, 185–86; voluntary, 29, 95–97, 125–26, 131
Deception, 69–70, 87, 108–9
Democracy, Athenian, 4–6, 7–8, 10, 75, 85. *See also* Imperialism, Athenian; *Isonomia*; *Nomos*
Democratic values, 68, 148; and Aphrodite, 56–57; and mortality, 41, 44–45, 123; transmitted through drama, 185. *See also* Endurance; Equality; Freedom; Reconfiguration of values
Democritus, 24, 65
Didactic theory, 4

205